Armistice Service at the "Angel" - November 2005. The late Mr. John Bassindale, of the Royal British Legion, who, for some years organised the Scunthorpe Armistice Day Parade and Service, is standing in front of the Memorial thanking everyone for attending.

This book is the result of work undertaken over several years by an enthusiastic group of local people who wish to ensure that the history of the Crosby "Angel" is permanently recorded for posterity in the annals of the Local History of the area wherein this unique World War 1 Memorial stands.

The research carried out has been as thorough and as meticulous as possible, and it is hoped that this book will be read for many years to come by those with an interest in the origin and early years of Crosby.

A perfect souvenir of the School's Centenary celebrated on

1st June 2008.

Cover Photograph
Mr. George Taylor, Headmaster, with his staff around the Angel Memorial circa 1923

Inside Front Cover
Congratulatory Letter sent on behalf of Her Majesty The Queen to Crosby Primary School Celebrating its Centenary

Book cover by
Roland J Proctor, graphic designer based in Dundee

The newly unveiled Angel Memorial, standing outside Crosby School, in 1923

THE CROSBY ANGEL

A Community's War Memorial

Researched and written
by
Ms. Susie Broadbent
Miss Rachel Butler
Miss Clare Midgley
Mrs. Jill Molnar
Mr. A Alan Mortimer
Mr. Stephen J Rimmington
Miss Patricia A Smith
Mrs. Margaret Stokes

"The Friends of the Crosby Angel"

Published by
"The Friends of the Crosby Angel"
Scunthorpe, Lincolnshire
2008

First published in the United Kingdom
by "Friends of the Crosby Angel" 2008

ISBN 978-0-9559674-0-5

British Library Cataloguing-in-Publication Data

A catalogue record for this book is available
from The British Library

Typesetting and Photograph enhancement Patricia A Smith

Printers G W Belton Limited Printers Heaton Street Gainsborough Lincolnshire
Telephone 01427 612291

THE CROSBY ANGEL - A COMMUNITY'S WAR MEMORIAL

Contents

INTRODUCTION

1.   The idea for this book came from Mrs. Marion Millest.

2.   Members of the group collected huge amounts of research material, not all of which can be used, as size and cost constrain us.

3.   Members wanted to honour all the 59 names on the Memorial, but it has proved impossible to collect material about every name so that all received an equal sized entry.

4.   Members of the group are indebted to relatives of most of the men who came forward with invaluable material, and their contributions are acknowledged under the biographies of the men to whom they are related.

5.   Where information is lacking, where researches have run into the sands, we have tried honestly to say so.

6.   Other former group members who have given invaluable assistance include Mrs. Helen Marris and the late Mr. Roy Gregson, who was a faithful member of our group until his death in October 2004.

Keith H Harrison B.A.
Tutor

FOREWORD

The statue of an Angel situated in the grounds of Crosby Primary School on Frodingham Road, Scunthorpe, is a well known landmark and memorial. It was erected from donations and collections at the instigation of George Taylor, the first headmaster of the school, in remembrance of 59 young men of Crosby who answered the "Call to Arms" and paid the supreme sacrifice during the First World War (1914-1918).

The publication of this book "The Crosby Angel" coincides with the centenary of Crosby Primary School. As a former pupil during the Second World War, I well remember time spent reading names on the Memorial and wondering who these people were.

Research into the lives and background of these young men has been painstakingly carried out by a group of local people. Although personal information from relatives of the majority of the men has been forthcoming, some of these Heroes died leaving no direct descendants to bear witness.

I commend this book to anyone interested in the history of Crosby in particular and Scunthorpe and North Lincolnshire in general. The proceeds are to help with the repair and maintenance of the Angel, which is unfortunately beginning to show its age. It would be sad indeed if this Historic Monument was allowed to fall into disrepair.

John E Odlin
President
The Royal British Legion, Scunthorpe Branch
July 2008

One of our Subscribers, Mrs. Kathleen Pegg, was for over 30 years the President of the Women's Section, Scunthorpe Branch of the Royal British Legion.

The Royal British Legion was founded in 1921 as a voice for the ex-Service community and over 380,000 members continue to ensure that this voice does not go unheard. Although the needs of ex-Service people have changed over the years, they are still there to safeguard their welfare, interests and memory. British service people are in action around the world every day of the year. They know that if they need their support - now or in the future - the Legion is always on active duty for them.

Legion Values

- **Reflection** – Through Remembrance of past sacrifice in the cause of freedom
- **Hope** - By remembering the past, a younger generation has the chance of a better future
- **Comradeship** - Through shared experience and mutual support
- **Selflessness** - By putting others first
- **Service** - To those in need and in support of the whole community

Mr. Robert Sheard, February 2008 celebrating the Chinese New Year at Crosby School, now in the centre of a multi cultural community.

The Angel War Memorial at Crosby Primary School

As we look forward to celebrating the centenary of this school in 2008, I feel privileged, as the Head Teacher of the school, to share some thoughts about the relevance and significance of the Angel War Memorial.

I had not been the Head Teacher for many weeks in 1994, before I was approached by two former governors of the school, the late Carol Abdi and Ken Tallentire, drawing my attention to the existence of the "Angel Memorial Fund." This had been established in 1987, with the explicit aim of restoring "The Angel." Well in excess of £1,000 was raised from donations from 55 friends of the school and local businesses who recognised the importance of "The Angel" as a vital local landmark and link with the past. A rededication service was held on Wednesday 11th November 1987.

The School Service of Remembrance remains an important annual event. Traditionally, it is held in the school on the Friday closest to Remembrance Sunday. Children from Year 4 attend as part of their study of life in the 1940's. They are joined by Year 6 and representatives from Henderson Avenue Primary School, together with veterans of former armed conflicts and their families. Whilst the service has been modified to make it more meaningful for the children, a sense of awe and wonder remains. As poppies are laid as tokens of remembrance by our pupils, they catch sight of the names on the Angel representing real people and families who worked in these very classrooms, walked the corridors and climbed the stairs to the Head Teacher's room!

The Angel is more than a landmark. It is a special piece of Crosby School history and an important part of this community's heritage.

Robert J Sheard
Head Teacher (1994 - 2008)

THE CROSBY ANGEL - A COMMUNITY'S WAR MEMORIAL

"The Friends of the Crosby Angel" wish to express their gratitude to those who kindly Sponsored and Subscribed to the Book prior to its publication as listed below:

SPONSORS (Donations of £50 or more)

Corus
Hinchliffe Hydraulics (Mr. Dare Hinchliffe)
Mrs. Sandra Curry (née Calvert)
Mr. David Calvert
Mrs. Sylvia Fenwick
Mrs Christine Mary Gow (née Calvert)
Miss Clare Midgley

SUBSCRIBERS

Armstrong, Mr Tony
Arnold Mr Brian
Atkinson Mrs Margery
Bailey Mr Christopher J
Bailey Councillor Robert
Baitson Mr Jeffrey V
Barnard, Mrs Edna
Barnard Mrs Pat
Bawden, Mrs Thelma (née Parrott)
Baxter, Mrs Christine
Beecroft Mrs Maureen
Bennett Mr Jack
Birkett, Mr Alan
Birkett Mr Steven
Birkett, Mrs Doris
Bottomley Mrs Julie
Bowden Mr Simon S
Bowden Mr Jeffrey A
Broadbent Mr Joshua R
Broadbent Mr Micah Jon
Broadbent Ms Susie
Brook Mr Peter & Mrs Caroline
Budworth Mr Max
Butler Dr Beverley J
Butler Miss Rachel
Butler Mr Richard Frank & Mrs Shirley Ann
Bycroft Mr Howard & Mrs Anne
Bycroft Mr William
Bycroft Professor Barrie W & Mrs Jean
Carr Mrs Jean
Chapman Dr L E & Mrs J E
Chennells Mrs Patricia A
Clark Dr Alan
Clipson Mr N T (Terry)
Cook Mrs Jean

Cooper Mrs Monica (née Parrott)
Corpse Mrs Polly
Cowling Mr David
Cox Mr Noel
Curry Mrs Sandra ((née Calvert)
Cuss Mr Steve & Mrs Rachel
Cuss Mr Tony & Mrs Maureen
Daddy Mr Paul
Dewhirst Dr Ian M.B.E.
Dickinson Mr & Mrs M J
Dodd Mrs Glenys
Dring Mrs Jean*
Driskell Mr Robert
Ellis Mr Stephen & Mrs Linda
Embling Mr Stanley
Fenwick Mrs Sylvia*
Ferenczi Mrs Jenny M
Fox Mrs Sheila
Frost Mr David
Fussey Mrs Barbara
Garcia Ms Isabel Estaben
Getley Mrs Jean (née Tallentire)
Goddard Mrs Patricia
Gow Mrs Christine Mary (née Calvert)
Green Mr John W
Green Miss Patricia Mary
Green Mrs Susan
Grinell Mr R H
Guesford Miss Marion
Harding Mr David & Mrs Pauline
Hardy Mr Stephen B
Hargreaves Mr Michael
Hargreaves Mrs Margaret
Hargreaves Ms Sharron
Harper Mr Ian

Harrison Mr Keith H B.A.
Havercroft Mr Nick & Mrs Gina
Havercroft Mr Tony & Mrs Elaine
Havercroft Mr Tony & Mrs Pat
Helliwell Mrs Ann
Hill Miss Margaret
Hinchliffe Mr Van
Hindmarsh Ms Lesley A
Hollingsworth Mr Richard
Horan Mr Chris
Hudson Mr Wayne & Mrs Samantha
Hunter Mr Roger and Mrs Irene
Isle of Axholme Family History Society
Kent Mrs Jennifer (née Thomas)
Kettleborough Mr Arnold
Kirk Mr F G
Kirkby Mrs Ann (née Thomas)
Knapper Mrs Sylvia (née Spencer)
Langton Mrs Janet
Lee Captain David John B.E.M. J.P.*
Leitch Mrs Mary C
Leeman Mr Donald
Lincolnshire Family History Society
Lockwood Mr Richard & Mrs Margaret
Lynch Mr Paul (Crosby Plant Hire)
Lyons Mrs Ann J
Manning Mr Dennis & Mrs Eileen
Marsh Mr Paul
Mason Sir John C.B.E. DL & Lady Margaret*
Maw Mr Patrick
May Mr Peter
Middlehurst Mrs Cath (née Staniland)
Middleton Mr Brian
Midgley Mr Ralph & Mrs Betty
Midgley Mr Stephen
Molnar Miss Carol
Molnar Mrs Jill
Molnar Mr Peter G
Moody Mrs S
Mortimer Mr Arthur Alan
Murray Mrs Joyce*
Newlove Mr John
Newstead Mrs Jane
North Lincolnshire Libraries
Norwood Mr David Alan*
Oliver Mr Duncan A.
Parrott Mr Geoffrey
Parrott Mrs June
Patterson Mr Alan
Pegg Mrs Kathleen
Pickup Mr Jim & Mrs Joyce T
Pittaway Mr David*
Pogson Mr David

Pogson Mrs Gloria
Pogson Mr Wilf & Mrs Chris
Polkinghorne Mrs Jean
Popple Mr Graham
Price Mrs Louise
Reeder Mr Rex & Mrs Dawn (née Harper)*
Rimmington Alison & Andrew Kirk
Rimmington Mr Gavin
Rimmington Mr Stephen J
Roberts Mrs Joyce
Robinson Leanne Broadbent
Robinson Mr David Stuart & Mrs Susan
Robinson Mr John
Roddis Mrs Diana Marjorie (née Spencer)
Rounce Mr Kenneth L M.I.S.M. F.I.S.M.
    F.F.Inst.Leadership & Management
    Hon.Instructor to Her Majesty's Forces
    (ex Sergeant Senior N.C.O.)
Scholfield Mr Sean*
Shaw Mrs Kathleen
Sheard Mr Robert J*
Sheppard, Mr Brian & Mrs Sherry G
Smith Mr Christopher J
Smith Mr Keith G & Mrs Pamela
Smith Mr Nicholas M & Mrs Georgiana A
Smith Miss Patricia A M.B.E.
Spencer Mr Thomas
Spindley Mrs Evelyn
Spriggs Mr Alan H
St Clair Mr Anthony
Stather Mr Alec
Steenken Mr J E*
Stokes Mrs Margaret
Sumpter Mr Tony
Tallentire Mr Kenneth (known as "Tally")
Thornley Mrs Sheila D.
Threlfall Mr Harry*
Wales Dr Richard
Wales Mrs Wendy*
Walshaw Ms Mandy Hinchliffe
Walters Mr Robert
Webster Mrs Marian
Whitelock Mr Derry A
Whitson Mrs Margaret A
Williamson Mrs June
Williamson Mrs Sheila
Woods Mrs Shirley

*Additional Donation received

Chapter One

The Crosby Angel

Detail of Panel Inscriptions

Panel 1

"THE LAST DESPATCH"
DUTY DONE
VICTORY WON
NOW FOR PEACE
EVERY ONE
CARRY ON.

A E WALTERS

Panel 2

THE ROLL OF HONOUR

IN BEAUTY OF YOUTH BUOYANT, SERENE
THEY STEPPED FROM THE SCHOOL TO THE BATTLE SCENE

RICHARD DAVISON
ERNEST HORNSBY
GEORGE HUDSON
WILLIAM LANGTON
WALTER MARTIN
JACK RIMMINGTON
WILFRED SHORT
JOHN ROBINSON

----

113 OLD BOYS JOINED HIS MAJESTY'S FORCES
1914-1918

*DULCE ET DECORUM EST PRO PATRIA MORI.
SIC ITUR AD ASTRA.

:--oOo--:

ALFRED GARRETT

(*It is sweet and fitting to die for one's country.
Thus do we reach the stars.)

Detail of Panel Inscriptions

Panel 3

OUR FATHERS
THEY HEARD THE CALL AND RUSHED TO FALL

A SACRIFICE FOR ALL

H BIRKETT	A NORWOOD
J BOOTHBY	E PITTAWAY
N BUDWORTH	T POPPLE
J W BOWERS	G ROBERTS
T W BOWDEN	E W ROBINSON
J BYCROFT	G H ROSE**
G COOK	W H RYLANCE
J COWAN	W SELBY
D CUNNINGHAM	C SHAW
J H COWLING*	L SISSONS
H S DANIELS*	G SIMMS
G CALVERT	F E SELLERS
J DALE	A H SELLERS
W H DYMOND	F SILVESTER
J FORREST	G W SMITH
C S FOSTER	J W STANDERLINE
A FROST	W STREETS
J FOWLER	G R STURMAN
G A HALL	W STOW
G HARLEY	W SPRIGGS
T G HARPHAM	A L WARD*
F HARE	A S WILSON
A HAVERCROFT	W J WELTON
J HAVERCROFT	W HARPER
A NEWSTEAD	J J POGSON

**This is actually ROSS—not established how the error occurred.   *incorrect middle initial.

Detail of Panel Inscriptions

Panel 4

DURING THE GREAT WAR THE SCHOOL BOYS COLLECTED
WASTE MATERIALS ALL OVER THE DISTRICT, AND WITH
THE MONEY REALIZED THEREON, BOUGHT WAR SAVINGS
CERTIFICATES, WHICH IN 1923 WERE CONVERTED INTO THIS
MONUMENT AS A HUMBLE TRIBUTE TO THE MEMORY
OF THE OLD BOYS OF THIS SCHOOL, AND OF ALL FROM
THIS PARISH, WHO SACRIFICED THEIR LIFE DURING THE
WAR

G. TAYLOR ***(INTER C.A. LOND) HEAD MASTER

"HIS UNWEARIED LABOURS, HIS LIFETIME OF PURPOSE
INSPIRED HIS PUPILS TO ERECT THIS MEMORIAL."

***should be "Inter B.A. (Lond.)"

ANALYSIS OF REGIMENTS/BATTALIONS/SHIPS WHERE THE MEN SERVED

Regiment/Service	Battalion/Ship	Name	Date Died	Day Died
Lincolnshire Regt.	1st	Hare F	1.11.1914	Sunday
	1st	Harpham T G	1. 8.1916	Tuesday
	1st formerly 5th	**Langton W**	3.11.1918	Sunday
	1st	Pittaway E	1.11.1914	Sunday
	1st	Standerline J W	22.10.1914	Thursday
Lincolnshire Regt.	1st/5th	Boothby J	3.11.1915	Wednesday
	1st/5th	Budworth N	13.10.1915	Wednesday
	1st/5th	Cunningham D	13.10.1915	Wednesday
	1st/5th	Daniels H A	30. 5.1918	Thursday
	1st/5th	**Davison R H**	20.11.1915	Saturday
	1st/5th	**Hornsby E**	13.10.1915	Wednesday
	1st/5th	Newstead A	13.10.1915	Wednesday
	1st/5th	**Robinson J**	9. 3.1918	Saturday
	1st/5th	*Simms G	23. 4.1921	Saturday
	1st/5th	Sissons L	1. 7.1917	Sunday
	1st/5th	Ward A E	13.10.1915	Wednesday
Lincolnshire Regt.	2nd	**Cook P	5. 1.1915	Tuesday
	2nd	Forrest J	10. 2.1917	Saturday
	2nd "W" Coy	Shaw C	25. 9.1915	Saturday
	2nd	Streets W	1. 7.1916	Saturday
	2nd 8th Div. 25th Bde	Sturman G R	23.10.1916	Monday
Lincolnshire Regt.	5th	Bycroft J	14. 8.1916	Monday
	5th	Cowling J W	9. 7.1915	Friday
	5th	Selby W	14.10.1916	Saturday
	5th	Stow W	28. 4.1915	Wednesday
Lincolnshire Regt.	7th	Birkett H	3. 7.1916	Monday
	7th	Frost A	9. 3.1916	Thursday
	7th	Ross G H	28. 4.1916	Friday
Lincolnshire Regt.	8th	Dale J	4. 8.1916	Friday
	8th	Foster C S	3. 7.1916	Monday
	8th	Fowler J	26. 9.1915	Sunday
	8th	**Martin W**	19. 4.1916	Wednesday
	8th	**Rimmington J W**	28. 4.1917	Saturday
Lincolnshire Regt.	9th	Sellars F E	26. 11.1915	Friday
Border Regiment	1st	Bowers J W	1. 7.1916	Saturday
Coldstream Guards	2nd : 3rd Company	Cowan J	15. 9.1916	Friday
Duke of Cornwall L.I.	6th	Harley G W	27. 4.1918	Saturday
Durham Lt.Infantry	19th	Spriggs W T	25. 3.1918	Monday
Grenadier Guards	1st	Calvert G W	24.10.1914	Saturday
Lancashire Fusiliers	11th	**Garrett A**	28. 5.1918	Tuesday
Machine Gun Corps (formerly in Lincolnshire. Regiment)	Heavy Branch Rec Depot Battalion -	Bowden T W	2. 2.1917	Friday
Machine Gun Corps	18th	Harper W	18. 6.1918	Tuesday

Regiment/Service	Battalion/Ship	Name	Date Died	Day Died
Machine Gun Corps	42nd (Infantry)	Smith G W	22. 8.1918	Thursday
Manchester Regiment	11th	Sylvester F C	30. 9.1916	Saturday
Royal Field Artillery	81st Brigade	Dymond W H	17.11.1915	Wednesday
Royal Field Artillery	"C" Battery 232 Brigade.	Pogson J J	27. 6.1917	Wednesday
Royal Garrison Artillery	71st Heavy Battery	Hall G A	16. 8.1917	Thursday
Royal Garrison Artillery	144th Siege Battery	Robinson E W	28.11.1917	Wednesday
Royal Scots	16th	**Hudson G A**	10.10.1917	Wednesday
Royal Welsh Fusiliers	13th	Roberts G	9. 2.1917	Friday
South Staffordshire	2nd	Norwood A	24. 1.1917	Wednesday
	2nd/6th (T/F)	Sellars A H	27. 4.1917	Friday
West Yorkshire Prince of Wales Own 10th .		**Short W**	20. 9.1918	Friday
West Yorkshire Prince of Wales Own "B" Company 10th		Wilson A S	11. 6.1918	Tuesday
Royal Navy	H M S "Aboukir"	Rylance W H	22. 9.1914	Tuesday
Royal Navy	H M S "Hawke"	Welton W J	15.10.1914	Thursday
Royal Navy	H M S "Queen Mary"	Havercroft A	31. 5.1916	Wednesday
	H M S "Queen Mary"	Havercroft J	31. 5.1916	Wednesday
Royal Navy	R N Division Howe Bn.	Popple T	4. 6.1915	Friday

N.B.

(a) *George Sims died after the end of World War 1 but was commemorated on the Angel War Memorial. His name is also spelt wrongly on the Angel Memorial as "Simms".

(b) **Parkinson Cook's name is not on the Memorial, but like others also omitted, probably should be, as he lived in Crosby Parish - see his biography for further explanation. He is not included in the total of 59 men listed below.

(c) The NINE names in **BOLD** were Old Boys of Crosby School.

Regiment/Royal Navy	No. of Men
Lincolnshire	34
Royal Navy	5
Machine Gun Corps	3
Royal Garrison Artillery	2
Royal Field Artillery	2
South Staffordshire	2
West Yorkshire	2
Border	1
Coldstream Guards	1
Duke of Cornwall's Light Infantry	1
Durham Light Infantry	1
Grenadier Guards	1
Lancashire Fusiliers	1
Manchester	1
Royal Scots	1
Royal Welsh Fusiliers	1
TOTAL	59

A DESCRIPTION OF THE MEMORIAL

Angel looking South along Frodingham Road from Crosby School Playground.

The "Crosby Angel" War Memorial has stood in Frodingham Road, Crosby, Scunthorpe, outside Crosby School, since 1923. It is entirely a First World War memorial and lists 59 names, all male. Nine are Old Boys of the School (the name of the ninth Old Boy, Alfred Garrett, was added after the Monument was unveiled), and 50 are men who were connected with the Parish of Crosby. There is also a glowing tribute to the Headmaster of the time, Mr. G. Taylor, *"His unwearied labours, his lifetime of purpose, inspired his pupils to create this memorial."*

The Memorial has some distinctive features. Most First World War memorials, particularly in small towns and villages, are either a simple cenotaph or cross, or have a statue of a soldier standing to attention, so the "Crosby Angel" is rather a dramatic memorial. The Angel is holding a wreath in her left hand and is bending forward, as if looking benevolently on future generations who will pass beneath.

The site of the Memorial, though not on a hilltop or rising ground, is also quite dramatic; it is right on the angle of the crossing of Frodingham Road and Sheffield Street. Diagonally opposite was a shop of the Scunthorpe Co-operative Society, a large store with several departments, so the "Angel" has always stood at the centre of a thriving community.

The Memorial is catalogued in the United Kingdom National Inventory of War Memorials (U.K.N.I.W.M.), kept at the Imperial War Museum, London, under reference number 35698. Here, the site is described as being *"in the playground on the south side of the school outside."* The type is listed as *"sculptured/cast figure"* as *"an angel with outspread wings, standing on a square pedestal, head bowed."* The material is *"marble-white"* and the ornamentation is *"laurel wreath held in the left hand of the angel."* The artist was the stonemason A. E. Walters of Crosby. The U.K.N.I.W.M. notes that the statue was repaired at a cost of £500 in 1987.

The Crosby Angel Memorial was one of as many as thirteen memorials of various types (this includes wall-plaques) produced in Scunthorpe and District in the 1920's. Research into the erection of these has been carried out by Mr. David Taylor of North Lincolnshire Museum, Oswald Road, Scunthorpe, and these two paragraphs of this chapter are based on his work, see his article in "Lincolnshire Past and Present" No. 21, Autumn 1995. As David Taylor says, *"There was no co-ordinated attempt to honour The Fallen in the Scunthorpe area as a whole, with the result that the town contains an assortment of different Memorials and Rolls of Honour."* The first was the printed Roll of Honour, compiled by W. S. Liddell and published by Scunthorpe Urban District Council in 1917. It was sold at 8d. each to raise funds *"for some Soldiers' and Sailors' Fund decided upon by Scunthorpe UDC."* Then there were the big memorials: the Scunthorpe and District War Memorial unveiled on Sunday 14th November 1926 (by General Sir Ian Hamilton, no less) which stood originally in Doncaster Road opposite The Old Showground, and was re-erected on its present site outside the Museum and Art Gallery in 1955; and the War Memorial Hospital formally opened on 5th December 1929.

THE CROSBY ANGEL - A COMMUNITY'S WAR MEMORIAL

As David Taylor points out, there are war memorials in Ashby, Crosby, Frodingham and Scunthorpe. Only Brumby is left out, but at the time it was part of the ecclesiastical parish of Frodingham. He points out that the situation in Scunthorpe District reflects the general confusion about the erection of war memorials throughout Britain in the 1920's, with pressures, sometimes conflicting, coming from church and chapel authorities, traditional landowning families (particularly in small villages), ex-servicemen's organizations, workmates, clubs and institutes, schools and relatives of The Fallen, (see, for example, the letter in the "Lincolnshire Star" of June 1925 from Mr. E. Burgess, Chairman of the War Memorial Committee for Scunthorpe and District, pressing for a Parish War Memorial, still not erected).

The more the members of the Local History Research Group studied the "Crosby Angel" War Memorial, the more it was realized how well it reflected the History of the First World War. It lacks, however, any women's names (not unusual in a memorial of the time) or any Air Force names. Nor are there any, as far as we can trace, who were *"shot at dawn."* Also, it is very much an Other Ranks memorial. There is no-one above the rank of Sergeant.

1. There is one man killed in the first weeks of the War, **William Henry Rylance**, who also seems to have been the oldest named, at 41.
2. The ages of the six killed in 1914 are notable: 41, 38, 36, and two aged 31. Very different from the 20 year olds (and younger) of 1917 and 1918.
3. There is one man killed in the last days of the War, **William Langton,** on 3rd November 1918. He was one of the 9 Old Boys of the School, aged 20.
4. There are a number of Regulars serving in the County Regiment at the start of the War: **John William Standerline, Fred Hare,** and **Edwin Pittaway**. Hare and Pittaway were both Lance Corporals in the 1st Battalion Lincolnshire Regiment, and died on the same day during the First Battle of Ypres (1st November 1914).
5. There are five killed on the same day during the Battle of Loos (13th October 1915): **Norman Budworth, Ernest Hornsby, Daniel Cunningham, Arthur Newstead** and **Albert Edward Ward.** They were all serving in a Territorial Battalion (1/5th Lincolnshire Regiment). Hornsby was an Old Boy of the School.
6. There is a Regular with a Guards Battalion: **George William Calvert.**
7. There are some who were Kitchener Volunteers: **John William Cowling, John Fowler, Frank Edward Sellars, Arthur Frost**, and **Walter Martin.** The latter was an Old Boy of the School.
8. There are two brothers killed at the Battle of Jutland (31st May 1916): **John** and **Alexander Havercroft,** who both went down on the same ship.
9. There are 2 who died on the first day of the Battle of the Somme (1st July 1916): **John William Bowers** and **William Streets**, as well as **Horace Smith Birkett** and **Charles Selwyn Foster,** who died on 3rd July.

The "Angel" stands at the junction of Frodingham Road and Sheffield Street.

18

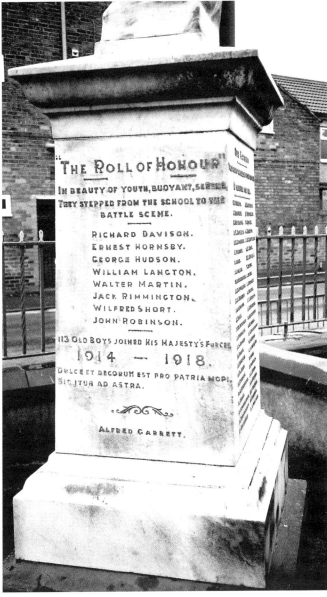

The nine "Old Boys" - note the name of Alfred Garrett at the foot of the Panel.

10. There are a number who served in new technical units developed during the war: **Thomas William Bowden, William Harper**, and **George William Smith**. William Harper, for example, joined the Lincolnshire Regiment, but was in the Machine Gun Corps at the time of his death.

11. There are, particularly in 1917-1918, a number who served in regiments completely unconnected with the local County or Guards Regiments: **Arthur Norwood, Gideon Roberts, Arthur Herbert Sellars,** and **George Allison Hudson** (another Old Boy).

12. There are some who would have been conscripts, joining the forces after January 1916:
Thomas William Bowden and **Thomas George Harpham** appear to have joined the Lincolnshire Regiment at the same time and are buried in their home district, Bowden in Scunthorpe Cemetery and Harpham in Crosby Cemetery, together with **George Henry Ross**, who had a military funeral and has a British and Commonwealth War Graves Commission headstone.

13. There was only one who would be counted as a "gentleman" by the standards of the time: **Arthur Shannon Wilson**, the son of the local Vicar, and born in South Africa.

There are also particular problems and mysteries, not untypical of First World War memorials:

14. The alphabetical order is not kept to throughout the list of 50. **Simms** is placed before **Sellars** and **Sylvester** before **Smith** and **Standerline**, and the last four on the list are completely out of alphabetical order: **Welton, Pogson, Harper** and **Garrett.**

15. There are some names where the connection with Crosby is unclear, so why they are on this particular memorial is uncertain, e. g. **William Henry Dymond.**

Something of the story of the erection of the Memorial, through a period of six years (June 1917-May 1923), comes wonderfully to light in two volumes of school log books. These were meticulously kept by George Taylor throughout his time as Headmaster, 1908-1933. There are two volumes, each 9¼ by 7½ inches in size, standard school log books, 300 pages in each, supplied by A. Brown & Co. Ltd., Scholastic Publishes, Hull. Unfortunately, however, the log books provide no information about meetings, discussions and decisions on the form of the Memorial or the names that should be on it.

The first mention of a school memorial is on 21st June 1917. (By this time, boys and girls had separate departments, after being mixed when the school originally opened in 1908.) The entry for that day reads,

"Our allotment is now in a very good condition. We have this week planted nearly 500 cabbage plants of various kinds. We have commenced to collect coppers from the boys with which to erect in school a marble monument to Old Boys who have laid down their life (sic) *for their King and Country.*

Today we forwarded 36 eggs to London." (This was for the Central Department, National Egg Collection for wounded soldiers and sailors. Collection at the school had begun on 18th June.)

Four Old Boys had died up to this date: **Davison**, **Hornsby, Martin** and **Rimmington**.

The inscription on the Memorial states that waste material was collected to pay for the erection.

This collection was well in hand in the early part of 1918. The log book records,
"Jan. 18 (Sat.) I spent today in school overhauling the waste material that children had collected in the Parish. Waste paper, bottles and tins. Owing to the snowy weather our collection was not a success during the holidays."

There was money from another source,
"Jan. 21 Owing to the difficulty of securing meal the managers decided that the School Pig (Mr. Taylor uses capital letters) *should be killed. Today he was transformed into pork. He weighed 15 stones and was sold at 17/6d. per stone to Mr. Mark Morgan, who presented the pig to the school. The money realised is to be divided between the Red Cross Fund and the Old Boys Monument Fund."*

Then on 2nd February 1918,
"From the Pig £3. 17s. 6d. will be invested in War Saving Certificates for the Monument Fund." (£4. 14s. 1d. went to the Red Cross Fund).

The 50 names on the Angel.

For months, for each Saturday, there are entries like these,
"Feb. 9 Spent all day amongst jam jars and bottles brought in by the boys (£2 5s. 9d.). We sent the jars to the Provincial Stores Co. in Scunthorpe and the bottles to the chemists and hotel proprietors. We have two or three tons of tins the boys have flattened out. I am waiting for information as to where I can send them."
"Feb. 16 I spent the day amongst jam jars, bottles and waste paper."
"Mar. 2 Spent the day amidst bottles, jam jars and waste paper."
"Mar. 16 Today we realised 11/3d. on jam jars and £2. 13s. 6d. on waste paper. I am now daily expecting to hear of a market in which I can dispose of our old tins of which we possess two or three tons. We now possess 51 certificates which we have purchased with money realised from waste materials and children's toffee half-pence. On Jan. 17th 1918 we had 13 certificates."
"Mar. 23 Today we got 15/6d. on jam jars. This week we have collected over 8 tons of waste paper. Today I was told that we must be prepared to put our tins into the market any day. We shall now begin a vigorous collection of tins. Already we possess four or five tons. We shall very soon make it ten tons. We now have 56 War Saving Certificates in the Monument Fund."
He was writing this two days after the start of the last great German offensive of the war, the

Kaiserschlacht, which was to lead to Allied counter-attack and victory. But, of course, at the time Mr. Taylor didn't know that.

"*Mar. 30 (another Saturday). During Easter Week the boys disappointed me in the collection of waste material. The weather was very wet and cold. Disappointed in number of boys who turned up for collection of waste materials.*"

"*April 27 This week we got £2. 17s. 8½d. for waste paper and pickle jars. Our Monument Fund now consists of 70 War Saving Certificates.*"

"*May 11 (another Saturday) Our Soldiers' and Sailors' Monument Fund has risen to 81 War Saving Certificates.*"

On 17th May it stood at 91, on 31st May at 99. But,

"*June 1 Very little collecting done today. It is very warm. Boys helping fathers on allotments.*"

Even Mr. Taylor began to feel the strain, but perhaps not from the waste materials collecting,

"*June 15 (the total was now 102 War Savings Certificates). We are now getting in funds for the "Prisoners of War." We already have more than £3 in hand. We wish to have £10 by next Saturday night. This means a big effort.*"

"*June 21 (this was a Friday) I have suffered from a severe bilious attack. I could not possibly walk to school. I had the mortification of hearing the school bell ringing and could not answer it. Absent from duty the whole day.*"

"*June 22 (Sat.) Today we have done nothing in the collecting line. I am too limp.*" (This would seem to prove the statement on the Memorial about Mr. Taylor's labour, "*inspiring his pupils to create this memorial.*" Without his supervision and driving power things didn't get done.)

He continues for this Saturday,

"*As we could not get meat we had to take ham from the Butchers last week-end. On Thursday I made a dinner of cold boiled ham with the usual consequence. As it is years since I had a severe bilious attack, I was beginning to think myself immune from them and ventured to eat what I regard to me as poison.*" (He does occasionally tend to use the log book as a personal diary.)

However, there were rewards,

"*July 26 As I was walking home a Crosby man stopped me and gave me a pound note for the Soldiers' Monument Fund because of the children's industry.*"

But also there were disappointments,

"*Sept. 27 (Fri.)* (By now of course, indeed since mid-August, the prospect of final victory had become clear.) "*We have today been advised that we can only realise 14/- per ton on the waste tins we have collected and flattened. This is a great disappointment to us as we were told we could get £14 a ton.*"

On 11th November 1918 (It was a Monday) is this simple entry,

"*Today is Armistice Day. The managers gave the boys a half-day holiday to celebrate the occasion.*"

There are brief mentions from time to time about the Memorial in the years immediately afterwards,

1919 "*Jan. 10 Today we received £3. 2s. 6d. from Messrs. W. J. Ward & Co. of Sheffield for a wagon load of waste tins that we supplied to them.*"

The following day he wrote this,

"*I wrote today to Mrs. Henderson, the Secretary of the Scunthorpe and District Red Cross Committee asking for permission to devote the money which we have recently raised for the Red Cross Fund to our "Old Boys" Monument Fund. I asked for this permission because the authorities at Head Quarters say that they have now sufficient money to meet all requirements.*"

He copied into the log book her reply,

"I think your scheme an admirable one and ought to appeal to the local people. Is it not delightful to think the fighting is over and funds are no longer required? I don't know anyone who had worked harder or with more enthusiasm than you and Mrs. Taylor and your family. You really have done splendidly and the Committee greatly appreciate your effort and the support you have given them."

He continues that day,

"We have already 111 War Saving Certificates and about £18 that we have collected from sources that usually go to waste. When the £18 have (sic) been converted into certificates we shall have 134."

Mentions of the War Memorial then go quiet for some time, though the Celebrations for the Declaration of Peace (Saturday 19th July 1919) are described in some detail.

Then, in January 1923,

"This morning I received permission to go on with the erection of the School War Memorial."

It was at a time when he was much occupied with school football. He wrote on 6th January,

"We are now at the top of the league again after the first round."

(And on 26th April he recorded, *"School closed to celebrate the Duke of York's wedding."* Presumably, he would have been surprised to learn that the bride from that wedding lived until 2002 - Her Late Majesty, Queen Elizabeth The Queen Mother, whose husband became King George VI.)

Finally, Wednesday 16th May 1923 (six years almost to the day since the idea was first mentioned),

"The School Monument to our 8 Old Boys who fell during the war was completely erected today by Mr. A. Walters of Crosby."

After the unveiling, the story of the Angel Memorial and George Taylor's involvement is still not quite finished,

"Aug. 3 1923 Closed school at mid-day for the midsummer vacation. Paid Mr. Walters, the monumental Sculptor, £152. 0s. 0d. as part payment for the monument. To do so I today received £146. 2s. 10d. from the Post Office after surrendering the War Saving Certificates."

On Sunday 18th November began the tradition of a ceremony at the Memorial about this time of year,

"The British Legion hung a wreath upon our War Memorial. The British Legion Band played Sacred Music and the Revd. Burton conducted a short religious service."

1923 *"Dec. 20 A School Concert took place in the Centenary School Room. It was a gratifying success in every way. The proceeds amounted to £11. 19s. 0d. which will be devoted to the completing of the War Memorial."*

1923 *"I paid Mr. Walters, the monumental mason, £10. This makes £162 that we have paid for the Monument. The Monument as it now stands is paid for. It requires walling in before we can consider it complete."*

Over the next four years (1924-1927) the log book records bits and pieces of work on the Memorial.

1924 *"Jan. 21 Professor Pacey gave an entertainment after 4 o'clock. He gave me 20% of the takings. That is I received 4/8d. which I have put to the War Memorial Fund."*

"June 19 This evening I washed and scrubbed the Monument from top to bottom."

The reason for this appears two days later,

DURING THE GREAT WAR THE SCHOOL BOYS COLLECTED WASTE MATERIALS ALL OVER THE DISTRICT, AND WITH THE MONEY REALIZED THEREON, BOUGHT WAR SAVINGS CERTIFICATES, WHICH IN 1923 WERE CONVERTED INTO THIS MONUMENT AS A HUMBLE TRIBUTE TO THE MEMORY OF THE OLD BOYS OF THIS SCHOOL, AND OF ALL FROM THIS PARISH, WHO SACRIFICED THEIR LIFE DURING THE WAR.

G. TAYLOR (INTER C.A. LOND) HEAD MASTER "HIS UNWEARIED LABOURS. HIS LIFETIME OF PURPOSE INSPIRED HIS PUPILS TO ERECT THIS MEMORIAL."

The name of Mr. G. Taylor, the Headmaster of Crosby School, was inscribed on the Angel.

"June 21 The Foundation Stone of Crosby New Church (that's St. George's) was laid by Sir Berkeley Sheffield. The Bishop of Lincoln, the Archdeacon of Stow and numerous clergy were present. I was invited to the lunch."
"Sept. 23 I paid Mr. Barratt £34. 10s. 0d. for work done on the War Memorial."

Mr. Taylor's name and the 59 names of men who died and were connected with the Parish of Crosby were not on the Memorial originally. This is shown by log book entries in 1925,
"Jan. 19 Today I paid Mr. Walters £8 for carving and blacking 51 names of (sic) the War Memorial."
Unfortunately he gives no information on how these names were gathered. Also on 3rd February,
"Mr. Walters, the sculptor, fixed a chain round the Monument."

On 11th June he copied into the log book a letter he had received saying that some of his friends thought that one significant name had been omitted from the Memorial, his own. They had paid for this to be done and forwarded the balance of the money they had collected to him for School Funds. So were his *"unwearied labours"* remembered.

There was further work done on the Memorial,
1924 *"Oct. 31 I paid Mr. Walters £9 for 5 white marble vases for the War memorial. I still owe him £1. the vases will be placed in position for Armistice Day."*
"Nov. 7 (Saturday) I spent the day arranging flowers around the Monument. We now have 6 (sic) marble vases around the Monument."

Further work was planned,
1925 *"Dec. 17 My daughter* (this was Phyllis Mary Taylor who was working at the school as a Supply Teacher. Staffing problems seem to have been at a critical level all the time), *and a party of boys went round the parish at 6 p.m. singing carols. They returned at 8 p.m. with £1. 1s. 2½d. This money will be devoted to the Monument Fund. We now purpose* (sic) *putting a marble floor around it."*
*"Dec. 18 The carol singers went out again tonight and returned with £1. 17s. 3d. Total realised = £2. 18s. 5½d." (*The meticulous accounting is typical).
The last entry about the Memorial (except for recording the Armistice Day ceremony every year) is in 1927,
"April 11 Paid Mr. Walters, the monumental stone mason, 15/-, the final instalment for the marble vases which stand around the Monument."
As George Taylor wrote on the Day of the Unveiling, the "Crosby Angel" (though he didn't call it that), it *"bestowed fitting honour upon the young lads who had fallen."*
Written by Mr. K H Harrison B.A.
History Tutor
Workers' Educational Association

The Last Despatch, Duty Done (the name of Stonemason A. E. Walters is visible at bottom left hand corner of the plinth).

The Stonemason: Mr. A. E. Walters
- an appreciation written by his son, Mr. Robert Walters

My father is on the left, standing alone, with the Scunthorpe Town War Memorial, erected after The Great War.

Albert Walters was born in Peckham Rye, London, in 1886. At the start of the last century he followed his father and brothers up to North Lincolnshire to help build the new town hall in Gainsborough. Although he would spend most of the rest of his long life in the Scunthorpe region, he never lost his distinctively London twang and, for Scunthorpe, his somewhat flamboyant sense of style (see photograph).

When the rest of the family moved back down south, Albert found lodgings in Dale Street with Julius and Charlotte Ellers. Many years later he would marry Dorothy, their daughter. However, during what came to be seen as the Edwardian heyday, there was no shortage of work for a skilled stone mason, as building projects mushroomed to keep up with the booming local iron and steel industry.

When the war came, Albert was rejected from active service because of what he described as his 'lack of inches', being only 4 foot 11 inches tall. If he'd been one inch taller he would have been enlisted in 'The Bantams', very few of whom survived. Despite his short stature he must have had a good head for heights – his war was spent on the steel works, building such things as the cooling towers. To reach the top, men had to climb up the outside and swing over the protruding rim at the top. He also installed the lightning conductor on the tower of St. John's Church.

After the war Albert had premises at Britannia Corner and on Ferry Road, as well as another in Skegness. He did the stonework on the Memorial Hospital and High Street premises such as Littlewoods and Barclays Bank. He supplied the stonework for many of the houses built in Scunthorpe between the wars, and was responsible for some prestigious projects such as the great gateposts at Normanby Hall.

However in the 1920s, most communities felt the need to honour the fallen of the Great War, and Albert supplied and erected most of North Lincolnshire's war memorials, including Scunthorpe War Memorial and, of course, the Crosby Angel. Where the memorials included carved figures, these were usually sculpted in Italy close to the quarries where the marble was sourced. This is almost certainly the origin of the Crosby Angel, shipped into Hull, probably imported by the stone merchants, Anselm Odling of Cleveland Street, Hull.

At about the same time as the Crosby Angel commission, Albert built 68, Old Brumby Street, as a guest house for Jennifer Revill, aunt and guardian of the now orphaned Dorothy Ellers. This was to become Albert's family home. He lived there until his death in 1972. After the Second World War the main focus of 'A. E. Walters' on Ferry Road had been personal tombstone memorials. He continued in the business well into his 70s, having trained most of the masons then active in the locality.

- Robert Walters, January 2007

The Angel at Crosby School

Forever and a day she stands
The angel with her wings outspread
Striking hard the memory chord
Of Crosby's sons, long lost, long dead.

Aloft she sweeps her sculptured arm
A smooth, fine figure pointing high
Her carved and silken visage, stone
Compassion in her transfixed eye.

A silent sentient message streams
From this noble, gracious form
"The candles of these earthly lamps
Have now to heaven gone."

Written in 2006 by Mrs. Pauline Wright, a local lady who died in 2007
(by kind permission of Mr. Jim Wright).

Chapter Two

Mr. G. Taylor

Inter B.A. (Lond.)

Headmaster 1908 - 1933

By

Rachel Butler

GEORGE TAYLOR: HEADMASTER OF CROSBY BOYS' SCHOOL
1908 - 1933

In addition to the sketches and character analysis of the Headmaster, George Taylor, adeptly undertaken by Keith Harrison, recently discovered information (in particular, the tracing of the autobiography of Mr. Taylor's daughter, Phyllis, **"The Noiseless Foot"**), means that we are now able to present a detailed biography of the man, including his childhood, and in-depth information about his teaching career at Crosby Boys'. The addition of **"The Noiseless Foot"** to our research means that we are also able to present glimpses of the private man, Mr. Taylor as 'Daddie', as well as detailing the formal aspects more commonly known and described.

Birth and Childhood

From the Crosby Boys' School Logbook, we find that George Taylor was born on the 14th March, 1869, in the village of Billinge, Lancashire, in the Parliamentary Division of Newton, and in the Administrative District of Lancaster.

He was the son of **Arnold** and **Margaret Taylor.** According to **"The Noiseless Foot,"** George's mother died suddenly in 1882, when George was just thirteen. This had a great impact upon him, says his daughter; "*His own development had been warped… by the sudden death of his mother. He was the youngest but one* (sic) *of a large family and henceforth was at the beck and call of his elder sisters, on whom devolved the task of running the village shop ...*" Indeed, from the 1901 census of Billinge, by which time George had 'flown the nest', we find **Arnold**, a widower of 68, running a shop at numbers 140 and 142 Upholland Road, along with his children **James, Jane, Emma** and **Margaret-Ann,** aged 34, 42, 28 and 24 respectively (George was 32 at this time). All of the daughters mentioned are listed as 'Grocer's assistant'. From **"The Noiseless Foot"** we gather that there were few academic choices for George in Billinge, and his family were too concerned with the shop to pursue 'book-learning' to any great degree; "*(His elder sisters) had scant patience for George's interest...and were for ever wresting him from his studies to fetch and carry, or to knead mountains of dough or tend the baby, until he began to despair of ever achieving his objective.*" What was mapped out for George in Billinge was to either take over his father's shop when the time came, or to join the main industry of the area; the coal mine. It is obvious from the 1901 census returns from Billinge that we have, that the local coal mine was pretty much 'the only alternative'. James Taylor, living at home and two years older than George, is listed as 'coal miner'; and in the four other houses listed on the same sheet, all of the males of working age, eight in total, are listed as some version of 'miner' or 'colliery-worker'. Phyllis Taylor talks about the very real "*... threat of the Pit,*" from which George desperately wanted to escape.

Sarah Morrell	Head	Wid		50						Warwickshire Middleton
Arthur G. do	Son	S	24		Grocers assistant		Worker			Lancs. Lpool Kirkdale
Charles Harrison	Brother	S	44		Barman		Worker			Shropshire Astley Abbotts
Geo Taylor	Boarder	S	32		Schoolmaster		Worker			Lancs. Wigan Billinge

The 1901 census for Walton on the Hill, Liverpool, Lancashire, shows George Taylor, aged 32 and single, working as a School Master, Boarding at No. 110 Walton Village at the home of Sarah Morrell, a Widow aged 50 with her son and brother.

Early Career and Marriage

"The Noiseless Foot," says it was the local vicar who helped George fulfill his academic ambitions. "*At fourteen years of age he became a Pupil-Teacher and at eighteen an Assistant Master in a large village* *school near Wigan. He was so keen that, during his pupil-teachership, after the labour of the day, he would walk to St. Helen's three miles distant, to attend night-school, and once a week go to Liverpool, eleven miles away, for more advanced instruction."* Phyllis Taylor says that *"In time he won a scholarship and was admitted to Chester Training College (where) at the end of his course of study he was appointed to a post as a Trained, Certificated Teacher, in St. Lawrence's School, Liverpool."* This, George's first certificated teaching position, was in 1893, for which he lodged in Liverpool - as shown on the 1901 census, where we find George Taylor, 32, residing at 110 Walton Village, Walton on the Hill, Liverpool, with a widower and her son, and as having been born at 'Lancs. Wigan, Billing (sic)'.

He was even at that early stage in his career, a very motivated, self-disciplined person, focused and willing to sacrifice pleasures for promotions in his beloved career. Phyllis Taylor mentions how he was well-known for resisting recreational activities such as going to the pub. *"He knew that in order to obtain his goal in life he must not spend money wastefully. He went to school every day with empty pockets so that he could not be tempted, for instance, to ride home on the tram-car."* This course of action did 'pay off'. *"George's sterling qualities were...appreciated by his Headmaster...and by the Chairman of the Board of Governors...The latter urged him to take a degree examination, advising him to aim for a Bachelor of Arts Degree of London University, and George immersed himself still more deeply in his studies. He would sit at the table in his lodgings, eating his solitary meals, with the lesson-books propped up against the teapot, and accept whatever the landlady put in front of him, so long as there was rice-pudding at dinner-time, and jam for tea."*

It seems that around about this time, George's thoughts turned to marriage; his focused and analytical reasoning towards even such events as courtship, companionship and marriage is apparent, *"He sought in a wife those qualities which had been so dear to him in his mother, uprightness, dignity, intelligence. None of the village girls, or the lady teachers on the school staff, filled his requirements."* However, reasoning can only take you so far; unexpectedly the unexpected happened, *"...suddenly he fell precipitately in love"* with a girl called 'Nance' (Mary Ann). According to Phyllis Taylor, George first saw 'Nance' in a Liverpool railway station, on a platform, *"...struggling to put on her cloak. Shyly, he offered his assistance. As she turned towards him and he saw the laughter in her eyes; the rose-petal cheeks; her curls, the colour of newly-minted pennies; his lurching heart was committed. They walked towards the exit, and when he learned that the lady was a young widow living with her sister in Southport... he was bold enough to ask permission to call on her."* These above sentences are far more romantic than the previous ones about searching for a 'suitable candidate'!

East Stockwith School - sadly now closed and up for sale in 2007 when this photograph was taken.

George married **Mary Ann Greetham** (née Breeden) in the September quarter of 1902. Mary Ann had been married since 1889 to Henry Oughton Greetham, a man of independent means, who sadly died at the age of 40 in 1898. Mary's parents, William and Jane Breeden, had been schoolteachers in Shropshire and Warwickshire. Mary was born in 1865, so was four years George's senior and would have been his perfect partner in every way.

Family Life and Children

After he got his intermediate degree, (Inter B.A. (London)) "...*he felt equipped to undertake matrimony.*"

His next appointment was across the country - in Retford (1902). His first child, **Joyce,** was born there. At this point, George decided to abandon plans for the completion of his degree, *"the responsibility of running a home and a school put an end to his hope of completing his degree*". Soon afterwards followed his first headship at East Stockwith, near Gainsborough, Lincolnshire, and, on 25th January, 1906, **Phyllis** was born whilst they were based there.

George's last child, **'Little Ena',** was born in East Stockwith, near Gainsborough, Lincolnshire, in May 1907. Phyllis recounts the sad tale of a baby that only lived for a year and a half, "*One day when I was three or four years old I became aware of a chill in the house. There were unusual comings and goings, and when the maid took me into the room where my parents were sitting I sensed that there was something between us… My mother held me tightly for a moment, and we returned to the kitchen. I wanted to know why my parents were dressed to go out, and I was told they were going to say 'Goodbye' to Baby. 'Little Ena', the youngest child, had died of meningitis at the age of eighteen months. This was a great grief to them.*" George's children obviously meant a lot to him; his Logbook records the sad events, "*December 21st 1908. My youngest child aged 19 months died from Acute Meningitis after 24 hours suffering. Have been in and out of school throughout the day.*" (her grave is located in the West Street Cemetery, Scunthorpe: Section B No. 79 "*Alice Ena Taylor died 21st December 1908 aged one year and seven months*".

Mr. Taylor on the extreme right wearing mortar board, with the school football team - the blackboard reads "*Boys of 1924 maintained the Honourable Record of 1921-22 Witness the 'Shield' and 'Four Silver Cups'*".

Crosby Boys' School

In 1908 George was told about a headship in Crosby, Scunthorpe, around 20 miles away. The post attracted him because it was for the first headmaster of a newly-built school, "*What an incomparable opportunity it would be to start a school, to build up his own traditions, to guide, through their school life, untutored minds along the paths of scholarship; to inform and inspire the young, and inculcate the*

THE CROSBY ANGEL - A COMMUNITY'S WAR MEMORIAL

Mr. George Taylor (centre front) and his staff in the 1930's
According to Mr. Taylor's Logbook entry dated 5th September 1930, the school staff were Mr. Norman Johnson, Mr. Hugh Gilgallon, Mr. Leonard Driskell (definitely identified front row extreme right), Mr. Frank Stott, Mr. Leonard Hassall, Miss G Fearon, Mrs. Gladys Carr, Miss D. Rushby and Miss Eleanor Parker.

right principles; to try to satisfy the thirst for knowledge without quenching it." After the usual round of interviews, George found himself on 1st June in charge of a brand new school, in a new town, with 375 pupils to care for.

Phyllis recounts how eager he was to teach his children, from infancy, in fun ways; with flash-cards, clay and sand etc, "*(The) Headmaster's study - (was) an upstairs room... to reach it you had to climb a flight of stone steps: it was almost an attic room... On the wall there was a photograph of the Headmaster's three little girls - Joyce, Phyllis and Little Ena.*" He even applied for special dispensation to teach his own daughters in his boys' school (Phyllis recounts some 'naughty' moments she had at the school, including walking on the roof outside the headmaster's study!).

A Typical Day at Crosby Boys' School

In **"The Noiseless Foot"** there is a wonderfully vivid evocation of a day at Crosby Boys' School. As a former pupil, Edward Dodd of Brigg remembers, "*For a full five minutes before lessons were due to begin George Taylor was out on the Frodingham Road corner ringing the handbell.*" Before the start of lessons "*... there was punishment of any late-comers, unruly pupils were dispatched to stand in the hall outside the headmaster's classroom. As soon as there were half a dozen or so gathered together, out he pounced like an avenging angel. No questions asked no excuse asked or given - if they hadn't done anything wrong they wouldn't be there, would they? Retribution was swift. Meant to be remembered.*" The hope was that once punished the pupil would never risk committing another misdemeanour.

"*After this a teacher who could play the piano would begin to hammer out a strain such as The Soldiers' Chorus. At this signal the classrooms would open and the hob-nailed boots would beat out a tattoo - Left! Right! Left! Right! as the boys marched to their places in the hall until the command HALT! was given.*" During assembly, Mr. Taylor led the 'Voice Training'. Morning lessons always included scripture, then, after a mid-morning break of ten minutes, there were lessons connected with Reading, Writing and Arithmetic.

Then it was dinner, "*At ten minutes to twelve a bell rang and a number of older boys in the older classes would stand up... leave the class and go racing down the road to their homes to collect a basket containing dinner for their father at the steelworks... At noon... a note was sounded on the piano. Then the 'Grace Before Meat' was intoned... (The classes at the far end of the corridor were likely to end up a few syllables ahead of the others).*" And the children marched out to the school yard.

After dinner, 'Grace After Meat' was said. The afternoon periods were given up to more recreational activities such as 'Hand and Eye Training'. Phyllis says that plasticene and painting were other "afternoon joys".

In the scholarship class, however, the afternoons were spent in solving problems in algebra and geometry, and in reciting French verbs and even Latin conjugations, because "*Mr. Taylor was determined that his scholarship winners should arrive at the Grammar School equipped to step off at a level with the fee-paying pupils...*". He often held '*night school'* for the brighter pupils, without any thought of extra pay.

"During the week, on most nights the aspiring scholarship winners would gather at seven o'clock for an hour of special coaching by my father. He undertook the extra work because he saw that some of his boys were intelligent enough to benefit from it - and because he loved teaching. Attendance at this 'night school' was entirely voluntary, but there was always a good muster of pupils - probably because my father succeeded in making learning fun. He relied chiefly on praise and encouragement..."

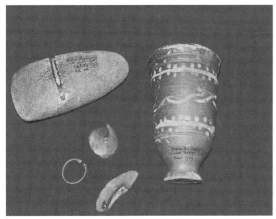

Some of the items donated by Mr. Taylor to Scunthorpe Museum before he retired from Crosby School.

Edward Dodd remembers that Mr. Taylor, *"...was seldom seen without his cane or mortar board… Joining the 'big boys' I found it was a different world, a place where iron discipline started from day one in Standard One...(but) it would be unfair to dub him simply as a disciplinarian... (he) was a dedicated teacher, and respected as such..."* Mr. Taylor's teaching style was not a brutal, meaningless aggressive one; he *"...believed that young people cannot mature properly without discipline. He also believed that discipline should not merely be enforced upon them...He himself, therefore, being a dedicated teacher, saw to it that he dressed neatly; worked conscientiously; attended punctually; spoke courteously; lived uprightly."* He lived as he taught.

Mr. Taylor's Collections

He was a great collector of historical items, which he used in his teaching, *"...my father had discovered Roman coins and pre-historic flint weapons* (at Risby Warren)...*pacing backwards and forwards over the sand, poking his walking stick at any piece of flint or stone or metal and picking it up to identify it… From time to time, too, someone would come to the school bringing a rare item of Roman pottery which had been uncovered during mining excavations...later a Roman lamp and brooch. The donor would hand over the item with his request, perhaps, that my father would pay the next quarter's rent for him..."* Phyllis states that, *"History and Geography were subjects that were brought alive by the display of prehistoric weapons picked up by the Headmaster...and exhibited in the school Museum Cupboard...as well as by expeditions to the church in...Broughton...or to Alkborough Hills...a picnic to Thornton Abbey. He knew all about wild-flowers, and often consulted ...one of the books that lined his study walls."* His daughter remembers that, *"In winter time he knew the names and positions of the constellations."* An article on Mr. Taylor's retirement from the **'Star'** dated 11th November, 1933, written by the curator of Scunthorpe Museum, Harold

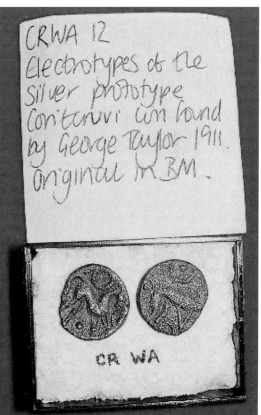

Facsimile of coin donated by Mr. Taylor to the British Museum.

Dudley, mentions that, "*With...retirement...Mr. Taylor decided to present the bulk of his collection to the town...(including) many excellent fossil sponges, corals, mammoth teeth, shark teeth, Saurian vertebrae belemnites, sea urchins, plant remains...crystals and minerals...flint implements...pieces of Bronze Age pottery… Roman and medieval pottery...good heads of buffalo, antelope and other horns...Indian spears, African amulets of ivory, a poisoned arrow of the Hottentots...an early miner's lamp, seventeenth century clay pipes, a horned cup and eighteenth century cutlery.*" Mr. Dudley mentions that some pieces were of such interest that they "*have found their way to the British Museum.*" Indeed, in the Crosby Boys' Logbook, there is an entry where George mentions that he, "*received a certificate from... (the) British Museum, acknowledging the [Iceni Tribe] coin which I sent on November 28*[th] *(1930).*"

Article from Hull Times 26th June 1915, *"Joyce and Phyllis Taylor, daughters of the headmaster of Crosby Council School, who have collected £? (in pence) for the Y.M.C.A. Children's Hut K? They hope, with the kind assistance of the public to get the same amount for the Red Cross Fund."*

The First World War

From **"The Noiseless Foot"** we discover how George Taylor first heard about the start of the First World War, "*The daily paper...plopped through the letter-box...mother (came) down the passage to pick it up. Suddenly she called out, 'George!' We sat up with immediate attention. When mother referred to Daddie as 'George' there was always urgency involved. Daddie was in the bathroom with his ears full of soap. 'GEORGE!' mother called again. 'Yes, my dear?' said Daddie, towelling his head as he emerged from the bathroom. 'George, Britain has declared WAR!' 'Eh!...' exclaimed my father, with a sort of long-drawn-out shudder, as he always did when he had been suddenly shocked.*"

Phyllis mentions the arrival of Belgian refugees in the town as the first visible effect of the war, "*The first impact of war on our community came with the announcement made in the town by the Roman Catholic priest, that a party of Belgian refugees was on the way to stay with us. It was decided that, to begin with, the families should be housed in some unoccupied buildings in Dragonby. The* noise of the blasting in the mines, however, *frightened the refugees so much that the older people would not take off their outer garments, thinking that the Germans were coming and they would soon have to be fleeing again. In the end, only a few of them remained in Scunthorpe.*"

Phyllis Taylor also discusses how keen her parents were to 'do their bit', "*My mother was very anxious to have a part in the war effort, but felt she had no skill to offer, until my father suggested that she should make use of her skill as a cook. So she embarked on a programme of making cakes and jam (to sell to the people who lived in the neighbourhood at a very modest charge). She limited the profits to a penny a cake and two pence on a jar of jam, keeping careful accounts and sending a cheque for the profit made to the local branch of the Red Cross at regular intervals. When sugar was in short supply she was allowed a ration of glucose with which to sweeten her jams. My sister and I acted as saleswomen, carrying our laden baskets from door to door on Saturdays and summer evenings… I would explore the tenfoots, delighting in the surprise offered by back gardens with chickens and rabbits in them: one old couple even had a donkey stabled in their back yard.*"

George Taylor had to see many of his former pupils go off to fight, "*As the war progressed it grieved my father to know that the lads who had so recently been his pupils, and who had in many cases shown promise in their first jobs, were now condemned to the life of the trenches; he wanted them to know that the old school was concerned for their welfare, and to this end established a rota for the posting of parcels to each one in turn. He invited the present pupils to bring to school magazines, cigarettes and chocolates, and to make contributions of pennies and halfpennies... Every contribution was recorded and accounted for, and the Headmaster, with the help of older pupils and staff, spent much time in packing parcels to send to camps and barracks all over Britain, and to the Army Post Office in France and later, to Prisoner of War camps. Letters from the grateful recipients of the parcels were read aloud to the school...*"

He was determined that the current crop of boys should not forget their forebears who had gone off to fight, and who paid the ultimate price for their country, "*The Headmaster also encouraged the boys to bring to school empty bottles, old tins, jam jars and scrap metal, and on Saturday mornings his young helpers would wash and crate and flatten the junk, and the proceeds of the sale of the salvage - together with profits from the school vegetable garden and from the sale of the two school pigs - were invested in War Bonds, the total of all these contributions was sufficient to purchase, after the war, a War Memorial in the form of an Angel of Peace in Carrera marble (as a Memorial for the whole parish of Crosby) which was erected in the school yard.*" The Memorial was erected and dedicated in May 1923.

It seems that Mr. Taylor took the plights, and subsequent deaths, of some of his 'old boys' in the 1914-18 conflict terribly personally, which is understandable, especially as the school had only been open six years when war broke out. "*During that war one hundred and thirteen boys of the parish fought in it, and nine names are recorded on the memorial of old scholars who died. So it became a shrine to the mothers, one of whom was especially distressed by the loss of her son who had been posted, 'Missing'. For a long time she lived in the faith that he would one day lift the latch and walk in on her unannounced, but at last she accepted the fact of his death, and brought her flowers to put with the others round the monument. She would look up to the statue of the angel, with its upraised arm pointing to heaven, and sigh, 'Poor owd Eernie! 'E wor a luvly lad!'*"

Mr. Taylor's bigger house - now Theodore Road Club, within cycling distance of Crosby School, which he did daily.

After the War: Removals and Retirement

The Taylors moved from 24 Gurnell Street, into a new and much bigger house in March 1926; a house with a plot and vista chosen by 'Nance', and designed by Phyllis, "*Mother had for some time been dreaming of moving into a house with a view. She had found the view, unobstructed for miles, on the crest of Crosby Hill...(a prospective council-house site). The Council, however, very kindly undertook to sell him a double-sized plot of land.*" In his Logbook, Mr. Taylor records the address of the house as 'Bryn Euryn', in Theodore Road. According to an article in **Nostalgia** dated 7th October, 1995, the house later became the Theodore Road Club.

"Hill Crest", West Malvern, Worcestershire, as photographed in 2007, George and Nance Taylor's last home to which they retired after George retired from Crosby School in October 1933.

In 1927 'Nance' had an operation for cancer. These health problems, and the fact that she desired to live 'in her own county' once again, quickened George's retirement. The **Scunthorpe and Frodingham Star**, 29th October, 1933 details the presentation given to him after 25 years of teaching, "*Dr. Armour (old scholar) said that he was greatly surprised that he :had been asked to make the presentation, because he thought that Mr. Taylor would leave the School in one of two ways - either on a stretcher or in a coffin. For energy, Mr. Taylor was unbeaten and for conscientiousness, unparalleled.*" He had been at Crosby from 1st June , 1908, to 20th October, 1933, with hardly a day off in between.

Mr. Taylor said a few words at his presentation. He talked about 'his boys', "*They have given me a fund of inexhaustible joy, and in my retirement I shall always have sources of happiness to draw upon. Scenes on the concert platforms, on the football field, and in the Classrooms can never fade away.*" He said that, "*My life's work has been done here in Crosby, and I have put my whole soul into it. I could not do more...I shall think of 'Dear Old Crosby, Crosby School Boys, and their parents'.*" At the Staff and Scholars presentation held at the School, Mr. Taylor, "*...at the end of his remarks, broke down, saying that he had never thought of his separation from the boys and the school.*" His oft-mentioned "*skill and devotion*" was acutely evident.

Soon after retirement, the Taylors moved to 'Hill Crest', West Malvern, Worcestershire. 'Nance' passed away there in 1946. George kept going until December, 1951, although his daughter said that he was totally distraught at the loss of his wife. The **Scunthorpe and Frodingham Star** dated 8th December stated that, "*a few days before admission to hospital he had sustained a fall in the kitchen of his home, by which he was found to have fractured three ribs, and the shock of which accelerated his death. He was active and mentally alert up to the end.*" He was 82 years old.

Mr. Taylor's Legacy

The most visually obvious legacy of George's time at the school is the Angel Memorial, which he spent many hours raising funds for so that his beloved pupils would never be forgotten. At his retirement it was said that, "*Those...interested in the School during the war knew the wonderful work Mr. Taylor did. Out of all kinds of waste material he and the boys collected a sum of money with the result that they had that wonderful Memorial in the School grounds. That would be a wonderful tribute to Mr. Taylor long after he had left the School.*"

Facsimile of actual page from School Logbook for November 1930 wherein Mr. George Taylor recorded the Armistice Day Commemorations around the Angel Memorial.

However, research makes it clear that there was a great deal of respect for Mr. Taylor simply as a man, and as a fine, encouraging teacher. One of the best 'obituaries' that could be given to George Taylor is his depiction in his daughter's memoirs. The following heart-warming couple of sentences from **"The Noiseless Foot"** concludes this biography of this significant and much-respected man, "*To me my father was a hero, ...it would give me great pleasure to hear the confident, 'Hello, Mr. Taylor!' from every child we met, and when some little fellow said proudly, 'I'm coming to your school when I'm a big boy, Mr. Taylor!' I shared his happiness in knowing that they loved him, too.*"

Bibliography:

The Noiseless Foot by Phyllis Taylor, First published in 1970 by
The Roundwood Press (Publishers) Limited, Kineton, Warwick
The Reminiscences of Edward Dodd (ex pupil of Crosby School)
Grimsby Telegraph 21st May 1923
Lincolnshire Star 19th May 1923

In Memory of Mr. George Taylor,
Headmaster of Crosby School 1908 – 1933.

A devoted Mentor of the Boys under his care.

Oh! Mr. Taylor What shall we do? …

There's blood and gore around us, the stench of wet and rot.
We're treading on the bodies of our comrades who were shot.
We dare not tell our mothers or families back home
This war's a living Hell like no man has ever known.
But don't you fret dear Mother, it will turn out fine we know,
Keep the parcels coming, we love and miss you so.

When we came home on leave the days were far too short.
We called on our Headmaster so dear and oh so smart.
He taught us right from wrong, gave his all us to inspire,
Unknowing of the horrors that "his boys" faced under fire.

We saw children in the classrooms, patriotic songs they sang
For brave young Crosby soldiers barely grown from boy to man.
We thanked them for the comforts sent to one and all of us.
For their hard work and their sacrifice but mostly for their love.

Thank you to our Mentor for remembrance of our call
For the lovely Crosby Angel that commemorates our fall.
So when you see our Angel remember if you will
And ask "where is the justice?" for boys sent out to kill.

Was this the War to end all wars? It ended our lives too
And left parents, sweethearts, children, wives, alone to struggle through.

By **Susie Broadbent**

Chapter Three

The Nine

"Old Boys"

The Men who had Attended

Crosby School

Biographies written by Mrs. Jill Molnar
Research: Ms. Susie Broadbent
Miss Patricia A Smith
Mrs. Margaret Stokes

Richard Henry Davison

Private 2600
1/5th Battalion Lincolnshire Regiment
Died: Saturday 20th November 1915 Killed in Action

Richard Henry Davison's great grandparents, **James** and **Eliza Davison,** lived in the Boston area of Lincolnshire where James was employed as an agricultural labourer. Richard was named after their youngest son, **Richard (**his paternal grandfather), and **Henry** after his maternal grandfather, **Henry Frow.** Henry Frow was a regular soldier in the North Lincolnshire Militia, with the rank of Sergeant, and died in 1903 (after holding the position of "Lincoln Cathedral Constable" - 1901 census) when young Richard was about seven years old. He would no doubt have regaled the boy with exciting stories of army life. Richard was thus probably inspired to follow in his grandfather's footsteps, especially on the outbreak of the Great War. Indeed, so the family legend goes, Richard was so keen to enlist that he lied about his age, stating that he was a year older than he actually was.

Richard Henry Davison was born in the Lincolnshire village of Waddingham on 4th December 1896, the first child of Police Constable **John Henry Davison** and his wife **Sarah Ann Beal Davison (née Frow).** On 12th December 1896 Richard was baptised at Waddingham Parish Church where his sister

Annie Elizabeth, was baptised two years later. His younger sister, **Fanny** was born in Scunthorpe, where their father now worked as a Security Officer at John Lysaght's Steelworks.

By 1901 the family had moved to Crosby, to 14 Mulgrave Street. Richard began his education at the Scunthorpe National School (Gurnell Street) but was transferred to the newly built Crosby School the day it opened, 1st June 1908. Fifteen months later the 14 year old Richard left school with an *"Exemption Certificate",* and became a working man in the Mill Department of John Lysaght's Normanby Park Steelworks.

In September 1914, as a result of Kitchener's phenomenally successful recruitment campaign, Richard Davison enlisted in the 1/5th Lincolnshire Regiment along with his contemporaries **Ernest Hornsby, Norman Budworth, Daniel Cunningham, Arthur Newstead, Albert Edward Ward** and his friend **Jack Rimmington,** and were sent off to their training camp until February 1915, when they were deemed ready to fight and were shipped out to France on overseas service. A month later their old Headmaster, Mr. Taylor, noted in the School Logbook a list of clothing sent to old boys, including two jackets to Billericay for the use of **Richard Davison** and Albert Hill. *"They are in Kitchener's Army."*

But Richard's army career lasted just nine more months; his pitifully short life was ended on 20th November that same year, a month short of his 19th Birthday. In the War Diary for the 1/5th Lincolns 20th November 1915 is written, *"weather was fine, wind N.N.E. work commenced* (sic) *as commenced* (sic) *on 19.11.1915 (work continued on parapets and communication trenches also in reserve dugouts in orchard north of H.Q.) Our artillery firing short. One shrapnel killed No. 3940 Pte. Thompson and* **No. 2600 Pte. R. Davison.** *Another shell burst close to H.Q. Relief by 6th Staffords complete at 7.30. Went into billets at Croix Barber."* In modern parlance, it would appear that Richard was killed by so-called *"friendly fire."*

The Commonwealth War Graves Commission entry records that, at the time of Richard's death, his parents were living at 82 Berkeley Street, Scunthorpe. Mr. Taylor's Logbook bears witness to his continuing concern for his former pupils.

After seeing Richard's mother, he made the following entry, *"November 27th 1915 (sic). This morning our charwoman asked Mrs. Taylor if I knew that Richard Davison had got killed. I have not heard from this lad during the past fortnight, hence I hurried at once to his home and asked his mother how he was getting on and why he had not written to me. Her face answered my question. She invited me inside. She said Mrs. Maw of 19 Dale Street had shown them a letter in which Mrs. Maw's son said that Richard had been buried in France. I consoled the mother as well as I could, for he was her only son a fine boy just eighteen years of age and more than six feet in height. I visited Mrs. Maw's house and asked to be allowed to read her son's letter wherein the death of Richard Davison was mentioned. The letter was at once produced and the exact wording of the significant part was "poor old Dick Davison is killed, he was buried at a little cemetery just behind our lines. I saw his body the night before". Those were the only words referring to his death. I propose writing for a full account. I remember his visit to school when on his final leave just prior to leaving for France. His last words were "If I get through this war alright I shall make soldiering my profession Mr. Taylor". He was a big fine lad, his grandfather was a non commissioned officer in Lincoln. His mother was born in Lincoln barracks."*

The Lincolnshire Star of **8th January 1916** ran this final tribute, *"Private R. H. Davison of 60 Burke Street, Crosby who served with the 1/5th Lincs. has been killed. He was only 18 years of age and prior to his enlistment was very popular with the youth of the Ironstone district."*

The Hull Times reported, *"Yet another Crosby home is saddened by the war, for on Monday last, Mr. and Mrs. John Henry Davison, of 60 Burke Street, were informed by the War Office that their only son, Private Richard Henry Davison, was killed in action on November 20th. Had he lived until Saturday last he would have been 19 years of age. Before the war Private Davison worked in the mill at Lysaght's, was a member of Mr. Symes' Bible Class, and most popular with the youth of the Ironstone district. Enlisting with the 1/5th Lincolns on September 4th, 1914, he went to France on August 15th (sic). A memorial service will be held at Crosby Parish Church on Sunday night."*

Even though his life was so tragically short, he lived five weeks longer than his contemporaries **Ernest Hornsby, Norman Budworth, Daniel Cunningham, Arthur Newstead** and **Albert Edward Ward**, who all lost their lives on the 13th October 1915 at the **Hohenzollern Redoubt.**

Richard Davison's grave in France.

In 2002, Richard's niece, Ann Lyons, visited his grave; sadly the original graves near Bethune were blown up during World War 1, and his remains moved to the beautiful cemetery at **Rue des Berceaux Military Cemetery** in **France.**

Richard is commemorated on the **Lysaghts 1914 Roll of Honour** as well as on the Crosby Angel Memorial.

Information from:
Mrs. A J. Lyons, niece

Alfred Garrett

Private 57143
11th Battalion Lancashire Fusiliers
Died: Tuesday 28th May 1918 Killed in Action

Alfred Garrett, youngest son of **Henry** and **Mercy Garrett,** was born in Yaxley, Huntingdon on 9th September 1899. His father was a brickyard labourer with six children to support, so it is likely that the family moved North for economic reasons after 1901. Work was plentiful at that time; bricklayers were needed to line furnaces at the steelworks. Opportunities were there to be seized. The Garrett family moved into 31 Mulgrave Street, Scunthorpe, and the young Alfred transferred from Yaxley school to the brand new Crosby School. He started there on 5th October 1908 and left on the 19th September 1913 *"over age."* Where Alfred worked for the four years between leaving school and enlisting at Scunthorpe in the 11th Battalion Lancashire Fusiliers is not known.

Yaxley War Memorial, Huntingdon.

He died on Tuesday 28th May 1918 killed in action. The following extract is from the *"History of World War I"* by Andy Wiest, *"...then the Germans would once again strike in Flanders against the British. On 27th May 1918 some 41 German Divisions struck lightly held French defensive lines on the ridge (Battle of Blucher-Yorck, France) and the attack came as a total surprise to the Allies. In addition, the French commander in the area, General Duchene, like Gough before him, had failed to ready his defences accordingly. By the end of the first day of the offensive, German forces had retaken the ridge and had advanced nearly 13 miles creating a gap almost 25 miles wide in the French lines. For the next three days the Germans made astonishing gains even reaching the River Marne*

for the first time since 1914, only 55 miles from the French capital."

Alfred Garrett has no known grave but he is commemorated on the **Yaxley War Memorial, Huntingdon,** where he was born. He is also on the **Soissons Memorial, Aisne, France** and commemorated on the Crosby Angel Memorial because he was an *"old boy"* of Crosby School. Alfred was only 18 years old when he died.

His cousin Samuel also died in World War 1 on 6th February 1915 age 24, and is buried in **Yaxley Cemetery** and commemorated on the **Yaxley War Memorial, Huntingdon.**

Information from:
Martyn Smith (Yaxley War Memorial Photo)
Sue Adamson and the late Henry Garratt
(researching Garrett family tree)

Ernest Hornsby
Private 2612
1/5th Battalion Lincolnshire Regiment
Died: Wednesday 13th October 1915 Died of Wounds

There had been Hornsbys living in and around the Crosby area since the 1500's. They were

Ernest with parents Jessie and Robinson Hornsby and younger brother.

probably the largest local family. In 1909 the following report appeared in the Frodingham Star of 2nd October,

"Family reunion at Crosby of the Hornsby Family" *"Nearly 100 relatives". "There were five brothers, George and William of Frodingham, James of Crosby, John a farmer of Barrow and Frederick of Scunthorpe. There were 4 generations present at the "Old Homestead", Crosby. George is 80 with 85 descendants, James is 76 with 21 living descendants, John also a septuagenarian with 31 descendants, Fred ten children living and 85 descendants. William one child and two grandchildren. James is a famous rat catcher and poet at Crosby and challenges the whole world to beat him at his profession. King Edward has been graciously pleased to accept some of his verses."*

Ernest Hornsby was the grandson of **George Hornsby** and the son of **Robinson Hornsby**, an

ironstone pit miner, and his wife **Jessie (née Fowler)** whom he married in the Spring of 1884. Ernest was born on the 20th July 1895, the second child of the family, to which eight more children would be born. Ernest and his siblings were Baptised at St. John's Parish Church, Scunthorpe, where their parents had married. In due course the children attended Crosby School along with a large number of cousins and other Hornsby relatives. Ernest started there on the 1st June 1908, transferred from Scunthorpe National School (Gurnell Street) and left in July 1909 *"over age"*. He went to work at a butcher's shop, W. K. Fletcher, Parkinson Road (now Frodingham Road), Crosby/Scunthorpe.

On 4th September 1914, Ernest Hornsby enlisted at the same time as **Richard Davison, Norman Budworth, Daniel Cunningham, Arthur Newstead** and **Albert Edward Ward**, school friends and neighbours all. Enticed by smart uniformed and beribboned recruiting officers who told them they were *"needed at the Front"*, thousands of such boys, eager to be turned into men, answered the call to arms. They had been brought up on battles, dates and victories at school; Empire Day was an important celebration when one third of the globe was coloured red, which denoted British rule, and most colonial wars had been successful. Defence of the Realm was paramount, doing one's duty automatic. The Regular and Territorial Army had only just been able to keep the enemy at bay. A new batch of Kitchener's men was needed to tip the scales in England's favour. Less than six months after enlistment, Ernest and his contemporaries were deemed ready for action and shipped out to France on 26th February 1915. They were part of the original 1/5th Battalion rather than a later draft/reinforcement.

Before he left for the front, Ernest was given a prayer book by Mr. R. A. C. Symes, whose Bible Class he had attended at St. John's Church. The prayer book is personally inscribed by Mr. Symes, a well known local solicitor who founded the Keenites Boys' Bible Class. According to family legend, Ernest's cousin's great-great grandmother bought a Bible in monthly instalments at a total cost of £8, a phenomenal sum at the time. She then walked to Epworth to have it bound. When it was completed, she walked there to fetch it home and carried it back on her head. Faith was strong for the majority of people and Christian certainty the norm.

Hull Times 31st July 1915, *"Crosby soldier's interesting letter. Private Ernest Hornsby, eldest son of Mr. and Mrs. Robinson Hornsby, of Crosby, spent Monday, his 20th Birthday, in the trenches. Writing to his Mother, he says: - "We are now in the trenches around Ypres and Hill 60, which, for us, is a very warm shop, but we keep giving the Germans 'Poll Thompson'. We are in for 18 days, and have had a bit of bad luck, but I hope we shall finish up all right. We have been wet through to the skin for 4 days, and our trench has been over the knees in water and mud, so you may guess what sort of form we are in. The sky is the only roof we have".* (N.B. the expression 'Poll Thompson' means to give someone a hard and difficult time). *"At the time of writing, we are pleased to say, he has not received a scratch. He has the 'Hull Times' sent every week, and would rather miss his Sunday dinner than his favourite paper."*

The dignity, humanity and humour in the moving detail of Ernest's letter is typical of so many young men facing death with great courage.

School Logbook 21st October 1915, Mr. Taylor wrote, *"16 old boys now in France. Five of them are wounded. Several of our boys took part in the charge for the Hohenzollern Redoubt. The Redoubt was captured but of the 750 5th Lincolns, only 102 returned for the roll call."*

School Logbook 24th October 1915, *"Today Mrs. Hornsby called at my house and told us that she fears her son Ernest was killed in the recent charge for the Hohenzollern Redoubt. Eleven days have now passed and she has heard nothing from him. Three trenches were captured and his comrades saw him roll into the third trench. Since then he has not been seen."*

School Logbook 15th November 1915, *"Ernest Hornsby is missing – his comrade dragged him into a trench and left him there. He was suffering*

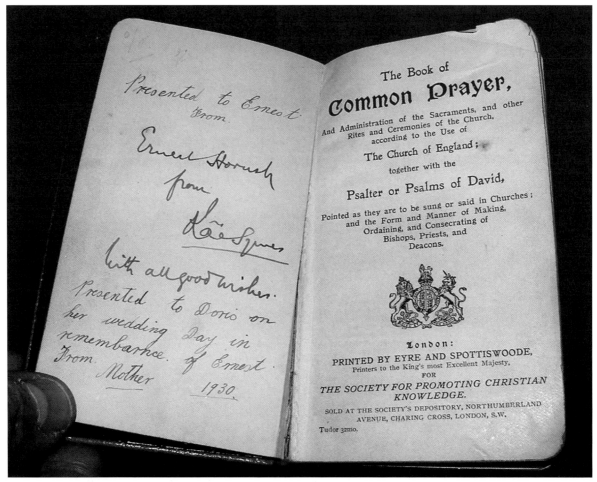

New Testament presented to Ernest by Mr. R.A.C. Symes, a local solicitor who ran a Boys' Bible Class known as the "Keenites" at St. John's Parish Church, Scunthorpe.

from a severe thigh wound. As the Lincolns had to retire from this trench we are hoping he is a prisoner in Germany, otherwise he may have died from loss of blood."

School Logbook 26th November 1915, "Herbert Bowers, one of our old boys who took part in the Hohenzollern Redout charge, and was gassed, called at the school today. I was astonished to find him looking so well, as he left Exeter Hospital only a few days ago. I asked him whether he considered Ernest Hornsby, who is missing, was a prisoner in chamber (sic). He replied 'I think we shall hear nothing more of him, Sir. Our Officers instructed us not to take any prisoners. Ernest Hornsby was dragged by a comrade into a German trench which we had just captured. We, however, had to retire from that trench and the Germans returned to it. Ernest had received a bad thigh wound and consequently could not retire with his comrades. We had given no quarter to the Germans hence we expect our men left behind receive none from the enemy. I have now given up Ernest as killed. I have seen a letter which a young man wrote to his Mother in Ashby, wherein he states quite casually that "he dragged 'that lad Hornsby, who used to work at the frozen meat shop in Scunthorpe into a trench from which we had to retire'." Mr. Taylor then wrote, "Albert Hill, one of my old boys, to whom I wrote asking for information regarding Ernest Hornsby, told me he was missing. Albert was wounded in the same charge."

School Logbook 24th January 1916, "Today I wrote to the American Embassy, London asking if they would kindly enquire into the fate of three Crosby lads who had been missing since the attack on the Hohenzollern Redoubt October 13th 1915". (America, at that time, a neutral country, was a conduit for knowledge as to the whereabouts of Prisoners of War taken by the enemy).

Hull Daily Mail 5th August 1916, "Mr. and Mrs. Robinson Hornsby, 58 Sheffield Street, Crosby, are very anxious about the fate of their son, Pte. E. Hornsby, No. 2612, for they have been informed by the War Office that he has been missing since the charge, at the Hobson gollern (sic), Redout on October 13th, 1915 (sic). For six years before the war he was a butcher at Messrs. W. and K. Fletcher's, High Street, and joined the

1/5 Lincs. on September 4th, 1914. He went to France, February 28th, 1915 and fought at Ypres and Hill 60, spending his 20th Birthday on the last-named famous hill with many boxes and parcels from home. Wednesday was his 21st Birthday, and if any of our readers could inform the anxious parents of his whereabouts they would be most grateful." This indicates that nearly a year later, his parents were unaware that their son had in fact been killed.

At the Battle of Loos, 13th October 1915 Ernest Hornsby died as he had lived, alongside the four other Crosby lads, **Daniel Cunningham, Norman Budworth, Arthur Newstead** and **Albert Edward Ward** at the Hohenzollern Redoubt. He was the first ex-Crosby schoolboy to die. His name was on the **Roll of Honour at St. Lawrence's Church, Frodingham** in 1915, where he was listed as *"missing"* (records at St. Lawrence's Church). Of the 59 men, Ernest is the only one listed on the **Congregational Church Memorial Plaque,** now situated in the new Congregational Church on Ferry Road West (Information from Memorial Plaque Record Book at Scunthorpe Museum). His name is on the **Dud Corner, Loos Memorial, Pas de Calais, France, Panel 31 to 34.**

Reverse of 1914-15 Star showing Ernest's Number, Rank, Name and Regiment.

The **Scunthorpe Urban District Council Roll of Honour dated October 1917** lists the following, who may have been members of Ernest's family:

| Harry Hornsby | New Santon | |
| | Lincs. | Pte. |

Harold Hornsby	2 Church Street
	H.M.S. Bristol Gunner
John Hornsby	54 Manley Street
	West Yorkshires Pte.
Herbert E. Hornsby	158 High Street
	Royal West Kents
	Pte.

Ernest's descendants are in possession of two medals, the 1914-15 Star and the Victory Medal.

Ernest Hornsby is one of the nine Old Boys whose name is on the Angel Memorial because he attended the School and lived in Crosby.

Ernest's Mother, Jessie Hornsby, remained at the family home, No. 58 Sheffield Street, until she died aged 85 in 1952, surviving her husband, Robinson Hornsby, by 29 years. She was profoundly deaf and used a blue ear trumpet. She went to Cleethorpes for a week every year, sometimes taking a grand-daughter Margaret with her. It is said that Jessie always wore black. A great deal of information and many interesting stories about the Hornsbys exist, including a wealth of social history and biographical detail. Many more Hornsby descendants still live in and around the Scunthorpe area.

Memorial Plaque in Congregational Church, Ferry Road West, Scunthorpe with the name of Ernest Hornsby inscribed thereon.

Information from:
Mrs. Margaret Hargreaves (niece)
The Late Mr. Desmond Hornsby (nephew)
The Late Mr. Leonard Hornsby (second cousin)
Mr. David Hornsby (second cousin)

George Allison Hudson

Private 270448
16th Battalion Royal Scots –
originally he was in the Highland Light Infantry
Died: Wednesday 10th October 1917 Died of Wounds

George Allison Hudson was born on Christmas Eve 1897 at Thornton Curtis, North Lincolnshire, and Baptised there in January 1898. His Father, **William Hudson,** an agricultural labourer, of Fossdyke Few, Boston, married **Rose Ann Allison,** who had been employed as a general servant on a farm at Ulceby, Lincolnshire, prior to their marriage in June 1886.

Their first three children, **Charles, Nellie** and **Gertrude,** were born at East Halton. **Elsie, Maud, George** and **Walter** were born at Thornton Curtis where the family lived for some years at 42 Hall Lane. Initially George attended the village school, but transferred to Crosby School on 3rd May 1909 where he remained until January 1912, when he left school *"over age."*

Three years later, in October 1915, he enlisted in the Highland Light Infantry.

"The Battle of Poelcapelle took place on 9th October 1917 – fighting had commenced on 4th October at the Battle of Broodseinde and the bad weather persisted. At 0520 hours on the 9th the attack was renewed on a front of over 6 miles

and the 11th Division fought its way forward in the face of great opposition to the eastern outskirts of Poelcapelle village. This battle was part of the Third Battle of Ypres which commenced on the 31st July 1917 until the 10th November 1917." (History of the Lincolnshire Regiment 1914 - 1918 by Major General C. R . Simpson, C.B.)

School Logbook, Mr. George Taylor, Headmaster, wrote, *"15th October 1917. Today I learned that Geo. Hudson, one of our old boys, had fallen in action. He was buried by the Chaplain in Mendinghem Military Hospital in France (sic) on October 10th. He was a private in the 16th Royal Scots."*

Hull Daily Mail Saturday 1st December 1916, *"Private George A. Hudson, Royal Scots Regiment, second son of Mr. W. Hudson, 50 Sheffield Street, Crosby, died of wounds received in action on October 9th. He was admitted into hospital but passed away on the following day. He was a milk dealer in Crosby and Scunthorpe previous to joining up in October of last year. Much sympathy is felt for his friends and the family. Deceased was 19 years of age."*

On the outbreak of War, George enlisted at Lincoln, was trained in Essex and spent two months in Ireland during the troubles in 1916. Sadly he was killed the very first time he went up the line to the Front.

George Allison Hudson died of wounds incurred in the Battle of Poelcapelle and is buried at **Mendinghem Military Cemetery Poperinge, West Vlaanderen, Belgium.**

He is commemorated on the Crosby Angel Memorial because he and his siblings attended Crosby School.

Soldier's cap badge - the star and cross are silver, the remainder gilt. The badge was introduced for the rank and file of the Royal Scots in 1890.

Infomation from:
Mr. Brian Fewster
http://www.theroyalscots.co.uk/badges.html

Military Cemetery, Etaples, France, where William Langton is buried. Also buried there is Thomas Ward, brother of Albert Edward Ward, whose name is also on the Angel. (See his entry later in this Chapter.)

William Langton

Private 21742
1st Battalion Lincolnshire Regiment
Died: Sunday 3rd November 1918 Died of Wounds

William Langton, like so many other young soldiers, came from a family of agricultural workers. Born on 29th May 1897 at 13 Belton Turbary, youngest child of **Frederick Sowersby Langton** and **Alice Emma Langton** of Westgate, Belton, Isle of Axholme. He was Baptised on 30th June 1897 at the Belton Primitive Methodist Church where his family were regular worshippers. But his was not to be an agricultural life. His education began at Scunthorpe Boys' School as the Langton family had moved into town, probably for economic reasons, and had taken up residence at 42 Grosvenor Street, Crosby.

When the brand new Crosby School opened its doors on 1st June 1908, William was transferred there. His education was completed in June 1911 when he left school *"over age."* Where William worked between leaving school and becoming a soldier is not known, or where he enlisted with the 5th Battalion, Lincolnshire Regiment.

That William was wounded is mentioned in Mr. Taylor's School Logbook entry 20th December,1916, *"Jack Rimmington, **William Langton** and Frank Standish today visited the school at 3 o'clock. The boys gave them a grand*

World War I Trench, Lincolnshire Regimental Museum.

*reception; **William Langton** is still suffering from wounds received in the Somme battle. Jack Rimmington who had never had a leave for 19 months told the schoolboys that their parcels and magazines were greatly appreciated by the old boys at the front."*

The wounded rarely had clean bullet wounds; most were inflicted by shrapnel from exploding shells. In soldiers shipped back to England for treatment, injuries to limbs were most common. Referred to as *"walking wounded"*, these men had a better chance of survival, which was both good news and bad as in William's case, because he was sent back into the firing line when he was sufficiently recovered, only to be killed.

William was wounded on 1st July 1916, the first day of the Battle of the Somme. Sadly this was also the day his elder brother, 32 year old married man **John Richard Langton, Private 18830 2nd Battalion Lincolnshire Regiment,** was killed, and buried in **Blighty Valley Cemetery, Authuile Wood, Somme, France**, just one of the 20,000 British troops who lost their lives on that fateful day. William's *"luck"* in living to fight another day finally ran out on the 3rd November 1918, just eight days before the Armistice. He was probably wounded on the 1st or 2nd November when the 1st Lincolns were at the Poix du Nord. It is recorded in the Battalion War Diaries there was one man wounded on the 1st November and seven on the 2nd. The 1st

Lincolns were relieved on the 2nd and moved back to billets in Vendeges, France. From historical information it appears that William may have been taken to a Military Hospital in the Etaples area prior to his death there.

Private William Langton was 20 years old. He is buried in **Etaples Military Cemetery, Pas de Calais, France.** Of those soldiers named on the Crosby Angel Memorial, he was the last man to die. He is also listed in the **Scunthorpe 1917 Roll of Honour** booklet as having been wounded once – home address given as 32 High Street, Scunthorpe.

William's Mother was spared the anguish of losing her two sons in battle. She pre-deceased both of them on 3rd June 1912.

Walter Martin
Private 11782
8th Battalion Lincolnshire Regiment
Died: Wednesday 19th April 1916 Killed in Action

Born on Christmas Day 1895, Walter Martin was the middle child of furnace man **William Martin** and his wife **Maud (neé Schofield)** of Park Street, Scunthorpe. Details of Walter's short life are scant, but it is recorded at the time of the 1901 census that he had siblings **Grace, John, William, Rose** and **Dorothy**. Walter was Baptised at St. John's Parish Church, Scunthorpe on 7th February 1896 and began his

Meaulte Military Cemetery, Somme, immediately south of Albert, France. John Cowan (also commemorated on the Angel) is buried at Meaulte, but at Grove Town Cemetery.

Military service was not new to the Martin family. In his younger days Walter's father, **William Martin,** had served in the army in the Egyptian campaign of 1882 receiving a number of medals. Walter's older brother, **John William**, died on 20th January 1913 whilst serving in the Royal Navy. John was an Able Seaman on the missing steam cutter *H.M.S. "Perseus"* in the Persian Gulf. He was a member of an expedition fighting smugglers in the East Indies. He and eight others lost their lives in mysterious circumstances, disappearing from their ship while carrying out their duty. His parents prized the medals he won and two old guns captured from the smugglers.

schooling at Scunthorpe National School (Gurnell Street) and, along with his contemporary **Jack Rimmington,** was transferred to Crosby School on 1st June 1908. He left school on 1st January 1910 *"over age"* to take up employment in the Blast Furnace Department at John Lysaght's steelworks, Normanby Road, Scunthorpe. (He is listed on the **John Lysaght's 1914 Roll of Honour** as a serving soldier.)

On the outbreak of war, Walter Martin enlisted at the same time as **Jack Rimmington** and **John Henry Dale** on 4th September 1914 as a result of Kitchener's call to arms. This was possibly the most successful *"hard sell"* of all time. The image of Kitchener's arm outstretched, with finger pointing, brought seven hundred and fifty thousand men to recruiting offices around the country in August and September 1914. War fever (or fervour) was contagious. In industrial towns like Scunthorpe many young men such as the Martins and Rimmingtons, Dales and Fowlers, and others, joined up en masse. For men who had played, worked and socialised together it was an adventure, a change from perhaps tedious work for a class and a generation who never expected to see the world any other way. And anyway, it would all be over by Christmas – wouldn't it?

Researchers have been unable to find a specific battle on or about the date Walter Martin was killed by a shell during bombardment.

Entry from **Mr. Taylor's Logbook of 26th April 1916,** *"Tonight Mr. Martin sent me word that his son Walter had been killed on April 19th and was buried on Good Friday in Meaulte Cemetery near Albert. I at once went to see Mr. and Mrs. Martin. They are bearing their trouble very nobly. Walter Martin was one of the nicest lads we ever had in school. He was tall, well built, well behaved and courageous. When he visited the school just before going to France his parting words were 'I consider every young man in Scunthorpe should join His Majesty's Forces.' These words were spoken in a deep bass voice very soberly in the early stages of the war. His life was a noble example."*

Walter Martin was killed in action almost a year before **Jack Rimmington.** He was 20 years old. He is commemorated on the Crosby Angel Memorial because he was a pupil at Crosby School. A record of his younger siblings **Wilfred**, **Leonard** and **Maud** attending the School has also been discovered, by which time the family had moved to 29 George Street, Crosby.

John William Rimmington

Private 11783
8th Battalion Lincolnshire Regiment
Died: Saturday 28th April 1917 Killed in Action

"Underline Jack" as discovered by his nephew
Stephen Rimmington.

JACK RIMMINGTON, as he is remembered on the Crosby Angel Memorial, was born on the 18th September 1894. At birth he was registered as John William Rimmington, the son of Frederick and Mary Rimmington, who lived at 91 Grosvenor Street, later, from 1925, at 37 Jackson Road.

Jack was the third of nine children, my father's eldest brother. All his brothers and sisters lived 50 years or more after Jack was killed on 28th April 1917, at the village of Gavrelle during the battle of Arras. My father, George Rimmington, was the last sibling to die, in 1996, 79 years after Jack.

Jack's brothers and sisters, my uncles and aunts, as well as my father hardly ever talked about

Jack. I knew of him and the circumstances of his death, but I had the strong feeling that you were not to ask about him! The only emotion, about either of the two world wars, that occasionally erupted, particularly from Jack's sisters was a strong anti-German attitude.

I never knew Jack, I was born 25 years after he was killed. It was only after my father's death in 1996 that I became the keeper of some family papers, photographs and heirlooms. These included photographs of Jack, medals he was awarded and letters; a dozen letters he wrote home, a few letters he received and a few letters written by others after his death. These, together with references to Jack in various documents, including a recently published book containing information about the battle at Gavrelle and a photograph of the small battle cemetery where Jack lies, give me a glimpse of the young man. He was 22 years old when he was killed.

Jack moved from the Scunthorpe C. E. School to the new Crosby Council School when it opened in 1908. He only attended Crosby School for a few months before he was granted an exemption certificate (still in my possession) on 12th July 1908, to leave school and take up the position of office boy, he was still only 13 years old.

Two weeks before his 20th birthday, on 4th September 1914, Jack enlisted, number 11783. Enlisting at the same time was **Walter Martin** (11782) killed in action April 1916 and **John Dale** (11786) died of wounds August 1916. The Hull Times, wrote in Jack's obituary, that as a lad he worked in the butchery department of the Scunthorpe Co-operative Society, but was in the boiler shop at Frodingham when he enlisted.

A letter Jack wrote home on the 10th September 1915, a year after enlisting, tells of his imminent embarkation to France. This is part of his letter, which begins '*Dear Mother and All*',

"We leave tonight Friday about 7 o clock for Southampton arriving in France early Saturday morning. But dear Mother don't trouble about me, if you only knew what we have gone through at this camp you would be pleased we are moving I can tell you. We are not sorry to leave and we have a special course of bayonet fighting to go through when we get to France so we shall not

be at the front for 3 or 4 weeks yet, so just think I have gone on a holiday to Blackpool or somewhere and am enjoying myself it will be a lot better than fretting about me and it would be a lot better for me, so cheer up, never say die. I shall come back alright, I might be home for Christmas dinner, perhaps before, you never know what is going to happen these days. Well I think this is all this time, so I will close with love to all, hoping you are all in the best of health.

I remain
Your loving son
Jack.

Many happy returns of the day and the best of wishes to my dear Mother on her birthday,

Jack"

The next letter I have was written on the 2nd October 1915 and tells of his first taste of action. The letter is not long, to quote it all helps to give a picture of the trauma of battle, his first contact with friends missing in action, and his attempts to reassure his family, and perhaps himself too, that he will see the war through.

"11783.Pt.J. Rimmington
D. Company
8th Service Battalion
Lincolnshire Regiment
B. E. F.

"Dear Mother & All,

"Just a few lines to let you know I am in the best of health and getting on alright under the circumstances. I expect you have been worrying yourself with not having a letter from me for so long. I have been started on this one about a week, but could not seem to get on with it, so I think it is time it was finished, by the way I have not had one from you lately. What is the matter.

"Well I am pleased to tell you that I have come through our first engagement without a scratch, how I managed it I don't know as I think it was one of the fiercest battles ever been fought, shells were dropping about us like rain. We were not in action very long, but long enough to make me remember it all my life, if I live to be 100 years old. Well, we are not allowed to say much, but don't worry yourself about me, as I shall come out of this lot alright, I feel sure. We

are having a rest now, to get reorganised a bit, how long we shall be before we go into action again I don't know, but I will write again before then. I am sorry to tell you my mate who I listed with is missing, also B. Wilcoxson, but I don't know what has become of them, so I would not mention it to Bobs mother yet. Well I think this is all this time so I will now close with love to all, hoping you are all in the best of health.

I remain
Your loving son,
Jack"

Jack was not allowed to disclose in letters home where he was fighting. The "History of the Lincolnshire Regiment, 1914 – 1918" by Major C. R. Simpson, gives us the details of the first battle Jack's battalion was engaged in. The 8th Lincolnshire Battalion was involved in the action known as the Battle of Loos.

The 8th Lincolnshires were called up as reserves on the afternoon of 25th September 1915 and began fighting between 7-00 p.m. and 8-00 p.m. They were relieved and withdrawn from the frontline at 4-00 a.m. on 27th September. Jack's first full day of fighting was 26th September 1915.

It was also the first day of fighting for John Kipling, Rudyard Kipling's only son. His first day, as an officer in the Irish Guards, was at the Battle of Loos, but it was also his last day. John Kipling was killed on 26th September 1915 and his body was never found.

Jack survived to fight a few more battles and live a little longer, unlike many of his comrades in the 8th Lincolnshire Battalion. In that first action at Loos, no less than 22 officers were killed, wounded or taken prisoner; of the other ranks, 148 were killed, 323 wounded or missing, a total of 493 casualties, half of the men in the battalion if it was at its full strength of 1000 men.

On 29th May Jack writes to *'Dear Sister'*. The only May he saw in France was May 1916. In the letter he refers to his sister **Harriet,** so it will have been written to **Florrie** or **Lucy**, sister **May** was only 6 years old so it would not be her, most likely to **Lucy.** There are a few family items of interest in the letter. Jack's father was chairman of the Crosby parish council and a school governor, so what trouble he got himself into I am not sure. Jack asks to be remembered to Harold, someone his sister was writing to. In a later letter Jack alludes to a romance between his sister and possibly Harold, but doesn't pursue the matter. Both letters are the only ones I have that he wrote to his sister Lucy, below is the first. **Lucy** never married, she spent her life teaching and will be remembered by many local women who went to Doncaster Road School as girls, where **Lucy** spent most of her teaching career.

Jack's Mother and sister Lucy 1903/04.

"May 29th Monday

Dear Sister,

Just a few lines in answer to your most welcome letters which I have duly received. I am very sorry I have not wrote before, but I have not had much time until this week and now can't seem to write at all. I don't know how it is, but sometimes I feel as though I could sit down and write letters all day and another time, which is nearly always, I feel as though I would rather do anything than try to write a few lines and I put

it off as long as possible, so if you don't happen to hear from me for a week or two don't trouble yourself about me, you will know I am only waiting for a writing fit to overtake me, don't think I have took (Oh dear your grammar Jack) I mean taken a fit now, because I haven't I am just trying to write a few lines to set your mind at ease regarding your last letter which I received today.

I don't know where you get all the yarns from but don't take any notice of them. Albert is alright but the others are absolutely wrong. Percy Glew as (sic) arrived back off leave and he tells me he has been to see you, so I expect he gave you what information you required, and you can take it for granted. He says it is grand to be home for a few days, I wish I could get my leave but I have given up thinking about it, still I shall get it sometime with a bit of luck, but I don't know when, anyhow I have it to look forward to.

Well, when do I think the war will be over. Well I haven't the least idea, but I believe the last two years will be worse than the first two, but to speak the truth I have no idea at all as it is very seldom I see a paper. What is the matter with Dad, it is surprising he does not know, I think he must be too busy with patrols etc he will have no time to study things. He is not too busy to get into wars I notice. I think it is about time he gave over such silly games. I hope he is better again.

As (sic) Mother got all the painting done, you must be a very busy lot nowadays. I expect Harriet will not feel in form for work she will be pining in despair, just fancy 7 weeks its awful isn't it, tell her she has my deepest sympathy and to keep smiling. I am very sorry to hear Harold is sick again, he seems to be having a very rough time and I think it would be best if they did send him home, just remember me to him when you write.

Well I shall have to close it is teatime and there is a fine boxing competition tonight which I must not miss seeing. If you happen to see Mr. Benson tell him I got the cigs alright and tell him I should be pleased to hear from him. Well I will close now, trusting you are in the best of health, best love to all,

I remain
Your loving brother
Jack."

David Monteith, Jack's brother in law 1915.

The horrors of war are reflected in these two final quotes from Jack's letters. One is to his future brother in law, **David Monteith,** who was to marry Jack's sister Harriet. David enlisted as a second mechanic in the Royal Flying Corps in March 1915, the letter is dated 10th February 1916. The other is part of an undated letter to his Mother. At all times Jack tries to be cheerful and positive, trying not to worry the family back home. In his letter to David he chides him for being pessimistic, and comments upon the Zeppelin attacks on the Scunthorpe and Crosby area, here is part of that letter,

*"Dear David,****************** I received a letter from Harriet today about the second since I have been out here and I have had a good laugh over it, I can tell you. You are a Job's comforter, keep smiling. Oh dear what a joke, I should liked to have been home the night the raid was on and seen the panic, it would be a sight of a lifetime, what say you. I would have had a laugh I bet, but all the same, it was a very rude awakening for them, and it would give them a very nasty shock. It is a mercy the majority of the bombs fell in the pit. There is one thing about it, it will make them*

realise what war is and give them a slight idea what it is like to be out here and if there are any slackers left it ought to move them. I wish we had only Zepps to contend with, it would not be so bad.

"I have had a few sensations since I have been out here, but none like I had a few days ago. The Germans blew a mine up about 50 yards in front of our trench, and you talk about shells and bombs, it isn't in it. It lifted the ground up, and made our trench rock like a cradle. I thought our time had come then, but we got over it and we still keep smiling, but when the ground starts to rock it makes you think things doesn't it.

"Well Dave I am pleased to hear you are keeping well, but I am sorry you did not get your leave, you are the same as me, you have it to look forward to, but that is not much comfort is it, but this lot can't last for ever can it. I am looking forward to another trip to Blackpool. Well I have not much time as usual, so I will close, trusting this finds you well, with best wishes. Keep smiling.

I remain
Your Old Pal
Jack"

An undated letter to his Mother describes the conditions in the trenches in the winter. I think it will have been written at the end of November 1915, as in the letter he writes of a Scunthorpe lad called Foster, *"killed last Monday".* Walter Henry Foster from Scunthorpe, a member of the 8th Battalion of the Lincolnshire Regiment, was killed in action on the 23rd of November 1915. He also writes of leave to come, but it was a whole year before he was given his one and only period of leave, in December 1916. This is an extract from the letter,

*************** "we are going away for a months rest, and we are going to start leave. I hope it is right, but I think it is too good to be true. Well we are still having it bitterly cold and wet, plenty of rain and hailstones, but no snow, which I think you have had. The Germans have sent more shells than usual these last few days, dropping several right in the trench held by one of our companies, several men being killed and wounded. We have not had one casualty this last week in our company. We were very lucky last Wednesday*

51

though, a whiz bang caught our trench and smashed it down, sending sand bags flying high, broke my mates rifle to bits and burying mine and another mates. We had been sat talking just where the shell came and had just got up about 6 yards away when the shell came, so I think we were very lucky.

"One Scunthorpe man, one of Dawny Fosters sons, who was drafted to us about three weeks ago, was killed last Monday, being shot through the head by a sniper. It is a life to lead is this, we have something to put up with. I have been called some fancy names today, I can't do anything right. Four of us messes together, I went this morning to draw our tea and sugar for the day and upset it all among the mud, so we have had mud tea today. To make matters better I did another nice trick, we had got a nice little fire and had got the water boiling for tea, when I caught my foot against the fire, upset the water and put the fire out. Oh dear I shall never hear the end of it.

*"Well, I think this is all this time. I want to get 2 or 3 hours sleep before midnight when it is our turn for guard. Just remember me to Aunt Rachel and family *********

I remain
Your loving son
Jack"

Jack did get his leave, and Mr. G. Taylor, headteacher at the Crosby School records the following in the School Logbook on the 20th of December 1916,

*"**Jack Rimmington, Wm Langton** & Frank Standish visited the school at 3 o'clock. The boys gave them a grand reception. **Wm Langton** is still suffering from wounds received in the Somme battle. **Jack Rimmington,** who had never had a leave for 19 months, told the school boys that their parcels & magazines were greatly appreciated by the Old Boys at the front. This Xmas time we have sent 27 parcels to our Old Boys."*

Before detailing the events leading up to Jack's death, during the Battle of Arras, it is important to note that Jack went over the top on the 1st of July 1916 at the start of the bloody Battle of the Somme. A friend, E. Blanchard, writing to **Lucy**

after Jack's death, recalls the event and his feelings at the later loss of his friend, ***** *"It is nearly a year since we went over the top together (come July 1st) and Jack had that miraculous escape, and although in pain he carried on until we were relieved. Truly a lad full of grit. Why should such a blow be dealt to us all when thousands of others, not a patch on him, are time after time spared. We know this, it had to be done as it was the Good God's will and I satisfy myself on one point, that if there is a heaven, Jack is in it."*

When Jack and his comrades in the 8th Battalion of the Lincolnshire Regiment went over the top on that Saturday,1st July 1916, at the start of the Battle of the Somme, the temperature was 72° F, and there was a clear blue sky, according to Chris McCarthy in his book *"The Somme – The Day-by-Day Account."*

"At 8-40 a.m., 10th York and Lancasters & the 8th Lincolns went forward in support. Both suffered from the machine gun in Fricourt. On the left, the Lincolns supported the Somerset Light Infantry, and led by bombers, cleared Lozenge Alley as far as the sunken road.

"By night-fall on the first of July 1916, the British had managed to advance about one mile on a sector three and a half miles wide. The modest first day gains cost the British 19,240 killed and 39,493 wounded."

On the 18th November, the day before the **Battle of the Somme** petered out, Jack's battalion was involved in the part of the Somme Battle which is called **The Battle of the Ancre**, named after the River Ancre.

"Saturday, 18th November, temperature 54° F & 8mm of rain. By dawn the 8th Lincolns had posts in Muck Trench ready to support the 32nd Division."

Bad weather brought the battle to a halt, the Official History, with rare candour, describes the appalling conditions.

"Here, in a wilderness of mud, holding water-logged trenches or shell-hole post, accessible only by night, the infantry abode in conditions which might be likened to those of earthworms

rather than of human kind. Our vocabulary is not adapted to describe such an existence, because it is outside experience for which words are normally required. Mud, for the men in line, was no mere inorganic nuisance and obstacle. It took on an aggressive, wolf-like guise, and like a wolf could pull down and swallow the lonely wanderer in the darkness."

From 1st July to 19th November 1916, the British and French managed to wrest a strip of territory approximately 20 miles wide by some 6 miles deep. This cost the British 419,654 casualties, the French 204,253, while estimates of German casualties range from 437,000 to 680,000.

Jack had his miraculous escape when a bullet grazed his chest on the 1st July 1916 at the Somme, but another bullet killed him on the 28th April 1917 at Arras.

Jack's last communication home was a Field Service Post Card, a standard issue card that was sent from the trenches. He had deleted all the set messages except for –
"I am quite well" and "Letter follows at first opportunity" – signed "Jack" and dated 22nd April 1917. Six days later, on the 28th April 1917 Jack was dead.

What record is there of the action in which Jack died? If we turn to 'The History of the Lincolnshire Regiment (1914-1918)', edited by Major–General C. R. Simpson, this is what we know, remembering Jack was in the 8th Lincolnshire Battalion which was part of the 63rd Brigade which was in turn part of the 37th Division,

"The 37th Division, on the left of the 34th, tried to carry Greenland Hill, and but for the loss of direction in the centre, might have done so. All three brigades attacked in line, i.e. 112th on the right, 63rd in the centre, and 111th on the left. Of the 63rd Brigade, the 8th Somerset were to attack on the right and 8th Lincolnshire on the left. The assembly trench for both battalions was Cobra Trench, and the first objective the German trench Cuthbert immediately east. Zero hour was 4.25 a.m."

(The remaining information relates to just the 8th Lincolnshire Battalion),

"The battalion diary for the 8th Lincolnshire for the 28th April 1917 contains no narrative of the operations, simply: "Battalion in attack. Left of brigade front" and then the casualties.

"The advance began punctually at zero hour, but owing to the darkness and smoke from the barrage, which completely enveloped the troops, direction was lost. Instead of attacking Cuthbert Trench, the troops must have turned north and north east, for the trenches they attacked were Whip and Wish.

"Gradually those who had advanced west of Cuthbert Trench returned as they were unsupported, and by nightfall the brigade was back in its original line.

"Four officers missing and one wounded, twenty-two other ranks killed, one hundred and sixty four wounded and one hundred and five missing were the casualties suffered by the 8th Lincolnshire in this attack."

Today, adjacent to Greenland Hill and cutting right across the Cuthbert Trench, in the area where Jack fought and was killed, is a motorway interchange, where the A1 and the A26 intersect south of Gavrelle. The T.G.V. high-speed train line, T.G.V. Nord, runs parallel to the A1.

Jack is buried in the **Chili Trench Cemetery**, which is sited in the commune (parish) of **Gavrelle.** It gets its name from a communication trench, Chili Avenue, that ran west to east just north of the cemetery. It contains 196 graves, 17 are unknown, 86 are represented by a special memorial, Jack's grave is number 13 on row E. The cemetery was started by the 37th Division (which includes Jack's 8th Lincolnshire Battalion) and their graves dominate the cemetery. Unusually all the original graves only span a few weeks of April and May 1917. The casualties end when the Battle of Arras ends (mid May). This is a battlefield cemetery and not a concentration cemetery.

What more do we know of Jack's last day? The following obituary in the Hull Times fills a few poignant gaps,

"The sad news of the death in action of Pte. J. W. Rimmington, eldest son of Mr. and Mrs. F. B.

Rimmington, 91 Grosvenor Street, Crosby, was received last week. As a lad he worked in the butchery department of the Scunthorpe Co-operative Society, but was in the boiler shop at Frodingham when he enlisted on September 4th, 1914. He went to France toward the end of 1915, just in time to celebrate his 21st birthday on French soil. He fought at Loos, in the big push July 1916 on the Somme, the Ancre, and was killed in the battle of Arras on the 28th ult. In a letter to Mrs. Rimmington, a Grimsby lad named Blanchard writes:-"The boys had done well, but there was a hot corner in the open. The only bit of cover available was shell holes, into which 'Johnny' and a pal got. Snipers were everywhere, and my dear old chum met an instantaneous death through a bullet hitting him in the cheek and glancing up to the top of his head … He was liked by everyone, was a fine chum, and a splendid soldier. On July 1st last he was grazed on the chest by a bullet, but stuck it out, and remained in the trenches five days … But for him I should once have been killed, for he bayoneted a German who had me down." Pte. Rimmington was home last Christmas on a ten day's leave. He was a member of the Scunthorpe Social Club."

In the Crosby School Logbook for the 7th May 1917, Mr. G. Taylor, the headteacher wrote,

*"I learned this morning that another of our "Old Boys", **Jack Rimmington**, has been killed in France. He was shot by a sniper whilst attacking the Hindenberg Line. This is the fourth of our Old Boys who have died valiantly fighting. They were amongst the earliest to go out, true volunteers."*

Jack's family, though devastated by his death, was proud of him. Our family has had a long association with Crosby and Scunthorpe, and some of us are still part of the community of North Lincolnshire.

Jack's father, my grandfather, **Frederick Butcher Rimmington,** originally a farm labourer and later an ironstone miner, was a well-respected member of the local community. Here is a pen picture of him published in *"The Wheatsheaf"* in April 1932, the Scunthorpe Co-operative Society's monthly periodical,
"An enviable record! Forty years' unbroken membership of our society – sixteen years'

continuous service as a member of the society's committee of management, during the last ten of which he has creditably filled the vice-chairman's position. Surely, credentials sufficient to ensure his inclusion in our monthly portrait gallery.

Frederick Butcher Rimmington, Jack's father.

"A citizen well worthy of the name, he has devoted the bulk of his leisure time to the interests of his fellow men, and has continuously been actively associated with the public life of the district since the introduction of the Parish Council Act. He was for many years a member of the Crosby parish council, and was in 1912 elected chairman, a position he held for six successive years. Since the amalgamation of the four parish councils into the urban district of Scunthorpe and Frodingham, our subject has many years to his credit as a councillor. But this is not all. Mr. Rimmington has been a member of the local education authority for the past 24 years. Is it to be wondered at that in April 1918, he received the well deserved honour of being appointed a justice of the peace? Verily an enviable record. Much as we appreciate Mr. Rimmington's public services, it is the man himself who makes the greater appeal to those who know him intimately. Judged from the standpoint of character F. B. Rimmington is an aristocrat. Though a man of few words, those few are weighty. Not quick to make a decision, his judgement is to be relied upon when he has

sifted all the facts. Any member or any employee of the society can confidently leave their case in his hands, always assured of justice. But whilst his judgement is tempered with mercy, his ruling and advice must be taken full notice of. He means what he says.

Fred Rimmington we raise our hats to you."

Jack's mother, **Mary Jane**, my grandmother, was as I remember her, a kindly woman, small in stature, but full of obvious pride in the children she and her husband had raised.

What of those eight brothers and sisters?

Harriet married David Monteith, who after the war worked at Lysaghts Steel works as a smelter. They had three children.

Fred Rimmington trained as a car mechanic and worked for a while for Laynes at Brigg. But either an accident or an illness caused him to be paralysed down one side of his body and I remember him keeping lots of chickens on an allotment off Normanby Road.

Two sisters and a brother were teachers, teaching for many years in local schools. **Lucy Rimmington** taught at the Doncaster Road Girls' School; **Eric Rimmington** at Doncaster Road Boys' School, and **Florrie (Tot) Rimmington** at Ashby Girls' School.

Vincent Rimmington, Jack's youngest brother worked for Scunthorpe Borough Council for many years, and like his father was involved with the Co-operative movement.

May Rimmington, Jack's youngest sister spent many years looking after her parents and the extended family who still lived at home. In her younger days she was a keen hockey player.

My father, **George Rimmington,** was a Scunthorpe Borough Councillor from its Charter year in 1936 until the Second World War, when he went away to serve in the Navy as did brother **Vincent. George** worked on the railways all his life, clerk at Scunthorpe, stationmaster at Grimoldby, Misterton, Kiveton Park, Althorpe and Penistone. Finally he was Yardmaster and area manager at Wath upon Dearne.

Three of Jack's brother, (L to R) George, Vincent and Fred. Early 1930's.

Teaching must run in the Rimmington veins as I taught in a number of local schools for 20 years before spending 16 years as headteacher of a Cleethorpes school.

My two daughters are both teachers, **Rachel** in London and **Alison** in Lincolnshire. **Alison Rimmington** might be better known to many locally through her fine soprano voice.

Finally, I recall one other key relative, Jack's cousin **George William Rimmington** (known as **Billy**), who came from Somerby, near Brigg, who also perished in that dreadful war. Although in the Royal Garrison Artillery, Billy was stationed very close to Jack and they met each other regularly. Billy managed to survive until the 1st September 1918, aged 21. He is buried at the **Bac-Du-Sud Cemetery** at **Bailleuval,** only 15 miles away from Jack. When Jack was killed, Billy wrote to Jack's Mother, his Auntie,

"May 8th 1917.
My Dear Aunt,

Just a line or two to let you know that I am in the best of health and hope you are keeping pretty well. Am sending two of Jack's letters home that I received a day or two ago, but did not send them as I thought I should be

hearing from you. The letter had been partly opened but the handkerchiefs were alright, I wanted one, so I am keeping them hope you don't mind. There's a letter from Eric as well. There was a letter from Dave last night with a photo in for Jack, so I wrote a letter to him and sent them back this morning. Poor old Dave, he will be shocked when he hears.

"But cheer up Aunt, you will miss him I know. I miss him a lot myself and if I live to come home it will be jolly hard to come back without him. I miss him most when I group for my pay, we used to always wait for both our names to be called out together, I used to follow him up. The other day I waited for him to be called out but he called mine instead.

"I sent a piece of newspaper home to mother, get her to show it to you, Jack was in it. Will send anything home that comes for him. I expect you will be hearing from the chaplain, he said he was going to write. Hope there'll be a letter before long, am longing to hear from you. Think that's all this time so will close with love to all at home.
"Your loving nephew
Billy. Cheer–up."

**Jack's cousin "Billy" -
George William Rimmington.**

In April 2004, I visited France and spent time at Jack's cemetery on the 28th April, 87 years after he was killed. I also visited Billy's cemetery. The accompanying three photographs show the gravestones of Jack and Billy, together with one showing me next to Jack's grave.

Billy was wounded three days before he died on 1st September 1918. He was an artillery-signaller, this involved a variety of duties. He could have been near or on the front line, relaying messages back to the battery. He may have been laying telephone wire or repairing breaks in the wire, each task having its share of danger. **Gunner 104086, George William Rimmington** was wounded on Thursday 29th August 1918 and subsequently died of his wounds at a casualty clearing station near or at **Bailleval** on Sunday 1st September 1918.

The young men of Crosby went to fight for king and country. Many returned whole, others wounded and for those who didn't return the angel is a reminder of their supreme sacrifice.

I am proud of Jack, the Jack I have discovered through researching his short life. He was a kindly cheerful soul, clumsy at times, but prepared to face the dangers of war bravely, both with and for his comrades.

Billy's grave at Bac-Du-Sud Cemetery.

Jack's grave in Chili Trench Cemetery.

This is me, the nephew, standing next to Uncle Jack's grave in the **Chili Trench Cemetery**, exactly 87 years later, to the day, when he was killed. The saddest thought I had, was that nearly all of the 196 buried in the cemetery, were in their twenties, a few younger and a few older.

Jack and Billy were cousins who lived about fifteen miles apart in Lincolnshire, Jack in Crosby and Billy at Somerby, near Brigg. In death, they are buried about fifteen miles apart in Picardy, Jack to the east and Billy to the west of Arras.

When I read one of Siegfried Sassoon's many war poems, a very short poem, entitled *"The General"*, I like to think he was writing about 'UNCLE JACK'. It was written in April 1917 about the battle at Arras:

*The General
"Good morning; good morning!" the General said
When we met him last week on our way to the line.
Now the soldiers he smiled at are most of 'em dead,
And we're cursing his staff for incompetent swine.
"He's a cheery old card," grunted Harry to Jack
As they slogged up to Arras with rifle and pack.
But he did for them both by his plan of attack.

* Copyright Siegfried Sassoon by kind permission of the Estate of George Sassoon.
Quote from *"Somme - The Day by Day Account"* by kind permission of the Author, Chris McCarthy.

John Robinson's sister Margaret (Meg) with Colin, the husband of her great niece, Christine Baxter. Meg was 85 when she visited John's grave. She died aged 94.

returned and took up residence at 23 Burke Street, Crosby.

John had a younger brother **Harold,** born in 1905, who also attended Crosby School. Harold would have helped to collect towards the comfort parcels sent by the school to each Old Boy who had gone to war.

Prior to his enlistment, John worked in the Mines Department of John Lysaght's Normanby Park Works. It is not known when John Robinson enlisted, or where, but at the beginning of 1918 he was serving with the 1/5th Lincolns in the Cambrian Sector in France. On 9th March 1918 at the age of 20, John Robinson died from wounds possibly received at the Bethune front.

He is buried at the **Chocques Military Cemetery, Pas de Calais, France.**

From **Mr. Taylor's School Logbook 14th March 1918,** *"I learned today that another of our old boys had made the supreme sacrifice in France, **John Robinson** of Burke Street. I do not yet know any of the circumstances of his death. His mother is dying of consumption and cannot be informed of the sad news."*

John Robinson

Private 241254
1/5th Battalion, Lincolnshire Regiment (also No. 4360)
Died: Saturday 9th March 1918
Died of Wounds

John Robinson was born on 14th October 1897, fourth child of an Irish father and Scottish Mother, **John** and **Margaret Robinson,** of 8 Grosvenor Street, Scunthorpe. His education began at the Scunthorpe National School (Gurnell Street) but he was transferred to the brand new Crosby school on 1st June 1908, where he studied until October 1910 when he left *"over age."* The whole family left the district in 1913, but later

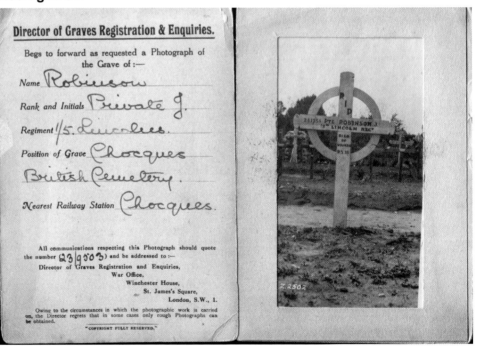

Advice sent to John's next of kin of his grave location, and a photograph of its original headstone before the Commonwealth War Graves Commission standardised headstones.

John Robinson is listed as a serving soldier on the **John Lysaght's Normanby Park Works 1914 Roll of Honour**, on **Scunthorpe Museum's outside wall** near the **Town War Memorial, the Lysaght's Memorial at Foxhills Club** and on **St. Lawrence's Church Memorial, Frodingham.**

Inscription: "J. Robinson 15 Platoon" - Hull Times 18th September 1915 : Pte. John Robinson won the snooker league championship. Was this the Award?

Information from:
Mrs. Pat Chennells (great niece)

Wilfred Short
Private 60484 (formerly 19142)
10th Battalion West Yorkshire Regiment
(Prince of Wales Own)
Died: Friday 20th September 1918 Killed in Action

Son of **John Walker Short** and his wife **Mary**, Wilfred was born on 9th April 1899 in Crosby and Baptised at St. John's Parish Church, Scunthorpe on 30th April 1899. He had three older sisters, **Lily, Jessie** and **Alice**. When Wilfred was five years old, his sister **Annie** was born in October of 1904. She was to become his greatest confidante and a significant influence to him for the rest of his life. Two more children were born to the family, **Herbert** in 1902 and **Horace** in 1906.

Like most young men of that era, Wilfred came originally from farming stock: many generations of his family had worked the land in various parts of Yorkshire and Lincolnshire. His father, **John Walker Short,** was an agricultural labourer who left the land to seek his fortune in the burgeoning ironstone industry, where he became an ironstone miner, living with his family at 15 Old Crosby, Scunthorpe.

When Wilfred was nine years old, he transferred from the Scunthorpe National School (Gurnell Street) to the brand new Crosby School, purpose built to accommodate the influx of children moving into the area from outlying districts. He must have been an especially bright scholar for it is recorded in Headmaster **Mr.Taylor's Logbook dated 8th April 1911** (the day before Wilfred's twelfth birthday), *"Percy Ibbiter and **Wilfred Short** sat for the Labour Examination at Crowle Council School."* And on April 18th, *"The Correspondent gave me the two Labour Certificates won by Percy Ibbiter and **Wilfred Short**."*

On April 28th 1911, Wilfred left school with an *"exemption certificate."* At the age of 17 years and one month, May 1917, Wilfred enlisted at Scunthorpe with the 10th Battalion West Yorkshire Regiment (Prince of Wales Own) and almost immediately began to write. That Wilfred's family was the very core of his existence is evident in the many affectionate letters that he wrote to his sister Annie to whom he was especially close. He sent Annie the photograph seen at the beginning of this biography and the words she wrote on the back have particular poignancy, *"Xmas 1917 first time out to France. 30th March 1918 wounded in left wrist and thigh. April 1918 In Aberdeen Hospital 18 weeks and then came home on leave and then came on leave again in August. He was*

Gauche Wood Cemetery, Villers-Guislain, Cambrai/ Peronne area, France, where Wilfred is buried.

drafted out to France a second time after only being out of bed about four weeks. Left Folkestone on 2nd September 1918 and was killed on 20th September. Poor kid he didn't last long enough for us to write back to him." (N.B. Wilfred's letters to Annie follow this biography; the originals remain in the care of his niece, Annie's daughter, Sylvia Fenwick (née Newlove) and her brother John Newlove, Wilfred's nephew, who treasure his artefacts.)

Scunthorpe and Frodingham Star 18th October 1918, *"News has been received by Mr. and Mrs. John Short, Old Crosby, that their eldest son, Private Wilfred Short of the West Yorkshire Regiment, was killed in action on September 20th. He was, this year, shot through the right thigh and returned to France six weeks ago. Previous to joining up in May 1917 he was employed at the Normanby Park Steelworks. He was only 19 years of age and much sympathy is felt for the family."*

Killed in Action, Wilfred appears to have died in the heavy fighting to regain the village of Villers-Guislain. He is buried in **Gauche Wood Cemetery, Villers-Guislain, Nord, France.** *"One of the prettiest cemeteries on the whole of the Western Front the remains of the trenches are still very visible in the wood."*

Wilfred's last job was in the Mechanical Department of John Lysaght's Steelworks, Normanby Park, Scunthorpe. He is commemorated on the **Lysaghts Memorial,** on the **Scunthorpe Museum Wall Memorial,** and the **Lysaghts Memorial at Foxhills Club.** He is commemorated on the Crosby Angel Memorial because he was an Old Boy and also because his siblings were pupils at the school. He is listed on the **Scunthorpe 1917 Roll of Honour** as a serving soldier of 3 Gurnell Street, Scunthorpe.

Wilfred's sister, Annie, married Clarence Newlove, and they lived in West Street, Scunthorpe. He became Mayor and Annie was Lady Mayoress of the Borough of Scunthorpe in 1954. They cared passionately for the town. Their daughter says Clarence was a man of great integrity and when the Councillors were first granted allowances and expenses, he resigned after 30 years' service, rather than accept any payment for his services.

Wilfred's sister Annie, as Mayoress of Scunthorpe, with her husband, Clarence Newlove as Mayor of the Borough 1954.

Information from:
Mrs. Sylvia Fenwick (niece)
Mr. John Newlove (nephew)

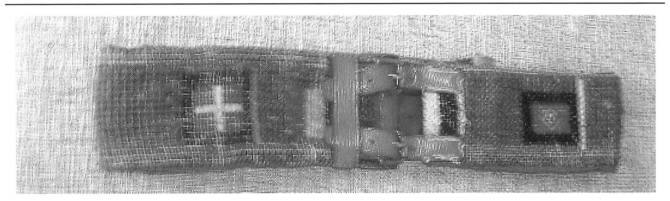

Belt made by Wilfred Short whilst in hospital recovering from wounds received when he first went out to the Front.

Wilfred Short's letters written to his Sister Annie and brother Horace:

Monday Night July 2nd.

Dear Annie just a word in answer to your letter which I received this morning & the 5 stamps. Well I will look out for the parcel which you say is coming & if there is any ham pasties in the same as the last I shall be highly pleased. I can tell you the others went down a treat. Well I am glad you liked the card I will see if I can get Horace a nice one, Well I am glad to hear you are all well as it leaves me, but this last week I cannot get full I always want to be eating. I went into the canteen the other night got sausage & peas 3½d. 5 cakes & a glass lemonade, & although there was a good plate of peas, I felt as empty as ever when I had got them eaten. Just tell Mother I don't think I have ever been down in the mouth over it, I'm as happy as can be, & there are hundreds of lads besides me I've got that consolation, & wherever we get to I shall always do my best sis no matter what it is, so just tell her to keep on smiling. I went down to Hednesford yesterday afternoon Sunday & got my photo took. I stood up beside a stand in about the same position as soldier Bills photo if you remember what that was like. Well they are 3/6 a dozen & they will be ready for next Saturday. I paid 2s. so I shall only have to pay 1/6 when I fetch them. You will have received the letter I wrote on Saturday & the broach *(sic)* I should think by now, & I enclosed Mr. Scotts letter so you will see what he is like. Young Wilf wrote and told me that the sphinx party was going to Empire wishing I could have been home & gone with him. I don't suppose Mother went but she ought to have done its a treat. Glad to hear the chickens are laying well also the pigs are growing. Well Jess Morley has picked a bad name for his kiddie I expect he will have more bounce on than ever now, Well I think this is about all the news this time, with the best love from your Brother   Wilfred x x x x x x

Wednesday Night.

Dear Sister Annie I received your letter this morning & was pleased to hear you are all well as it finds me in the pink. Well I wrote and told Alice last night about that 5ˢ. and I asked her if she was pulling my leg. She wanted to know if I thought the elastic had broke & let her fall from a Xmas tree. I am glad to hear Dad has got to work again & his leg is alright. Just tell him to be careful & not get trapped no more. I expect he will think me a cocky young devil telling him to go careful but you know I've got to put something on the paper. Well Joe has got his papers has he well he will not go by himself & sometimes I think it is all sham about him frightened of going. Still there are some who are frightened of getting there *(sic)* tickets punched & he might be one of them. Well Alice told me in a letter I got from her last night that you had a conversation with soldier Bill. I am glad Mother has altered her opinion of him I always told you when at home that he was a fine little fellow. Will you please send me a little parcel as soon as you get this letter & don't forget to put me a (dozen hooks and eyes) for my tunic then I can sew them on. I have kept looking for some in these places down here but I have not seen any & if I wait much longer I shall have my leave before I get them & I want to come to Scunthorpe smart as I can so don't forget. I shall look for the parcel about Sunday night. Should you have posted one when you receive this make a packet of the hooks & eyes & send them along. Well I received a few lines from Charlie Hill this morning asking me how I was getting on. His people wanted him to remember

THE CROSBY ANGEL - A COMMUNITY'S WAR MEMORIAL

China Cooking Range ornament with Kettle with motto: *"Keep the Home Fires Burning - Till the Boys Come Home"* - a gift from Wilfred, sent whilst in Staffordshire.

them to me & that if I had a photo to spare would I let him have one. He said him and Bob often thought how I liked soldiering when they were talking together but he says never mind I have something to be proud off as I was the last(?) out of the village. When I have finished this letter I shall have to write him & tell him he will have to wait a bit for a photo. I am sorry to hear the hens (have slacked of) laying perhaps it is the wet weather. Well I think I have about told you all the news this time with love from your brother Wilfred.

x x x x

Monday Afternoon Aug 6th 1917
Dear Annie I received your welcome letter this morning & was pleased to hear from you. Well we have all been grumbling this morning thinking we had to go on parade this afternoon. We had got our harness on & was ready when they yelled no Parade so we are having a half day off. There are some sports on Thursday & we shall have the afternoon off so we shall not do bad this week. Well I will look out for the parcel & don't you

forget. I feel liking eating a bit of nice cake again. So Joe has got up in the north has he well he will be alright he has nothing to worry about. They will be a bit different twang for him up there just the same as there is down here. He will be a smart little chap when you see him again just take my tip. I am sorry to hear about Herbert's little kiddie its hard lines & bye *(sic)* the way, how is he going on I have never heard much about him since I left home. Madge has got to say Dad has she I'll bet she's a fine kid and that Gladys is too. also sorry to hear Horace is off his grub I hope by the time you receive this that he is himself again. Glad to hear you have got your holidays I hope it will keep fine weather for them it has done nothing but rain down here of & on for the past week. Glad to hear the hens keep laying I should think you are getting a couple of fine pigs by now. They used to shift some grub when I was at home so I don't know what they will want now. Well I am not going to talk about getting home no more I am damn sick of hearing the yarns as I have this last 3 weeks. They say some are going on Saturday but as I tell you, you cannot believe anything you hear. How to stop him and Alice going on about the same I hope. Well I think I have about told you all the news this time hoping you are all well as it leaves me in the pink I remain your loving brother

Wilfred x x x x x x
If I get the parcel tomorrow do not write in answer to this until you get a reply to the parcel & then the two can come in one. I have not heard from any of the lads for the past fortnight I think I shall have to liven them up a bit. when I see them which I hope for the lords sake will not be long as I have been more restless this last fortnight talking about getting leave than any other time. Just remember me to Grandmother & all the rest of them not forgetting Mother.

Tuesday Aug 14th 1917
Dear Sister Annie I received your welcome letter this morning & was pleased to hear you are all well as it found me in the pink. Glad to hear you are getting another parcel ready. I have got the other one eaten except a bit of cake. I had the tin of pineapple for last Sat's tea it went down a treat. In fact I like it better than salmon. Well do you know whether Stephen has got the letter I sent him telling him to keep out of the army if there was a possible chance. I told him that if he was offended he need not be afraid to let me know, as it came into my mind in a minute & I wrote right away . Well I cannot say when we shall get home, I think we are going to be transferred this week, so I will let you know whether I shall have to go. Do not send anything of value till you hear from me, then if we move & I do not get it, it will

62

be alright. I don't think we are going out of the camp, I think we shall go into another battalion. Well we have had some rotten weather down here for the past fortnight, in fact it is raining and thundering now. I shall have to see if I can send Gladys a bit of something. Pleased to hear Jessie and Madge are all right. Well I think I have about told you all the news this time hoping to hear from you soon I remain your loving Brother Wilfred, with a kiss for Mother. x x x x x x

Dear Horace I am pleased to hear you are getting a bit better, & that I am enjoying myself as much as is possible down in this wilderness of huts. What are you doing with an absess (*sic*) in your mouth, it is not tooth ache is it. I'll bet it is rotten, both for eating & everything else, but I hope by the time you read this it will have done a flit. Glad to hear the hens are laying well, I have just a picture in my mind as I write this, of our garden & the old chicken hut, & mother & us all looking at them. Well I shall be pleased when I can spend a few moments in the garden again, I don't think it will be long now. Sorry to hear Mr. Rat has evaded that trap of yours, but keep on he will find it some night. Well I don't think there's any more to say hoping to see you soon with best love & a kiss from your loving x x x x x x Brother Wilfred

Wilfred's "dog tag" - identity disk worn round his neck at the Front - this would be returned to his parents with his other belongings when his body was recovered.

ps. Excuse scribble it has gone 8 o'clock & I want to clean my belt, ready for Church Parade, in morning also to have a few minutes in canteen before ½ past nine so I wish you Good Night.
I shall be pleased when I can have a night in that bed of yours and get off these hard boards.

Saturday Night, Aug 19th.
Dear Annie I have just received your welcome letter & I am pleased to hear you are all well, as it found me in the pink. Well please tell Dad, that he can rest assured, that when I get home, I shall not go on the top of Dicky's hill & start drilling, as I can get plenty of that down here at Rugely. Still I am glad to hear he is alright & that I hope he sleeps well. For the first 3 weeks I was down here, I heard the bugle every morning at 6 o'clock., but to tell you the truth I have not heard it a dozen times since. I believe if they would not chuck us out of bed, I could stay till dinner time. So Joe is going to beat me in getting home the first is he, well I wish him luck, but I don't think we shall be long. We are finishing our firing this next week, commencing Monday morning & then we shall not be long. Well I had a letter from R. Morley. He told me that George Hill is in hospital at Leeds severely wounded, so I hope he will go on all right. He said that he had been talking to Charles Hill, & C had said he had started to write 2 letters to me, but he could not finish them. Sorry to hear you got wet coming from Alkboro, I expect you ought to be well pleased if it kept fine all the fore part of the day. It has not been fine 2 days together down here this last fortnight. Well we have been shifted about this last week. Several of the lads have been moved into other battalions, but me and another lad has been shifted 4 huts lower down the row so if you write to the underneath address it will be alright. The others I shall have to tell as I hear from them. I have only got to slip up and see if there are any letters come for me, to no 6 Hut. Well I think I have about told you all the news this time, so will conclude now with the best love from your affectionate Brother   Wilfred.
No 19142 Pte. W. Short,
No 1 Platoon,
A Coy, No 2. Hut
5th J. R. Battn. Rugely Camp
Cannock Chase
Staffordshire.

This letter was written by Wilfred to his Father:

Thursday May 9th (1918)

Dear old Dad

You cannot tell how pleased I was to see your old handwriting again this dinner. Glad to hear you are all in the pink as it found me. Leg is going on nicely but I'll not be able to leave my bed yet awhile. It's a year yesterday since I left you only 9th is Thurs this year. It's been a long 12 months since but I hope I'm home before the next passes. Well Dad I've have (sic) been saving a little present for you ever since I left Poo-jee (sic) land. You will see on the lid who presented them to us. We all got one as soon as we had been made comfortable aboard. There was this pipe & tobacco 4 packets of Woodbines. I used the cigs but I made my mind up that I'd send the rest to you. I think it a nice pipe & I know you will enjoy it. It will be the same way I expect. Oh I'll launch this on Sun. Well Dad I thought I would not tell any of you when at home that I was booked for across, but it's alright. It was a lovely ride that afternoon across the channel. Two great transports of us & all the beautiful but deadly looking destroyers each side of the two boats. It was very choppy when we got well out & you would have laughed if you had seen the chaps running to the side to be sick. I was not sick myself but I had an empty feeling bottom of my stomach I tell you. I watch (sic) the cliffs of England until they faded from view then I said to myself (you have done it now) when shall you see them again. Of course that question had to go unanswered for the present. We were 2 hours going across & when we came in sight of Bologne (sic) it was a fine sight. Seems to be standing on an hill & all the big, prominent buildings looked great. It was about 1/4 past 3 when we planted our feet on French soil. We walked off the boat into the town where we were formed up & marched to a resting place built for troops. The women & kiddies came running up to us selling chocolate & I asked how much a bar & she said (seespence sir) I believe I spelt that as much like as it was said, at any rate I offered her ½d. then 2 & then 3 pennies but no not having any. When we had had our tea & an hour's rest we were marched to a station where we were put in cattle trucks & told not to leave them. After about 1½ hrs wait we commenced our lovely ride jog, jog, jog, talk about getting on your nerves I had heard a lot about those trains but I did not think they were that slow. One thing was it gave us a good chance to look at the surrounding country through which we were passing. It was a treat & we jumbled along until 10 o'clock when we came to a town on a kind of big hill. We were on the outskirts of it though we afterwards learned. Then we were marched or I should say followed the crowd to a small camp of tents. This was a place called Etapes. (sic Etaples?) That was Mon night of course. Here we were put in tents small bell tents you know 14 in each & got our packs off. Then damn my eyes if they did not fall us in & and have a roll call by the aid of a stable lamp, & didn't we say something. We then went back to our tents & I can tell you we were full up. Blankets we had none nor ground sheets to lay on so we lay down on the wet sand. Twice that night I was up to stretch my cramped limbs & all the lads were laid there, some awake and our teeth chattering in our heads. Next night we managed to get a blanket (a bit better) & we stayed there until Thursday morning when we packed up, got 170 rounds ammunition and an iron rashing (sic ration?) & set off again to station. Cattle trucks again & we set off. I remember a lot of places we passed through but too many to put down. Suffice it to say we pulled up about 3 in afternoon. We were formed up each party for its own Batts. We then were within sound of

Dedication to Wilfred after his death in his sister Annie's own handwriting.

the guns, & I believe our hearts beat a little faster as we realised what we were going to and getting very near 'em too. We set off then & marched about 5 miles to where the remains of 7th N Y were and which were in a village called Vauchelles. As I have said before when we got there we had a biscuit soup supper, & what muck too. We were told that we were going into the line Sun. night straightways, & we asked if we could write letters home & they said yes, but when we got 'em wrote on Friday, we were told no letters were going & we were going in the line Sat instead Sun. That put damper on us I tell you. Sat afternoon came & we set off about 4 o'clock. Walked about 4 miles then we got into motor lorries. Then we had a ride & I should guess it to be 9 o'clock when we pulled up. Then we opened our eyes for all along the battle front as far as we could see was continuously blood red flashes of bursting shells, varie lights & a hundred other things. We set off walking again pitch black save for these flashes, & we kept on, & it was raining torrents, no coats, so you see our position was extremely nice & to be envied by lunatics only. It seemed a never ending road but at last we came to

Next of Kin Disk, known as "Dead Man's Penny" as it was sent to the relatives when the soldier was killed.

all that remained of a village. When we had passed through we came across the first signs of the war zone. The road began to be full of shell holes with plenty of water kicking about. Still we kept stumbling on blindly cursing when we dropped into a shell hole full of water. At last it grew so bad we got into single file & you passed the word, back, every two yards, mind shell hole, mind timber across road, & so on. The road led through what had been a large wood, only stumps standing remainder torn and twisted into fantastical shapes such as only a continuous bombardment can do. Here was a battery of our own guns barking fit to burst your ears, & here it was that we came under shell fire for the first time. Jerry sent them over fast as rain & shrapnel was bursting above our heads & you could hear the large pieces of metal, buzzing and flying like so many great bees. At last we stopped in some reserve trenches about 1½ miles from front line. I should say it was midnight now or perhaps later & we bundled into a trench with a foot of mud in. I managed to get with 2 more of our lads in a hole about 2ft. (*sic feet*) 6 (*sic inches*) squre (*sic square?*) scrudged up we were, & rain running out of our sleeve ends. At any rate we was out of the rain & I had a smoke good as a meal. I kept dropping off to sleep and waking when a shell burst near. One fell into the trench & buried 4 chaps & everything they had, & poor devils had to be dug out nearly suffocated. At last dawn broke with a watery sun peeping out & it looked down mercilessly on as tired and mud stained lads as ever you saw. It was Sun morning & at about 6 we had our fill of cold tea & rations. At about 8 officer came round with the rum first rum ration I had, I'll always remember it. It is rum mind, black firiery (*sic*) stuff burns you, but after being wet through & starved with cold we rejoiced at that. I don't think you would want much of it to stop you walking far. We stopped in there all Sun & Jerry kept sending 'em over just to let us know he was alive & kicking, managed to pepper 3 of us with dirt pebbles etc. On Sun night we fell in to go up to the front line to relieve. Now Dad I've told you all up to then & I'll not put the rest on paper. I hope you like the present & that this letter finds you all at Crosby in the pink. I don't think I've mentioned Mother in here, but here is my best love and kiss to her & the kiddies & the letter is yours Dad. More I'll say when I see you. No need to worry no bones fractured in leg, although it will be a bit stiff when I first get going. Just let 'em all read it & Alice closing now with best love to all I remain your ever loving Son

xxxxxxx Wilf

PS Write back & let us know what you think about letter, I've read it through & I think I've made it a bit romantic. I could go on & fill a book but I've been a good hour scribbling now. Well so long & keep smiling, hope you are having decent weather & Xby (*sic Crosby?*). Fine up here but I think we shall have a drop of rain before long. I'll perhaps dig you a few potatoes when I come again & help to eat 'em so Good Byee, hoping garden turns out well.

Chapter Four

The Fifty

The Men whose families or relatives attended Crosby School
and those who lived in the Parish of Crosby

Biographies written by Mrs. Jill Molnar
Research: Ms. Susie Broadbent
Miss Patricia Smith and Mrs. Margaret Stokes

THE CROSBY ANGEL - A COMMUNITY'S WAR MEMORIAL

Believed to be Horace Birkett taken in 1915 with the 1/5th Lincolns.

Horace Birkett

Private 18793
7th Battalion Lincolnshire Regiment
Died: Monday 3rd July 1916 Died of Wounds

Born at Brigg, Lincolnshire in 1891, Horace Birkett was the fourth son of general labourer **Robert Birkett** and his wife **Charlotte.** His elder siblings were **John** (born 1883), **Robert Henry** (born 1884), **Frances Hallsey** (a sister, born 1885) and **Albert** (born 1887). The Birkett family appear to have lived for generations in the North Owersby/South Kelsey area of Lincolnshire, employed as agricultural workers. His grandfather, **John Birkett**, was a shepherd.

Wages were low in rural areas, especially for men without a trade, but Scunthorpe had become a boom town offering better jobs and higher wages. Along with many other families in their situation, the Birketts moved into town. It is recorded that in 1901 they were living at 7 Trafford Street, Scunthorpe.

Ten year old Horace now had a sister, **Veda** (born 1895), and two younger brothers, **Percy William** (born 1897), and **Clarence** (born 1901). His eldest brother, **John**, worked in the steel industry with their father **Robert.** In due course Horace followed them into heavy industry and became an engine cleaner at the North Lincoln Ironworks.

On 23rd March 1914, his brother, **Donald Leslie** (born 1909), was admitted to Crosby school. The Birkett family had taken up residence at 10 Buckingham Street, Scunthorpe.

Horace's career was cut short when he enlisted in the town in August 1915. His time as a serving soldier was to prove equally brief. After six months' combat training he sailed to France with his unit, the 7th Battalion Lincolnshire Regiment.

It was January 1916. The 7th Lincolns were in the 17th Division. On July 3rd 1916 near Fricourt Wood, they advanced at 0900 hours and came under heavy machine gun fire against a Prussian Infantry Regiment, consisting of hundreds of personnel, who eventually surrendered. About 900 German prisoners (including their Colonel) were taken. This attack was known as *"the great push".*

Early in the afternoon Railway Copse was captured by the British. The 7th Lincolns had suffered heavy casualties, the Battalion losing three officers and 30 other ranks killed. Six officers and about 160 other ranks were missing or wounded. Among these was Horace Birkett, shot in the abdomen on the third day of the infamous **Battle of the Somme.**

He was buried the same day in the **Mericourt-l'Abbay Military Cemetery, France.**

Mericourt-Ribermont Station was a railhead used chiefly by field ambulances. Horace possibly died there before he could be taken to a Military Hospital. He was 24 years old. His parents, then living at 62 Mulgrave Street, Scunthorpe, were duly informed. His death was also reported in **The Hull Daily Mail.**

Horace is commemorated on the Crosby Angel Memorial because he had lived in Crosby and his younger brother, **Donald Leslie**, and nephews and nieces (children of his elder brother **John)** all attended the school. His brother, **Robert Henry Birkett,** also served in the Great War but fortunately survived, and it is possibly his name that is inscribed on the North Lincoln Ironworks Memorial Plaque as "R.H. Birkett".

Information from:
Mr. Alan Birkett (great nephew)
Mr. Sean Scholfield researcher Lincolnshire Regiment.

Lincolnshire Regimental Insignia - a Sphinx, recalling the Egyptian Campaign of 1801 during the French Napoleonic Wars 1793-1815.

James Boothby

Private 2201 "C" Company
1/5th Battalion Lincolnshire Regiment
Died: Wednesday 3rd November 1915 Died of Wounds

Named after his father, James Boothby, born in 1887, was the eighth child of **James Boothby** and his wife **Mary Ann,** who were both described as farm labourers on the 1881 census, living at Leasingham, Lincolnshire. His Service record reveals that his sister, **Sarah Jane**, and her husband John Dodson moved from there to live at 47 Grosvenor Street, Crosby some time after the 1901 census. James came to live with them there, and worked in the Smelting Department of John Lysaght's Steelworks.

He enlisted at Scunthorpe on 1st September 1914, with the 1/5th Lincolns, a Territorial Battalion, the Regiment with whom he had already served 4 years as a Volunteer - "time expired". As their service numbers were close together, it is possible that **Norman Budworth, Ernest Hornsby, Albert Edward Ward, Arthur**

Newstead, Daniel Cunningham and **Richard Henry Davison,** all enlisted at the same time. He went to France on 1st March 1915. His Medal Roll lists his entitlement to the 1915 Star, British War Medal and the Victory Medal..

His Service Record states that he was 5 feet 2 inches tall, weighed 126 lbs. and that his total service was one year and six days at the time of his death.

He was reported missing on 13th October, 1915, the first day of the **Battle of Loos (Hohenzollern Redoubt)**, and was on the German List of Prisoners of War released to the British Authorities through the American Embassy on 23rd June 1916. While a Prisoner of War, he had died of his wounds at Guardecourt, France on or before the 3rd November 1915. He was 27 years old and was buried in the **Rue Petillon Military Cemetery, Fleurbaix, Pas de Calais, France**.

It is believed that James survived three weeks longer than most of his contemporaries; the last man of the group to die was **Richard Henry Davison,** seventeen days later.

He is commemorated on the Angel because he lived in Crosby, and three of his sister's children, Gladys, Phyllis and John, attended Crosby School.

Rue Petillon Military Cemetery, Fleurbaix, Pas de Calais, France where James Boothby is buried.

Thomas William Bowden

Private 205724
(formerly 21248 Lincolnshire Regiment)
R.E.C. Depot Battalion Machine Gun Corps (Heavy Branch)
Died: Friday 2ⁿᵈ February 1917 Died of illness sustained in the Trenches at the War Front

Thomas William Bowden, second son of Cornish baker George Bowden and his wife Annie, was born in Leeds, Yorkshire in the spring of 1891. Ten years later the Bowden family were to be found living at 74 West Street, Scunthorpe, where Annie started the bakery business, making tea cakes and bread in the front room of the house. The business, which was founded in 1898, moved in 1904 to newly built premises at 236 Frodingham Road. The 1901 census lists the seven Bowden children, two boys and four girls, ranging in age from 13 years

to two months, **Edward, Mary, Thomas, Lavinia, Clara, Beatrice** and **George Ernest**.

Eventually, Thomas became a partner in his father's business and may well have enrolled in the Derby Scheme, introduced by the Government early in 1915. Men were offered the opportunity to join up but remain at their jobs until the Army specifically required them. Soaring casualty figures adversely affected voluntary recruitment. Conscription was introduced in 1916 when the age of enlistment was expanded from 19 to 38 years to 18 to 41 years. Newly trained soldiers were then drafted to the front, along with veterans who were returning to battle after convalescence.

Thomas Bowden enlisted on 11ᵗʰ February 1916 at the same time as **Thomas George Harpham**, and the Bowdens lived just three doors away from **Frank Clifford Sylvester,** two others who are commemorated on the Angel. Thomas was originally in the Lincolns, but transferred to the Machine Gun Corps, possibly to make up a shortfall of men.

The families must have known each other well: as children, Thomas and Frank probably played and went to school together, Frank's Mother would have bought her bread from George Bowden's shop. **Frank Sylvester** was killed five

Thomas William Bowden (arrowed) with the Machine Gun Corps - he and several other men still have their Lincolnshire Regimental Badge on their Caps. Vickers Maxim and Lewis guns are shown.

months earlier than Thomas Bowden, who died of trench fever on Friday 2nd February 1917, almost exactly one year after enlistment.

The following account appeared in the **Hull and Lincolnshire Times** dated 10th February 1917, **"Scunthorpe Soldier's Death and Funeral."**
"Sympathy is felt with Mr. and Mrs. George Bowden, 236, Frodingham Road, Crosby, in the sad loss they have sustained through the death of their second son, Private Thomas W. Bowden. He was 26 years of age, and a partner with his father in the business of baker and confectioner. He joined the army on February 11th, 1916 and became attached to the Machine Gun Corps. On August 11th he went to France, and after taking part in five engagements on the Somme he contracted trench fever. On December 28th last, he was brought to England and conveyed to the Middlesex County Hospital, Knapsbury, near London. He gradually became worse and died last Friday. Private Bowden was well known in the ironstone district, and his death has come as a shock to his many friends. He was a member of the Scunthorpe Social Club and the Crosby W.M. Club, Frodingham Road. Mr. G. W. Lefley had the funeral arrangements in hand and the body arrived at Scunthorpe by the one o'clock train on Tuesday. The funeral took place on the same afternoon at Crosby Cemetery, and many sympathisers were present. The mourners were:- father and mother, Private Hugh Rose and Mrs. Rose (sister), Mr. and Mrs. E. Bowden (brother), Master Ernie Bowden (brother), Miss Clarice, Olive, and Winnie Bowden (sisters), Mrs. F. Foster and Miss Foster (Leeds), Mr. and Mrs. M. Geary, sen. (sic), Bert Geary, Mr. Arthur Geary, Miss Ada Geary, Mrs. B. Bowskill, Miss Dorrie White, Miss Post, Mrs. Jarratt, Mrs. Bainton, Mr. and Mrs. R. Fox, Miss Sue Bedford, Miss Cissie Hillerby, Mrs. Hillerby, Mr. W. T. Milner, Mrs. L. Ayre, Mr. Beaman, and Private G. Vickers. There were many beautiful floral tributes."

Thomas William Bowden is commemorated on the Angel Memorial because he lived in the Crosby district. He is buried in **Crosby Cemetery,** and his father George was a baker with his own shop in Crosby.

The bakery business expanded to include several shops in Scunthorpe town centre. It also supplied bread and cakes wholesale to shops and villages in the local area. Sadly, the business closed in 1972, when Tommy's youngest brother, **George Ernest,** retired. He had run the business since the death of his father.

Information from:
Mr. Jeffrey Bowden (nephew)
Mr. Simon Swaby Bowden (great nephew)

Thiepval Memorial, France.

John William Bowers
Private 10350
1st Battalion Border Regiment
Died: Saturday 1st July 1916 Killed in Action

John William Bowers was born at Northwich, Cheshire in the winter of 1892, son of **Matthew Bowers** (who was a twin) and his wife **Betsy.** John's forebears were Lincolnshire people from the Broughton/Appleby area. In 1896 Betsy Bowers died aged only 36, probably in childbirth when their daughter **Rachel** was born, leaving Matthew with six children to raise, the others being **Alice Ann, Joseph Henry, Arthur** and **Benjamin** . This, sadly, was not uncommon.

It is not known where John William Bowers went to school or where he worked afterwards, only that he enlisted with the 1st Battalion Border Regiment at Carlisle, date not known.

He died on Saturday 1st July 1916, the first day of the infamous **Battle of the Somme** at **Thiepval.** It was a warm day, 72 degrees Fahrenheit, and the sky was clear and blue.

The battle began at 0720 hours and they advanced shoulder to shoulder in line, one behind the other, across the crater torn waste of *"No Man's Land"*. Weighed down by 66 lbs. of equipment each, they advanced slowly towards the waiting German guns. They were held up on uncut barbed wire and it was a wonder that any man could remain unscathed more than one minute in the inferno of fire that swept across the exposed slopes. They got 100 yards from the front line but were caught by three machine guns' fire. It was over by 0805 hours. The British casualties on this day were 57,470, of which 19,240 were fatal.

John's eldest brother, **Joseph**, is recorded as living at 27 Fox Street, Scunthorpe and as being his next of kin at the time of his death. John's name is on the **Thiepval Memorial**, along with those of Crosby men **William Streets** (who was killed on the same day), **Jacob Forrest, Charles Selwn Foster** and **Frank Clifford Sylvester**.

"Opened on 31st July 1932 by the Prince of Wales, the Thiepval Memorial to the Missing was and remains the largest British war memorial in the world. The memorial contains the names of 73,357 British and South African men who have no known grave and who fell on the Somme between July 1916 and 20th March 1918. 150 ft. high and dominating the surrounding area, the memorial was designed by Sir Edwin Lutyens."*

(*Interestingly, on 1st July 2006, it was the present Prince of Wales, H.R.H. Prince Charles, Duke of Cornwall, who was at Thiepval to commemorate the 90th Anniversary of the Battle of the Somme.)

John Bowers' name is entered in the **Scunthorpe Urban District Council Booklet 1917 "Roll of Honour"**:- *"27 Fox Street, 1st Cumberland Borderers Private Missing"* with his brother **Benjamin**, at the same address, as *"Yeomanry, Trooper."*

He is commemorated on the Crosby Angel Memorial because he lived and probably worked in the area. He could have been related to Bowers families whose children attended the school.

Information from:
http://www.firstworldwar.com/today/thiepval.htm
(Michael Duffy)

Norman Budworth

Private 2588
1/ 5th Battalion Lincolnshire Regiment
Died: Wednesday 13th October 1915 Killed in Action

Norman's family seem to have come to Frodingham in the 1870's, as his **Uncle Harry** is recorded on the 1881 census as having been born there. Norman's father, **Samuel Thomas Budworth,** and his grandfather, **Samuel Budworth**, were born in Dudley, Worcestershire. Norman's great great grandfather, **John Budworth,** was born in Wirksworth, Derbyshire, and moved to Worcestershire about 1835.

Norman is commemorated on the **Dud Corner Cemetery, Loos Memorial, Pas de Calais, France**, together with **Daniel Cunningham, Ernest Hornsby, Arthur Newstead, Albert Edward Ward,** and **John Fowler,** who died later than the other five men.

Norman Budworth, born 29th December 1896, was the eldest child of well known Frodingham sportsman **Samuel Thomas Budworth** and his wife **Florence** at King Street, Scunthorpe, Lincolnshire, being the eldest of six children. By 1901 the family had moved to Dunstall Street, Scunthorpe. Young Norman showed early promise as a sportsman himself. A photograph taken between 1910 and 1912 shows Norman as a proud member of Canon C. T. Rust's St.

Norman is seated second from left middle row in Frodingham Church Football Team. Canon C. T. Rust is seen second left standing back row. He was the Vicar of St. Lawrence's Parish Church, Frodingham from 1908 - 1948.

Lawrence's football team. He was also a prominent member of Mr. Sharp's Bible Class.

After leaving school Norman followed his father into heavy industry, finding employment at the North Lincoln Ironworks.

Meanwhile, the Budworth family had moved house several times, to 4th Street North, New Frodingam, 37 Trafford Street and Norman's last address, 85 Diana Street.

When war broke out he immediately volunteered his services to his King and Country along with **Richard Davison, Ernest Hornsby, Daniel Cunningham, Albert Edward Ward, John Fowler** and **Arthur Newstead,** who all enlisted in September 1914, probably as a result of Kitchener's patriotic call to arms. These were men specifically recruited to prepare the 5th Lincolnshire Battalion for overseas service. When Private Norman Budworth sailed for France in February 1915, he was among friends, all Crosby lads on the brink of what they thought was a great patriotic adventure.

A report in the book *"The History of the Lincolnshire Regiment"* by Major General Simpson, stated on the incident of that day, Wednesday 13th October 1915, *"At 12 Noon the artillery bombardment began and at 1 p.m. the wind became favourable, gas was projected on the German lines and smoke bombs were thrown which produced clouds of smoke to hide the advance of the infantry. All these arrangements went like clockwork. As soon as the enemy observed the discharge of gas and smoke clouds, he began in earnest to bombard the British trenches and the first support and reserve lines were heavily shelled. Violent machine gun fire also swept the ground over which the infantry was to advance. At 2 p.m. the 1/5th Lincs. with others of attacking infantry left the trenches and advanced against the enemy. All accounts agree that they advanced with great gallantry. The wire in front of the Redoubt had been well cut by the artillery, and both battalions swept over the west face with but a few casualties. They reached the Redoubt which was blown to pieces and captured a small number of Germans. A further advance was impossible as the Brigade on their right was held up on the wire in front of "Big Willie" and they were being heavily bombarded on their right flank. Attempts were made to get to Fosse 8 both over the open and up communications trenches, but the intensity of the German machine guns made efforts impossible. The attackers got across No Man's Land and into the Redoubt splendidly and then advanced on Fosse Trench 8 only to be mown down by violent machine gun and rifle fire."*

With the exception of **John Fowler**, who was spared a little longer, Norman and his companions were all killed in action during the attack on the **Hohenzollern Redoubt** on Wednesday 13th October 1915. Norman is commemorated on the **War Memorial at St Lawrence's Parish Church, Frodingham to those who died in the Great War.**

He is commemorated on the Angel because his family lived in Crosby at the time of his death.

Information from:
Mrs. June Parrott and Mrs. Wendy Wales (nieces)

Commemorative Lincolns Post Card.

John Bycroft
Private 4441
5th Battalion Lincolnshire Regiment
Died: Monday 14th August 1916 Killed in action

John Bycroft was born in Grimsby, Lincolnshire in 1897, second son of **John Tom Bycroft,** a milk dealer, and his wife **Mary**. The Bycroft family had been farmers at South Reston, Market Rasen back to at least the 1841 census, but by 1891, John's grandfather, **Henry Thomas Bycroft**, was working as a milk dealer and living in Louth, Lincolnshire.

In 1901 John's parents and siblings were living at 41 Ravenspur Street, Grimsby, and their family had increased. John, and his elder brother **William** had two sisters, **Mary Elizabeth** aged 2 years, **Edith** who was 1 year old, and a baby brother **Henry Thomas,** just three months old. Sisters **Kate** and **Emily,** who were born later, completed the family.

Little is known of John Bycroft's early life except that in the September quarter of 1910, his father died aged only 41 years. Life must have been hard indeed for his mother, a widow with five children to support. She did, however, marry again on 31st March 1914 at St. John's Parish Church, Scunthorpe, to Horace John Cracknell who had probably come to Scunthorpe because work was plentiful.

Certainly prior to his enlistment, John Bycroft was working in the burgeoning steel industry with the fitters at Frodingham Steelworks. He lived with his family at 51 Mulgrave Street, Crosby.

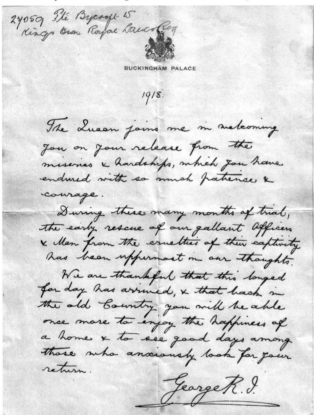

Letter from King George V to William Bycroft, John's brother. This was sent by the King to all those who survived World War I.

In the late autumn of 1915, probably November, when the Lincolns recruiting campaign was held in the area, both the 18 year old John and his older brother **William** enlisted at Crowle.

John's life, like his army career, was brief: both were swiftly ended by a bullet through the brain on Monday, 14th August 1916. Commemorated in perpetuity by the Commonwealth War Graves Commission, he is buried and remembered with honour at **Berles Position Military Cemetery, Pas de Calais, France.** Another of the men whose name is inscribed on the Angel, **William**

Selby, is also buried in the same French Cemetery, having died on 14th October 1916.

A report from the **Hull Daily Mail 9th September 1916** stated that, *"Mrs. Cracknell, 51, Mulgrave Street, Crosby, was officially informed last week that her second son, Private John Bycroft, was killed while on listening post duty on the night of August 14th. He was only 19 years of age and had not been more than 5 months in France. He joined the Lincolnshire Regiment last October when the Lincolns made their successful recruiting march in the ironstone district. He was shot through the brain, and was buried some 100 yards behind the then firing line. Before he enlisted, he was with the fitters at the Frodingham works and enjoyed the respect of a large circle of friends."*

*"Mrs. Cracknell's other son by her first husband, **Private William Bycroft**, who went to France last week, has recovered from wounds in his chest and left arm received while with the Lincolns in the Suvla Bay Landing (Gallipoli)."*

John's sister **Emily**, who is recorded as having attended Crosby School, worked for many years with the Scunthorpe Co-operative Society china and crockery department.

World War I Tank found near Cambrai, France and now preserved nearby.

Information from:
Mr. Howard and Mrs. Anne Bycroft
Professor Barrie W. and Mrs Jean Bycroft
(nephews and nieces)
Grimsby and Cleethorpes Directory 1910/11
St. John's Church Parish Records, Scunthorpe
St. Lawrence's Church Parish Records, Scunthorpe

George William Calvert

Private 11288
1st Battalion Grenadier Guards
Died: Saturday 24th October 1914 Killed in Action

George's paternal grandparents, **John** and **Sarah Calvert,** were born in Loughborough, Leicestershire, where John was employed as a lacemaker, moving later to Nottingham, where George's father, **Arthur,** was born.

George William Calvert was born in Holbeach Lincolnshire, in 1883, eldest son of **Arthur,** who was a board schoolmaster, and his wife **Lucia Calvert.** They were living at St. John's, Jekylls Bank in Holbeach, Lincolnshire.

At the age of 17 George was working as a pattern maker in Boston. The family had moved to Whaplode, South Lincolnshire, where his mother was also working as a teacher. Unusually tall and well-built for a man of that era, George was ideally proportioned for the Grenadier Guards, with whom he enlisted in London at the age of 20 years and 4 months, initially for three years and eight years in the reserve.

It is through his Army Service Record that we know he was 6 feet 1½ inches tall and weighed 170 lbs. (12 stone 2 lbs.) On 26th October 1904, he extended his service to complete eight years with the Colours. On 23rd January 1906 he was granted service pay of 6d. per day, and on 15th December 1909 transferred to Reserve Section B with his consent, before the expiration of his period of army service.

After leaving the army, George Calvert met and married **Ethel Louisa Warner**, daughter of George Warner, at the Parish Church, Croydon on 5th January 1911, in the presence of his younger sister **Hilda Calvert,** and George Warner. Perhaps the young couple came north in search of work; there was plenty to be found at Scunthorpe where, after serving as a police constable, he became licensee of the Reform Club in Cross Street, Scunthorpe. There he settled down to married life with Louisa and their baby son, **John Arthur**, who was born on the 19th October 1911, probably at 57 Mulgrave Street, Crosby, recorded in the 1914 *Willard and Kenning Directory* as being their address.

The 1st Battalion Grenadier Guards were based in Warley, London District in August 1914. George Calvert was re-mobilised on 5th August 1914, the day after the Great War was declared. The Guards were attached to 20th Brigade, 7th Division. The 7th Division was formed during September and very early October 1914 by the bringing together of regular Army Units from various parts of the British Empire.

George Calvert was part of the original contingent of his battalion rather than being a draft to replace casualties. Originally moved to Belgium, they landed at Zeebrugge on 6th October 1914 to assist in the defence of Antwerp. However, by the time they arrived the city was already falling, and the 7th were ordered to hold certain important bridges and other places that would help the westward evacuation of the Belgian army. Once the Belgians were through, the Division was moved westwards, where they entrenched in front of Ypres. They were the first British troops to occupy that fateful place, where it played a central role in the first defensive battle there.

The 1st, 2nd, 3rd, and 5th Cavalry divisions were very heavily engaged in these early days of the war; indeed by the close of the **First Battle of Ypres** they were all but destroyed. They took great pride in their achievements, and were always known as the *"Old Contemptibles"*. This was the title proudly adopted by the men of the British Expeditionary Force who saw service before 22nd November 1914. They were the originals, and most, like George William Calvert, were regular soldiers or reservists.

George Calvert in his Police Constable's Uniform with his father Arthur Calvert.

On Saturday 24th October 1914, only 23 days into the war, George William Calvert died of wounds received at the **Battle of Langemark (21st to 24th October)** in the lead up to the 1st Battle of Ypres.

Part of the British Expeditionary Force (B.E.F.) were moving north to the Channel coast. Depleted and exhausted, they were trying to hold a thinly defended portion of the Allied line. Around 24th October, the 1st Battalion Grenadier Guards were fighting near Polygon Wood and the village of Langemark.

Hull Times 14th November 1914, *"A SCUNTHORPE WAR VICTIM." "News reached Scunthorpe on Saturday of the death of George*

Calvert of the Grenadier Guards, a Scunthorpe Reservist who was killed in action. He will be well remembered as a member of the Police Force. Latterly he was Watchman at Lysaghts, and Steward of the Old Social Club, Cross Street. He did not leave England until October 9th. He was severely wounded and died in a French Hospital. The flags of the Constitutional Club, the Iron and Steel Smelters' Club and the Reform Club were down at half mast."

"Members of the Reform Club attended the evening service at the Parish Church on Sunday when the Vicar expressed sympathy with the family in their bereavement."

He is buried in **Ypres Town Cemetery, West Vlaanderen, Belgium.** He qualified for the 1914 Star with Clasp as he was in the firing line before 22nd November 1914, the British War Medal and the Victory Medal. His total army service is stated in his documents to have been 10 years and 277 days (Home – including Reserve – 10 years and 254 days, Expeditionary Force - 23 days.)

George Calvert's name is inscribed on the War Memorial at Whaplode Drove, South Lincolnshire, where his parents probably still lived at the time of his death.

At the time of his death, George's wife and three year old son John were living at 8 Long Road Crosby. As John later became a pupil at Crosby School, his father George William Calvert's name was included on the Crosby Angel War Memorial.

Information from:
Mrs. Sandra Curry (grand-daughter)
Mr. and Mrs. Tony Bratley, Whaplode, South Lincolnshire
The Long Long Trail Website (Battle Information) -
    http://www.1914-1918.net/

G. Cook's name on the Angel Memorial.

Research has failed to reveal with certainty the identity of this soldier. The following two biographies are possibilities:

George Cook

Possibly 1st Battalion Lincolnshire Regiment Private 7008
Survived the War

Born on 27th May 1892 at Barnard Street, Brigg, George Cook was the second son of **Arthur H. Cook** and his wife **Betsy** (formerly **Ward**). As well as his older brother, **James Ward Cook,** George had three younger sisters, **Ada, Ivy** and **Annie.** Their parents, Lincolnshire born and bred, came from long established local working class families. The children's maternal grandfather was the Captain of a vessel called *"The Walton."*

It is not known where George Cook went to school, but it is understood that he worked on the railway. It is recorded that a *"G. Cook No. 7008 of the 1st Battalion, Lincolnshire Regiment"* embarked for France on the 13th August 1914.

Informant, the late **Mr. Derry C. Cook,** son of George Cook, was born on 30th April 1921. Derry Cook was admitted to Doncaster Road Boys' School on 7th January 1929 and remained there until 31st August 1931. Shortly before his death in 2006, researchers of this book met with Derry Cook who said that his father was reported missing and was mistakenly commemorated on the Angel Memorial. George Cook married in 1919 and Derry went to Crosby School, therefore everyone would know when the Angel was erected at Crosby School in 1923 that George Cook was alive and had survived World War I.

As there was a large number of people named Cook in the area at that time, it is not possible to be absolutely certain which Cook is commemorated on the Angel Memorial.

Information from:
The late Mr. Derry C. Cook (son)
Mr. Derry Whitelock (grandson)

Blyton War Memorial, near Gainsborough

Parkinson Cook

Private 9699
2nd Battalion Lincolnshire Regiment
Died: Tuesday 5th January 1915 Died of Wounds

Parkinson Cook was born on 16th November 1895 at Blyton, Lincolnshire to foreman bricklayer **Charles Henry** and his wife **Mary Hannah Cook.** Parkinson was the second child of the family; he had three sisters, **Charlotte Ruby, Mary Elizabeth** and **Julia Rebecca** and one brother **Frank.** At the time of the 1901 census, the family lived at Park Street, Winterton and Parkinson's grandfather, who was also called **Parkinson Cook,** lived in Appleby, the next village.

It is unfortunate that so little is known about young Parkinson Cook, no details of his schooling or employment having been found. Because there were a great many Cooks living in the area, it has not been possible to positively identify any but the immediate family. It is recorded that Parkinson enlisted at Gainsborough, Lincolnshire, but no more is known of him until the following notice appeared in the **Hull Daily Mail 6th February 1915,** *Private P. Cook of the 2nd Battalion Lincs. Regiment late of Scunthorpe and Blyton whose death was recently announced in the Times. He was 19 years of age and was killed by a gunshot wound through the head on January 5th."*

He is recorded as having been killed in action but this was probably by a sniper as there appeared to have been no fighting at the time. He is commemorated at the **Boulogne Eastern Cemetery, France.**

Parkinson Cook's name is inscribed on the **War Memorial** at **Blyton,** where he was born.

Parkinson's name is not on the Crosby Angel Memorial, even though he lived in Crosby. No relationship between Parkinson Cook and the *"G Cook"* commemorated on the Angel has been proved.

John Cowan
Private 16017
3rd Company 2nd Battalion Coldstream Guards
Died: Friday 15th September 1916 Died of Wounds

John Cowan was born in Golborne, Lancashire in 1881. According to census records, his grandfather, also called **John Cowan**, was born in Douglas, Isle of Man about 1820, and came over to Lancashire where he found work on the railway in Golbourne. John's father, also called **John,** farmed some acres of land in 1881. He married farmer's daughter **Ellen Taylor** in 1875.

Young **John**, like his father, worked on the railway and came to Lincolnshire, after meeting his future wife, **Rose Ann Waterlow**, listed on the 1901 census working as a servant with her sister **Ruth** in a household at Chorlton-cum-Hardy, Lancashire. Perhaps Rose Ann wanted to settle down near her parents, who lived in Roxby-cum-Risby located between Scunthorpe and Winterton. John and Rose's marriage took place at St. Mary's Parish Church, Roxby-cum-Risby, on 8th December 1908. Her father, **Samuel Waterlow,** was an iron miner. John Cowan was then 27 years old.

(**John Green**, John's grandson, recalls that Rose Ann's employer's self portrait, given to the couple as a wedding present, used to hang in the house of his grandmother whom he visited in the 1950's.)

John's Widow received this from his Regiment - it states that he *"Died of Wounds received in Achory on Sept 15th 1916.*

John Cowan moved with his bride to 73 Sheffield Street, Crosby. The couple soon produced four children, **William**, born in 1910, **Margaret** born in

1912, **Hilda** born in 1913, and **Donald** born in January 1915. They were all to become pupils at the newly opened Crosby School. John Cowan's two sons were to serve in the army during World War II – **William** with the 8th Army in North Africa and Italy as a driver, and **Donald** in Northern Ireland with an Irish Regiment. Fortunately, they survived and found jobs in Scunthorpe - **William** at Clugstons, and **Donald** at John Manners, Gentlemen's Outfitters, in Scunthorpe High Street. Both remained unmarried.

After John Cowan enlisted in the Coldstream Guards at Lincoln in May 1915, he was never to see his newly born infant son, or any of his family again. Following his training period, John went to France in February 1916.

On 15th September 1916, the British Expeditionary Force once again undertook a major offensive on the Somme, the **Battle of Flers-Courcellete.** This time the infantry was guarded by a creeping barrage and by the few available tanks which caused terror among the German defenders.

It is recorded that the mist cleared to a bright day, temperature 72 degrees Fahrenheit. Ten tanks were to take part and there was heavy machine gun fire, but they pushed on, and by 11.15 a.m. had taken their objectives, the village of Flers-Courcelette. The French 10th Army was commanded by General Alfred Micheler. Despite using tanks for the first time, Micheler's twelve divisions gained only a few kilometres, six miles of territory, at a cost of 30,000 casualties. The British Expeditionary Force were not under French overall command until 1918.

It appears that John may have been wounded and taken from the Somme Battlefield to a casualty clearing station called locally *"La demie leuve,"* where he died from his wounds. In September 1916 the 34th and 2/2nd London Casualty Clearing Stations were established at this point (Meulte). Known to the troops as Grove Town, it dealt with casualties from the Somme Battlefields.

The Hull Daily Mail 14th October 1916 carried the following report, *"Private Jack Cowan, who leaves a widow and four children at 73 Sheffield Street, is another Crosby hero to give his life in the war. Until May 1915 he was working at Frodingham but he then joined the Coldstream Guards, and went to France last February as a bomb thrower. About three months ago he was transferred to the R.A.M.C., and it was while ministering to some of his old comrades during the famous charge by the Coldstreams on September 15th that he was shot in the abdomen and died the next day. He was 35 years of age. Private Cowan's sister-in-law is the wife of* **Sergeant A Sleight of the Lincs.** *"Somewhere in France"* (sic).

John's widow remained in Sheffield Street and took in lodgers, including theatrical people visiting Scunthorpe to appear at its two theatres, one on the corner of High Street and Manley Street (destroyed by fire in the 1940's) and one in Cole Street (demolished in recent years.)

Sergeant Albert Sleight married Rose Ann Cowan's sister, Ruth Waterlow in the June quarter of 1911. He survived the Great War.

John Cowan is commemorated on the Angel Memorial because his children went to Crosby School.

Information from:
Mr. John Green (Grandson)

John William Cowling's name is on the Althorpe War Memorial, North Lincolnshire.

John William Cowling

Private 2352
5th Battalion. Lincolnshire Regiment
Died: Friday 9th July 1915 Died of Wounds

Campagne 1914-1915
BOULOGNE-sur-MER — Cimetière de l'Armée Anglaise

Boulogne in 1919 - Later, the Commonwealth War Graves Commission introduced standard design headstones with no distinction made between military or civil rank, race or creed.

There were a number of Cowling families who originated from the Blyton/Scotter area of Lincolnshire. John William Cowling was the son of **William Cowling**, a Scotter-born ironstone quarry man, and his wife **Martha.** John William was born at Althorpe on 8th June 1893 and baptised on 30th July 1893 at St. Oswald's Parish Church, Althorpe. His sister **Florence** was two years older than he, and his two younger brothers, **Redvers** and **Joseph** were all recorded on the 1901 census.

Little more is known of his early life until he enlisted with the Lincolnshire Regiment at Scunthorpe on 4th September 1914. His service record indicates that he was 5 feet 8 inches tall and weighed 11 stones 4 lbs.

John William's days as a serving soldier were few, being 304 days in total. He was in "C" Company who were involved in the charge in the lead up to the **Hohenzollern Redoubt.** On 30th June 1915, the 5th Battalion relieved the 1st Battalion of the Lincolnshire Regiment to the east of Sanctuary Wood, which is in the Southern area of the Ypres Salient. He received a gunshot wound in his neck, and was moved to a hospital in Boulogne where he died aged 21 on Friday, 9th July 1915. He is buried in **Boulogne Eastern Cemetery, Pas de Calais, France.**

Lincolnshire Family History Society Magazine volume 6 No. 2 June 1995, *"The County's Blackest Day"* by Eric Walker, Liverpool,

"A pattern of life in the trenches was soon established with occasional fatalities and regularly wounded men. "C" Company had seven men killed up to 'Gallant Charge' on 13th October 1915, amongst them, Private Cowling, a fireman (N.B. possibly at the railway depot at Keadby) from Scunthorpe, who was wounded in action, and died on 9th July 1915."

John William Cowling probably lived in Crosby prior to his enlistment because it is recorded that his brother, **Redvers Roberts Cowling,** attended Crosby School until 1913, his address being recorded in the School's Admissions Register as 15 Frodingham Road.

St. Oswald's Parish Church, Althorpe, where John William Cowling was baptised - the Church was a focus for the village spiritual and social life.

John William Cowling is commemorated in **St. Oswald's Church, Althorpe,** on the **Memorial to Those Who Died in the Great War.** His name is also on the **War Memorial** situated in the main street at **Althorpe (Keadby with Althorpe Parish)** and on the Crosby Angel Memorial.

Information from:
Mrs. Vicki Whittaker (great great niece)
Mr. David Cowling (nephew)

Daniel Cunningham

Private 2592
1/5th Battalion Lincolnshire Regiment
Died: Wednesday 13th October 1915 Killed in Action

Born in 1895 at Rawcliffe, near Goole, Yorkshire, Daniel Cunningham was the fourth child and second son of **Daniel** and **Jane Cunningham**, who were both licensed hawkers.

In 1901 (census information) the family also consisted of three other boys, **Thomas, Joseph** and **Walter**, and two girls, **Grace** and **Ada**. They lived at Peat Moss Villas, Crowle, Lincolnshire. The family later moved into Crosby, possibly for more secure employment as the iron and steel industry began to flourish. Young Daniel found work at John Lysaght's Normanby Park

Steelworks as a washer *(sic)* prior to his enlistment in Scunthorpe. **Richard Davison, Ernest Hornsby, Norman Budworth** and **Arthur Newstead** all enlisted at Scunthorpe at the same time. Teenage boys were being recruited en masse. Regardless of the 19 to 38 years age of enlistment rule, thousands of under age boys *"slipped through."* The demand for recruits spawned a new kind of unit, uniquely made up of men who worked and/or socialised together, schoolmates, neighbours and relatives. Of such men as these, were the *"Pals Battalions"* formed.

Daniel Cunningham and his contemporaries were recruited specifically to bring the 5th Lincolns ready for overseas service. Daniel, with **Norman Budworth, Ernest Hornsby, Albert Edward Ward** and **Arthur Newstead** died, as they had lived, together, on Wednesday 13th October 1915 in the charge at the infamous **Hohenzollern Redoubt**.

Daniel Cunningham is commemorated on the **Loos Dud Corner Lincolnshire Regimental Memorial Panel, Pas de Calais, France,** with the four named above, plus **John Fowler**, another of the Crosby lads, who died later. Another Crosby lad, also included on this Memorial is **Albert Edward Ward** who, although he did not enlist at the same time, died on the same day as the other four.

Daniel was 20 years old at the time of his death. 13th October was certainly a tragic day for the Cunningham family.

Daniel's cousin, **Jack Cunningham**, is recorded in Scunthorpe's Roll of Honour, 1914 – 13th October 1917 as *"Cunningham, John, born in Stackyard, E. Yorks. V.C."* Jack's photograph is featured with the following write-up, *"Born in the Stackyard, on June 28th 1897. He was awarded this distinction for most conspicuous bravery and resource during operations. After the enemy's front line had been captured Pte. Cunningham proceeded with a bombing section up a communication trench. Much opposition was*

Daniel Cunningham's name is on the Loos Memorial at Dud Corner, Northern France - also inscribed on the same panel are the names of Norman Budworth, Ernest Hornsby, Arthur Newstead, Albert Edward Ward and John Fowler - all on the Crosby Angel.

encountered, and the rest of the section became casualties. Collecting all the bombs from the casualties, this gallant soldier went on alone. Having expended all his bombs, he returned for a fresh supply, and again proceeded to the communication trench, where he met a party of ten of the enemy. These he killed and cleared the trench up to the enemy line. His conduct throughout the day was magnificent."

The following (undated) report from the **Hull Daily Mail**, *"THE HULL V.C. – Private John Cunningham, 'the Hull V.C.' is the cousin of Mr. Daniel Cunningham of 76 Sheffield Street, Crosby. The Cunningham family is a very patriotic one, over 70 members of the family are serving with the colours: 23 of his nephews are in France, and a cousin is a prisoner of war in Germany."*

*"Two of Mr. Cunningham's sons enlisted in 1914 and **Daniel** (Junior), of the Lincolns, was killed on October 13th 1915, when the Lincolns made their memorable charge on the Hohenzollern Redoubt. Before joining the Army, he was employed at Messrs. Lysaghts as a washer, he was only 20 years of age when killed. Tom Cunningham, the other son, who was following a similar occupation as his father, that of a hawker, is in a machine gun section attached to the Lincolns and has been in the trenches since last August. Another cousin of the V.C., Private Jack Forrest, has been in France ten months and married Dan's eldest daughter Grace. Mr. Daniel Cunningham, who is a native of Rawcliffe in Yorkshire, has been hawking in the Ironstone District for 30 years, and the father of the V.C. hero, Mr. Chas Cunningham once lived in Winterton, but has stayed in the old Stackyard for 12 months at a*

*time. The new V.C. has several times visited the town. Mr. Cunningham's son, **Daniel,** who was killed, was recommended for the D.C.M."*

Mr. Taylor noted in the **School Logbook** dated 10th December 1915, *"13 sweaters and 13 pairs of gloves sent to old boys in the Forces including **Tom Cunningham**."* Tom Cunningham survived World War I.

West Street Cemetery, Scunthorpe, Section E10, *"The child of Daniel and Jane Cunningham died 25th March 1907 aged 18 months also **Daniel** son of above killed in action at Hulloch (sic) 13th October 1915 aged 20 also **Jacob Forrest** husband of Grace Forrest and son in law of the above killed in action in France 10th February 1917 aged 22."*

Daniel's cousin Jack was the only Scunthorpe man to win the V.C. during the Great War.

Daniel is commemorated on the Crosby Angel Memorial because his three brothers attended the school.

It is also recorded in the **School Logbook** that, *"2nd June 1930: Mr. R. Jones C.C. and J.P. presented a gold medal to **Fred Cunningham**, one of our old boys. He was working on Dorchester House, in Park Lane, London a building 7 stories (sic) in height. His brother was lying badly hurt and unconscious on a platform 23 inches wide. Fred saved his brother from this perilous position by risking his own life. Thousands of people gathered together and stood gazing; expecting to see Fred dashed 95 feet to the ground. News of this gallant feat was published in all the leading papers of the country.*

*The children's newspaper company sent us several numbers of the paper containing an account of the heroic deed for distribution amongst our boys. The boys and teachers bought a gold medal bearing the inscription **"For Courage on Dizzy Heights from Crosby Council Boys' School."***

"Mr. Jones, Mr. Cutts, Mr. Hornsby local Magistrates
Mr. Mark Morgan (C.C.) Mr. Thurston School Managers
Mr. Hornsby School Attendance Officer
Mr. and Mrs. Cunningham, parents of the Hero
Fred Cunningham and Joe Cunningham, brothers, present on the occasion."

Private John "Jack" Cunningham, V.C.

"The Superintendent of Police – Mr Hutchinson – was also present. We invited the Police to this ceremony because Fred when 16 years of age, offended the police by a high spirited action. They were pleased to show to present boys and old boys how much more delightful it is to them to deal out rewards and commendations than fines and reprimands."

Fred and Joe were two of Daniel's brothers.

(N.B. "The Stackyard" was situated in Manley Street, off High Street, Scunthorpe, adjacent to the Blue Bell Hotel, now demolished.)

A PATRIOTIC FAMILY.

Pte. JOHN DALE, 8th Lincs. Regiment. Died of wounds in France August 4th, 1916.

Pte. EDWIN DALE 2/5th Duke of Wellington's Regiment Serving in France.

Pte. ERNEST DALE, 6th Lincs. Regiment. Died of wounds at Dardenelles, August 10th 1915. Sons of Mr. and Mrs. Henry Dale, Churchtown, Belton.

John Henry Dale

Private 11786
8th Battalion Lincolnshire Regiment
Died: Friday 4th August 1916 Died of Wounds

The Dale family have been traced back to the early 1800's living in Church Town, Belton, North Lincolnshire. **Matthias Dale**, John Henry Dale's great grandfather, was farming several acres of land there, which passed to his son **Samuel**, whose son **Henry** was John Henry's father.

Like thousands of other young soldiers, John Henry Dale thus came from agricultural stock. Born on 2nd March 1893, he was baptised on 31st March at the Primitive Methodist Church at Belton, Isle of Axholme, Lincolnshire where generations of his father's family had worked the land. John's grandfather, **Samuel Dale,** is described as *'Farmer of nine acres'* (1881 census) and would have been a man of some status in the little community. Rural life had altered little during the preceding one hundred years but the cruel catalyst of war was about to change the lives of everyone, regardless of their social standing.

In 1901 John's parents, **Henry** and **Ann Maria Dale** were living at Church Town, Belton with their six children **Ann-Maria, Alice Mary, Laura, Ernest, Edwin** and **John Henry,** who was the second son. Although extensive research has been carried out, nothing more is known of the thirteen years of John's life between the ages of 8 and 21 years, except that for eight years of them he was organ blower at Belton Parish Church.

Eager for experiences different from those of their fathers and grandfathers, young men fired up by patriotism, martial music and the spirit of adventure, left their homes in droves, most of them never to return. Kitchener's phenomenally successful campaign drew thousands of volunteers from farming communities, recruiting them into the Service Battalions. John Henry Dale enlisted at the same time as **Walter Martin, Arthur Frost, John Fowler, George Henry Ross** and **John William "Jack" Rimmington.** He may well have already been living in Scunthorpe, following the lure of independence, a better paid job in the iron and steel industry, or perhaps he just came specifically to enlist.

John's elder brother, Ernest, also answered the call to arms, although it is not known where he enlisted. The following report is from the **Epworth**

Belton, near Epworth, Lincolnshire - town War Memorial whereon the names of brothers Ernest and John Dale are inscribed.

Bells dated **Saturday 21st August 1915,** **"Belton lads at the Dardanelles."** *"Private E. Dale, 6th Lincoln Regiment, who is with the Mediterranean Force, writes to his cousin (Mrs. F. Johnson, Churchtown, Belton):- 'I am all right at present. We have been in the firing line and just come out for a day or two's rest. We were six days without having a wash, so you will guess how we felt. We are somewhere near the Dardanelles. The firing trenches are only 50 yards from ours. The snipers are good shots; if you show your head above the trench they have you. Am sorry to say we had about fifty casualties in our regiment, and thank God that along with all the other Belton boys, I have escaped. Hope we shall all come back home again. We shall be able to tell you something then. We cook our own meals in the trenches. Writing material is bad to get here. I shall be pleased when I get the Woodbines, as they are not obtainable.'"*

A month later, **Epworth Bells** dated **18th September 1915,** *"The late Private E. A. Dale"* – *"On Sunday morning last a memorial service was held at the Parish Church. There was a large congregation. Besides the parents and other members of the family, the Old Volunteer Corps, numbering 26, attended the service. – At the end of the war a Parish Memorial will be erected to all from this Parish who fall in their country's service."*

And on **25th September 1915,** also from the **Epworth Bells, "*Letter of Condolence*"** *"Mr. H. Dale has received a letter from Mrs. Elkington, 68 Princes Gate, London who is at the head of the Central Registry for the 6th (Service) Batt. Lincs. Regt., referring to the death of Pte. E. Dale. She*

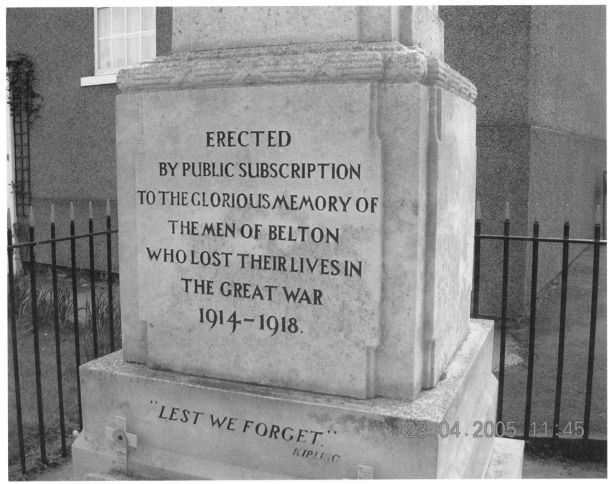

ERECTED
BY PUBLIC SUBSCRIPTION
TO THE GLORIOUS MEMORY OF
THE MEN OF BELTON
WHO LOST THEIR LIVES IN
THE GREAT WAR
1914-1918.

"LEST WE FORGET."
KIPLING

23.04.2005 11:45

Inscription at the base of Belton Town War Memorial whereon the names of John and Ernest Dale are inscribed.

writes: *'Please accept my very deep sympathy. I have only just got the lists from my husband and he tells me the men were splendid and fought magnificently; he was so proud of them. The poor regiment has suffered so badly, but they were all so brave. Yours truly, Kathleen Elkington.'"*

Later, Henry and Ann Maria Dale's second son, **John Henry Dale,** was killed at the **Battle of the Somme**, "**Epworth Bells Saturday 12th August 1916: Belton Soldier's Death.**" *"News has been received of the death of Pte. J. Dale, of Blyton, son of Mrs. Henry Dale. He enlisted in the 6th Lincolns soon after the outbreak of war. His brother, Pte. Ernest Dale died on August 10th 1915, from wounds received in action at the Dardanelles. Mrs. Dale has not yet received official intimation of her second son's death, but a note from the Sister in charge of the Casualty Clearing Station, who says he was brought in at 2 o'clock on the morning of August 4th, just breathing his last from a fatal wound in the back,*

and passed peacefully away. It was such a severe wound that he must have lost consciousness at once and could not have suffered any pain. Great sympathy is felt for Mrs. Dale and family in their second bereavement within a year."

And on the **19th August 1916,** "***BELTON – THE LATE PTE. J. DALE – Mrs. H. Dale has received further particulars of the death of her son Pte. J. Dale 8th Lincolns. Sergt. W. H. Cook writes: 'It is with deepest sympathy I am writing these few lines to you with regard to the death of your son Jack, of which no doubt you will have been informed by now. It happened this way. On the evening of the 3rd inst about 2 p.m. our company was "straffing" (sic) the Germans with trench mortars. We were all watching them, when something came through the air and hit a corporal on the head and Jack in the small of his back. They were both seriously wounded and both died sometime between then and next day* dinner time. I am sorry enough to lose Jack, because I was his Platoon-Sergt., and also one of his pals before the war broke out. He was well liked by all in his platoon and all who knew him in the company. He was a good and one of the bravest men in his company. He was a platoon bomber and did some good work in the big advance. You have the one consolation that he died doing his bit for King and Country. Please accept the sincere sympathy of myself and all his comrades.' Coy-Sergt. Major Henson has also written expressing sympathy and says: 'We are all sorry to lose your son. During the time he has been in my company I have found him a willing, reliable and good soldier. He died a brave soldier and credit, not only to his King and country, but to his parents'."

The Military Medal was Awarded to Edwin, younger brother of John Henry Dale

John Henry Dale is buried in **Barlin Communal Cemetery Extension, Pas de Calais, France**. The extension was designed by Sir Edward Lutyens. The Cemetery was used for burials by the Sixth Casualty Clearing Station.

A Memorial Service was held at the Belton Parish Church, **Epworth Bells Saturday 26th August 1916: "BELTON** – MEMORIAL SERVICE – A memorial service for the late Privates C. Hunt, (killed Sept. 25th 1915), and **J. H. Dale** (died from wounds August 4th, 1916) was held at the Parish Church on Sunday evening. There was a very large congregation and besides the bereaved families, the Epworth and Belton (old) Volunteers attended the service. Pte. Hunt was an enthusiastic member of the Belton Volunteers … An appropriate service was well rendered and the Vicar preached a suitable sermon from St. Matthew 8, v. 10 "I have not found so great faith, no, not in Israel." The organist played the Dead March and the service was concluded with the National Anthem."

The anguish of the Dale family is unimaginable during the next two years as their third son, **Edwin,** was also a soldier fighting in France: **Epworth Bells dated 14th September 1918,**

"MILITARY MEDALLIST: BELTON MAN'S GALLANTRY Mr. and Mrs. H. Dale of Churchtown, Belton, have received the following letter: 'No. 241045 Pte. E. Dale. I beg to inform you that the Corps Commander under Authority delegated to him, has awarded you the Military Medal for the following acts of gallantry:- "For great bravery on July 20th 1918, when his company were caught under heavy shell fire on a road and many casualties were sustained. He assisted in the collection of the wounded, and went out into an open field to help to bring in a wounded officer at great personal risk." K. Sykes Captain and Adjt. 5th Duke of Wellington's Regt. 5th August 1918.'"

As far as can be ascertained from research, Edwin survived the War.

John Henry Dale is commemorated on the Crosby Angel Memorial, presumably because he had lived in Crosby at some time, perhaps to be near his work. His brother, **Ernest's** name is on the **Helles Memorial, Dardanelles;** he was **Private 13577 of the 6th Battalion Lincolnshire Regiment**. Both John and Ernest are commemorated on the **War Memorial** and on the **Roll of Honour in the Parish Church of All Saints, Belton**.

The School Admissions Registers list a George Dale, living in Sheffield Street who had children who were pupils at Crosby School. It is possible that he was related to John Henry Dale's family at Belton.

Information from:
Isle of Axholme Family History Society Roll of Honour Book
Epworth Bells newspaper
First World War website:
http://www.firstworldwar.com/

FOUQUIERES CHURCHYARD EXTENSION, near Bethune, Pas de Calais France where Herbert Alfred Daniels is buried.

Herbert Alfred Daniels

Private 5814
1/5th Battalion Lincolnshire Regiment
Died: Thursday 30th May 1918 Killed in Action

Herbert's father, **Alfred Daniels** (whose father, **William,** was a *"gold beater")*, was born in St. Pancras, London. However **Alfred** became a schoolmaster, and married **Maria Winser**, also a schoolteacher, in 1876. Maria's parents and her Aunt Maria were all schoolteachers.

Herbert was born in 1881 in Cocking, Sussex, where he and his twin sister, **Ethel Mary**, had one sister, **Florence,** who was two years older. They lived in the school house with their relatively affluent lower middle class parents **Alfred** and **Maria Daniels**, who were both school teachers and as such were able to afford to employ a *"general servant."*

Alfred and Maria Daniels were living in Willingham, Lincolnshire on the 1891 census, by which time another two children, **Henry** and **Margaret,** had been born, in 1882 and 1890 respectively.

Herbert seems to have broken with the family teaching tradition, as on the 1901 census he is listed as being a 20 year old soldier based at Lincoln Barracks.

The family moved north to East Stockwith near Gainsborough, Lincolnshire, almost certainly a career move, as the couple appear on the 1901 census as Headmaster and Headmistress respectively of East Stockwith School.

In the period 1904-5, information gathered from local authority Teachers' Salary Books tells us that Mr. and Mrs. Daniels, described as Certified Teachers, had a nett monthly salary of £12 (£144 per annum). Their daughter **Margaret,** is described as *"Candidate on Probation,"* in other words Teacher in training, which she began on 2nd January 1905 with a gross annual salary of £8.

On 1st February 1905, Headmaster Daniels was replaced by a **Mr. George Taylor,** who was later to become Headmaster of Crosby School when it opened in 1908. It is likely that the twins, Herbert Alfred and Ethel Mary Daniels, and their siblings all attended schools where their parents taught, although no recorded proof of this has been discovered.

Herbert enlisted at Gainsborough, his 1916 entry into the Territorials indicates that he may have been a pre-war regular soldier in the Boer War era.

Mr. Taylor's Logbooks for Crosby School, *"March 19th 1917 Mrs. Margaret Musgrave **(Miss Margaret Daniels)** assumed duties as a supplementary teacher to act as a stop gap in the position Mrs. C. Cutts has resigned. We have not yet received a single application for Mrs. Cutts' vacated post. Miss Margaret Daniels was formerly a probationary teacher in East Stockwith C. School."* And on page 294, *"April 5th 1917 Mrs. Musgrave terminated her connection with the school on the 5th April 1917."*

The next and last mention of the Daniels family was the sad news of their only son Herbert's death. He was killed in action on Thursday, 30th May 1918 and buried in **Fouquieres Churchyard Extension, Pas de Calais, France,** where he is commemorated as *"son of Alfred George and Maria Elizabeth Daniels of Ferry House, East Stockwith, Gainsborough, native of Cocking, Sussex. Died aged 37 years."*

Herbert is commemorated on the Crosby Angel Memorial because his sister was a teacher at Crosby School.

Information from:
Teachers'. Salaries Books, held at Lincoln Archives:
1904-5 East Stockwith School, Boys

Royal Field Artillery Badge
Ubique - **Everywhere**
Quo Fas et Gloria Ducunt - **Where the Right and Glory Lead.**

William Henry Dymond

Gunner 72164
81st Brigade Royal Field Artillery
Died: Wednesday 17th November 1915 Died at Sea

Sadly, more is known about the death of William Henry Dymond than his life. That he lived in Crosby at the time of his enlistment at Scunthorpe is recorded on the *'Soldiers who Died in the Great War'* CD.

From what scant evidence remains of his life it may only be surmised that he was a stranger to these parts who had come here to work, as there are no other Dymonds recorded in the area.

Nothing more is known of William Henry Dymond except that he died at sea when the hospital ship H.M.S. *"Anglia"* struck a mine in the channel en route to Dover from France.

The total number on board the Anglia was 13 Officers and 372 Other Ranks, of whom about 300 were rescued by a patrol boat. One survivor had a miraculous escape when the *"Anglia"* went down with the loss of 72 lives. The following account is given in his own graphic words,

"I was aboard the hospital ship Anglia. We left Bolougne (sic) at 11 a.m. and all went well until we sighted the cliffs of Dover. It was then 12.40 p.m. About a minute later a very loud explosion occurred. We knew what that meant. Everybody did what they ought not to have done – run about and do all sorts of things. Meanwhile the ship took a very nasty tilt, the front part was already under water. Everybody rushed for the boats, but alas! They did not know how to manipulate one until two of the seamen went up and lowered one full. There was a bad swell on at the time, so half of them got tippled out into the water. As far as I remember there was only this one boat lowered. Coming towards us at full speed was a gunboat. She ran right alongside of us, and some of the lucky ones managed to jump onto her as she went by. She came back, and floated about twenty or thirty yards away, and anybody who could swim, swam to it. Of course there was a great many of us who could not swim, so we stuck to the ship, and watched those who could. The ship gave another nasty tilt, and she now had her stern high in the air. Well, I managed to get a life belt, and slipped this on. I thought if I could not swim I would float. It was a terrible sight to see the wounded men crawling up the gangway onto the deck lying there to go down with the ship, some with legs off, others with arms off. We could not help them. As luck would have it, I saw a lot of life belts in a cabin, so I started dishing these out to them. Meanwhile, another boat had come quite close and started picking some up. She managed to save quite a lot, when, just as she was breaking all records, up she went. In my opinion, we were both torpedoed. Well, I stuck to the old ship, and she gradually started to go, foot by foot. Up came a great big wave, and this polished her off – also me for the time being. What a sensation! All my breath was squeased (sic) out of my body, and I gave myself up. Down, down, down – what a depth, and how I did struggle! It seemed years! At last I came up, caught half a breath, and clung to a box. Then I got dashed against an upturned boat, and almost let go my box. I had lost my life

The *"Anglia"* prior to her being converted to an Auxiliary Hospital Ship.

belt. Wave upon wave came and absolutely drowned me. Well I kept hold as long as I could, but my strength was almost giving way when something banged my head, and I was grasped by the hair and lifted up, then someone else collared hold of me, and between them they got me into the boat, and I don't remember anything until we landed back at the gun boat. I managed to struggle up the gangway, and they carried me down into the mess room. I very soon got into a blanket after being rubbed down and am now very much at home in hospital."

The sinking of the *"Anglia"* on 17th November 1915, was the first case in which a hospital ship carrying wounded was sunk. Following the first thrill of horror at the fate of those who lay helpless in the vessel when she was struck, came a deeper sense of gratitude to the Navy for the marvellous manner in which it had afforded protection during the hundreds of voyages which had been made by the hospital ships since the outbreak of war.

William Henry Dymond was probably wounded at the Battle of Loos. He is commemorated on the **Hollybrooke Memorial, Southampton,** where personnel with no known graves are recorded.

His Medal Roll has the following information on it: Medals: 1915 Star, British War Medal and Victory Medal. This would indicate that he went out to France before December 1915 – he was either a regular soldier or a Territorial.

1915 Star: for service in all other theatres of war, 5th August 1914 and 31st December 1915: and for service in France and Belgium, 23rd November 1914 – 31st December 1915.

William is named on the Angel Memorial and on the **Crosby Parish Roll of Honour** as he had lived in the Parish of Crosby.

Information from:
MacKenzie J. Gregory's Ahoy - Mac's Web Log - Naval, Maritime Australian History: http://ahoy.tk-jk.net/index.html

Jacob's name on the Thiepval Memorial, France.

Jacob Forrest

Private 40512
(also shown as Private 4457 Lincolnshire Regiment)
2nd Battalion Lincolnshire Regiment
Died: Saturday 10th February 1917 Killed in Action

Jacob Forrest was born in 1885 at Ilkeston, Derbyshire, first son but second child of **Hamilton** and **Ann Forrest**. His sister **Ann** was two years older than him. **Thomas** and **Jane** were their younger siblings.

At the time of the 1891 census the family were living at Railway Arch Ground, in the Parish of St. Paul, Deptford, Greenwich, London. This may have been a rest place for itinerant people as they traded their way around the country. Given that Jacob and his siblings were all born in different counties and that generations of Forrests had been pot hawkers or *"dealers in earthenware"* this is probably the case, or they may have been replenishing their stock in that area. It is not known where, or if indeed, any of the Forrest children went to school, but Jacob eventually settled at 75 Sheffield Street, New Crosby after the death of his father, Hamilton Forrest.

On 11th June 1911, Jacob Forrest, then 27 years old, married **Grace Cunningham,** also aged 27 at the Glanford Brigg Registry Office. On the Marriage Certificate, his occupation is described as *"Pedlar."* Grace Cunningham was the

daughter of Daniel Cunningham, a hawker who had traded in the ironstone district for 30 years. Scunthorpe Market was opened by Rowland Winn, the Second Lord St. Oswald, on 2nd March 1906 and there is evidence of the Cunninghams working there as market traders for many years.

Jacob enlisted at Grimsby, Lincolnshire; the rank and number Private 4457, Lincolnshire Regiment, would indicate that he enlisted about the 13th October 1915.

*(A 5 digit number beginning with a 4**** was most common for, although not exclusively so, a man drafted from another Regiment into the Lincolns, so it is not certain how Forrest got this number 40512 and came to be in the 2nd Lincolns at the time of his death. Possibly he was transferred to another regiment/unit from the 5th Lincolns then came back to the Lincolns where he was issued with a new number. He may have been wounded, discharged and rejoined.)*

According to the **History of the Lincolnshire Regiment,** the 2nd Battalion had a quiet month in February 1917, so it is not known how Jacob Forrest met his death on Saturday 10th February 1917. The Medal Roll shows his entitlement to the British War Medal and Victory Medal, which indicates that he was not among the initial wave of British Expeditionary Forces, but probably among the reinforcements after the B.E.F. had been decimated at Loos in September 1915. The 2nd Battalion were at Rancourt in trenches on 10th February 1917, after the **Battle of Mallrepas Ravine** on the third of that month, in which five other ranks were killed and ten other ranks were wounded.

In the **Hull Times** dated **20th January 1917,** it is recorded that Jacob's younger brother, **Private 3599 Thomas Forrest** of the **62nd Field Ambulance R.A.M.C.** had lost his life five months earlier, when he was struck in the neck by a bullet while gallantly carrying wounded under heavy fire. He died immediately. He was 22 years old.

Jack Cunningham, a cousin of Jacob's wife, Grace, was the only Scunthorpe man to win the Victoria Cross in World War I. **Daniel**

Cunningham Junior, age 20, brother of Grace Forrest, was also killed in action on 13th October 1915. It is recorded that there were seventy men from this large patriotic family fighting for their country during World War I. Jacob Forrest and his brother Thomas are both commemorated on the **Thiepval Memorial, Somme, France,** together with Crosby men **John William Bowers, Charles Selwyn Foster, William Streets** and **Frank Clifford Sylvester.**

West Street Cemetery, Scunthorpe, Section E10, *"The child of Daniel and Jane Cunningham 25th March 1907 aged 18 months, also Daniel son of the above killed in action at Hulloch (sic) 13th October 1915 age 20, also **Jacob Forrest** husband of **Grace Forrest** and son-in-law of the above killed in action in France 10th February 1917 age 32."*

The widowed **Grace Forrest** married William Fewster at Glanford Brigg in the winter of 1923. It is understood that the couple sold pots and crockery in Scunthorpe Market until the 1960's, and then emigrated to Australia where Grace died in her 90's.

Jacob's name is on the Angel Memorial and on the **Crosby Parish Roll of Honour,** as he lived in Crosby.

Information from:
Monumental Inscription, West Street Cemetery, Scunthorpe
Jacob Forrest's Marriage Certificate
North Lincolnshire Magazine DIRECT May 2006

Lincolnshire Regimental Colours

Charles Selwyn Foster

Private 15604
8th Battalion Lincolnshire Regiment
Died: Monday 3rd July 1916 Killed in Action

Charles Selwyn Foster was born in Frodingham in 1892, the third son of **Joseph** (described as a *"stationary engine driver"*) and **Beatrice Foster,** who, on the 1901 census, lived at 4th Street, New Frodingham, later named Winn Street, with their five children **Edith, Albert, Algernon, Charles Selwyn** and **Frederick.**

Charles Selwyn enlisted at Scunthorpe as a recruit to the regular/service battalions of the Lincolnshire Regiment, probably in January 1916.

Charles was killed in action in the offensive for the village of **Thiepval, France** on Monday 3rd July 1916, the third day of the infamous **Battle of the Somme,** the same day as **Horace Birkett,** and two days after **William Streets.**

The Germans offered an unexpectedly fierce resistance and allied losses were catastrophic. It wasn't until the end of September 1916 that Thiepval was finally captured.

At the time of his death, Charles Selwyn Foster's address was 33 Trafford Street, Scunthorpe. Although Scunthorpe was home to a great many Fosters, some undoubtedly related to Charles Selwyn, a degree of uncertainty exists in the absence of reliable documentation being found.

However, the **Scunthorpe and Frodingham Star** dated **20th February 1930** reports, *"Funeral of Frederick Foster age 33 of Cliff Street Frodingham. Deceased, who was a native of Scunthorpe, died in the Scunthorpe War Memorial Hospital. His wife died three years earlier. Mr. Foster lived in Sheffield for six years and came back to his parents' home one and a half years ago. He had not been well for a few months…"*

Frederick Foster is recorded on the **1917 Roll of Honour for Scunthorpe** as serving with the Royal Field Artillery as a driver. It states that he had shell shock, which probably accounts for his early death – address: 33 Trafford Street, Scunthorpe. Frederick Foster was a brother of Charles Selwyn Foster.

Because Charles is commemorated on the Crosby Angel Memorial, it may be assumed that some of his siblings were pupils at the school. Charles Selwyn Foster is recorded on the **1917**

Scunthorpe Roll of Honour as having been killed. He .is also commemorated in St. Lawrence's Church, Frodingham on the Memorial to those who died in the Great War 1914-1918, and on the Thiepval Memorial, Somme, France, together with his contemporaries John William Bowers, Jacob Forrest, William Streets and Frank Clifford Sylvester. Charles Selwyn Foster was 24 years old at the time of his death.

Charles Selwyn Foster's name is recorded on the Crosby Parish Roll of Honour which consisted of 4 or 5 framed vellum documents, only some of which have been located at St. George's Parish Church, Crosby and are in a poor state of repair.

Alastair Fowler, great nephew, holding John Fowler's War Medals.

John Fowler

Private 12384
8th Battalion Lincolnshire Regiment
Died: Sunday 26th September 1915 Killed in Action

John Fowler's exact date of birth is not known, only that he was born in 1894 in Elton, Huntingdon, son of **Henry** and **Ann Fowler**. Ann (maiden name Smith) had previously been married to John William Eayres, a heavy smoker, who died of either heart disease or cancer of the tongue. The couple had one child, **John William** (known as William), who later took the surname of his step-father, **Henry Fowler**, his mother Ann's second husband.

The Fowlers had five more children, **Ellen Elizabeth**, **Martha Ann**, **Richard**, **Edward Henry,** and **John**, who was the youngest. When John was only fifteen months old, Henry Fowler died too, leaving the unfortunate Ann a widow for the second time with six dependent children; the eldest two were working, (John) William as a cycle polisher and Richard as a butcher's boy.

The family perhaps left Huntingdon for Scunthorpe due to the following quirk of fate. In the June quarter of 1906, John's half brother (John) William, eldest of the family, married Lily Birch in the Peterborough district. The day after the wedding, Lily's mother turned up with a young boy, Wilfred, who was Lily's illegitimate son. Although (John) William had no knowledge of this boy prior to the wedding, he brought the child up as his own son.

To look for work in his trade, or to escape questions about the boy, or perhaps both, (John) William moved with his wife and adopted son to Barton-on-Humber, Lincolnshire, where he got a job at the Hopper Cycle Factory. When (John) William told his brother, Edward, who was next in age to the younger John Fowler, son of Henry and Ann, that there was work in Barton, Edward moved from Huntingdon to lodge with them in Newport Street, Barton-on-Humber.

When his sister-in-law's attempt to pair him off with her sister failed, **Edward** moved on to Scunthorpe into lodgings on Sheffield Street. He took a job in the blastfurnace at Lysaght's Steelworks. The landlady's daughter took a fancy to Edward which was not reciprocated so he moved again to another house, No. 29 Sheffield Street, which he rented from shopkeeper Billy Hunt. He sent for his mother, **Ann,** to look after the house for him, bringing the remaining family still living with her, **Martha Ann** and young **John**. On their arrival in Scunthorpe, John may well have been considered too old to attend Crosby School as no evidence exists of his presence there, but he did start his working life at John Lysaght's Normanby Park Works, probably with the help of his half brother (John) William. Young

John became a Kitchener recruit to the service battalions in the late summer of 1914, along with **Arthur Frost, John Dale, George Henry Ross** and **John William "Jack" Rimmington**. He was 20 years old and about to embark on what so many young men of his generation hoped would be their great patriotic adventure.

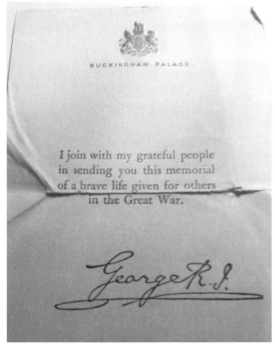

Letter sent by King George V to the bereaved.

Basic training over, the 8th Lincolns arrived in France on 11th September 1915. Later that month, John's mother, **Ann,** received a letter from him announcing his arrival there. The 8th Lincolns were part of the 21st Division, and the whole of the 21st Division had been in France scarcely 14 days, so they were quite inexperienced and lacking in knowledge of the enemy's methods, which other Divisions had gained. The Division as a whole had never been under fire.

The 8th Lincolns remained in billets until the 21st September, when the Division set out on a long approach march until the **Battle for Loos** began on the 25th September 1915. The troops were not marching "*light*." Full equipment was carried by both officers and men, even to great coats, which in the drenching rain became heavier and heavier. The Battalion was tired, wet through and hungry as the men trudged in the direction of Loos. For three hours they waited until at 8 p.m. orders came for the advance.

The advance was difficult, carried out in pitch darkness, first across the old British front line and then over the original front line German trenches, battered and ruined as they were by shell fire and littered with the dead and dying. For three hours, the Lincolns pressed on amidst the rattle of rifle, machine gun fire and the screaming of shells and explosives. Ahead of them they saw Loos in flames, the twin towers of the great mine standing out like the great towers on a burning oil field.

They pushed on and spent the night improving the trenches they had reached. About 8.15 a.m. on the morning of Sunday 26th September, they began to fire with great success at the Germans who were retiring in full view. However, this disclosed their position to the enemy's artillery, which bombarded them, killing one man. Four officers and 50 other ranks were also wounded. The Germans then began pushing through in large numbers, and there was a heavy rush of hostile troops. Trenches were quickly overwhelmed, some companies falling back in confusion. Three companies of the Lincolns retired in perfect order to the support trench, losing heavily both from their own and the enemy's shell fire. Hand to hand fighting and two or three bayonet charges took place but without success.

The casualties of the 8th Lincolns in this, their first battle, were terrible. Twenty two officers were killed, wounded or taken prisoner, other ranks losses were 471 killed, wounded or missing, of whom 148 were killed or died of wounds. John Fowler was one of that number.

A **Hull newspaper** report with photographs, dated, probably, 1916 records, *"After over twelve months of anxious suspense, Mrs. H. Fowler, 29 Sheffield Street, Scunthorpe, has been informed that her youngest son, Private John Fowler, is dead. When the war broke out, young Fowler was a car driver at Lysaghts. He immediately enlisted with the Lincolns at 20 years of age. Eleven days after his arrival in France, he was reported missing after the Battle of Loos and nothing has been heard of him since. His elder brother is a gunner with the R.F.A. in France."*

The majority of British troops killed at Loos were members of the Northern Pals organisations, men who had grown up together, attended the same schools, worked together, were neighbours or were from other social groups.

John Fowler was killed 17 days earlier than his contemporaries who are also commemorated on the **Dud Corner Memorial, Loos: Daniel Cunningham, Norman Budworth, Ernest Hornsby, Arthur Newstead** and **Albert Edward Ward**. He was 21 years old. He is also commemorated on the **John Lysaght's Works Roll of Honour 1914,** and on the Crosby Angel Memorial because he lived in Crosby. John's name is also listed on the **Crosby Parish Roll of Honour,** formerly displayed in St. George's Parish Church, Crosby.

Information from:
Mr. Alastair Fowler (great nephew)

Arthur Frost
Corporal 10973
7th Battalion Lincolnshire Regiment
Died: Thursday 9th March 1916 Died of Wounds

Arthur Frost was born on 19th February 1885, second son, fourth of twelve children (**George, Lily, Nellie, Frank, Sarah A., Harry, Betsy, James, Herbert, Walter** and **Elsie,** only six of whom lived to adulthood), of **Frank** and his wife **Sarah (née Ward) Frost** at 3 Engine Street, Brigg. The family moved around several times within the area, where Arthur's father was employed variously as a groom, a horse driver, a drayman, and a horseman at the Oil Mill in Brigg.

The family came to Scunthorpe when his father **Frank,** died of Phthisis (tuberculosis) in 1903. Although we do not know which school Arthur attended, it is recorded that his brother **Herbert** transferred from Scunthorpe National School (Gurnell Street) and started at Crosby School at its opening on 1st June 1908.

When war broke out, Arthur was employed at the John Lysaght's Normanby Park Works as a hoist driver in the Blastfurnace Department.

Herbert, his younger brother who was born in 1897, tried to enlist with Arthur, but as they stood waiting at Scunthorpe. Herbert was pulled out of the queue as he was too young but intended to lie about his age, as did many young men in their enthusiasm for adventure. Arthur became a Kitchener recruit to the Service Battalions in late August 1914, along with his contemporaries **John Henry Dale, George Henry Ross, John William "Jack" Rimmington** and **John Fowler.**

Hull Times 18th March 1916, *"Another local lad to be fatally wounded on March 2nd was Corporal Arthur Frost, second son of Mrs. Frost, 96 Buckingham Street, Crosby. On that date he received several gunshot wounds in his right arm and died (it is believed while undergoing an operation in Wimereuse Hospital, Bolougne (sic).) When the war broke out Corporal Frost was a hoist driver at Lysaghts, but in August*

Wimereux Cemetery, Boulogne, France, where Arthur Frost is buried (In 1919 it became the General Headquarters of the British Army.)

1914, he enlisted in the 7th Lincolns, and went to France, the following August. Corporal Frost fought at Loos, and in many battles in and around Ypres without being hurt. He was 31 years of age."

He died a week later, on Thursday 9th March 1916 while undergoing surgery at the Wimereux Hospital, Boulogne. He was 31 years old. He is buried in **Wimereux Communal Cemetery, Pas de Calais, France.** From October 1914 onwards, Wimereux was part of an important British Hospital Centre. The Medical units buried their dead in the communal cemetery, the right half being set aside for British graves.

Arthur Frost is commemorated on the Crosby Angel Memorial because he lived in Crosby and his brother **Herbert** went to Crosby School. He is also commemorated on the **Lysaghts Works Memorial Plaque, the Foxhills Club Memorial Plaque** and the **Crosby Parish Roll of Honour.**

Information from:
Mr. David Frost (nephew)

George Alexander Hall

Sergeant 27989
71st Heavy Battery Royal Garrison Artillery
Died: Thursday 16th August 1917 Killed in Action

A native of Leicestershire, George Alexander Hall was born in Coalville in 1889, first child of **George Alexander Hall (Senior)** and his first wife **Elizabeth,** who died in childbirth when George's brother William was born. George's father was a steam engine fitter and the 1891 and 1901 census records show the family living in Workington, Cumberland and Tinsley, Rotherham, Yorkshire respectively.

No evidence relating to young George's early years has been found, except that prior to his enlistment at Doncaster, he had worked at some time at John Lysaght's Normanby Park Steelworks in the Blastfurnace Department, and is commemorated on the **Works 1914 Roll of Honour.**

He was obviously a regular soldier who saw service prior to the Great War breaking out (see below).

"The first major attack of the Third Battle of Ypres was on the 31st July 1917 when the B.E.F. went "over the top" into No-Man's Land. Although they suffered heavy losses, initially they made great gains but the Germans counter attacked striking the B.E.F. whilst at its weakest. As a result, General Gough lost the vast majority of his gains and the attack was a failure. Making matters worse, that night the rain struck transforming the battlefield into a sea of mud and water-filled shell holes. The troops were allowed to recuperate waiting for the weather to break."

Hull Times 12th September 1917, *"During a heavy bombardment of his battery position on the night of the 15th inst., Sergeant George Alexander Hall, Heavy Battery, R.G.A. and a comrade, were instantly killed by splinters from an enemy shell. The news of his death was conveyed to his parents, Mr. and Mrs. George Hall, 200, Frodingham-road, Crosby, by his Commanding Officer, and the Chaplain, and their letters contained striking tributes to his character and abilities. Officers and men attended his funeral at a Military Cemetery behind the line, and all spoke of him in the highest terms of praise, for he was universally popular. Major Whittingham describes him as full of pluck, intelligence and self-sacrifice. 'He has done most excellent work under fire on many occasions, and in an emergency was certainly my very best Sergeant.' The Chaplain writes, 'in addition to skill in gunnery, he had a sterlingness of character and a devotion to duty which command* *the respect of all.' When a boy, Sergeant Hall was an electrician at North Lincoln, and became a soldier nine years ago, when he had just turned 17. He joined the R.G.A., and was six years with a heavy battery in India. In 1914 he came home on short leave and then went to France. His younger brother, **William,** served two years and four months in France with the Lincs., and is now working on munitions somewhere in England."*

Sergeant George Hall was buried in **Canada Farm Cemetery, Ypres, West Vlaanderen, Belgium.** The Cemetery was designed by Sir Reginald Blomfield, and took its name from a farmhouse used as a dressing station during the 1917 Allied offence on this front. Most of the burials are of men who died at the dressing station between June and October 1917.

George Alexander Hall's name is on the Crosby Angel Memorial, because his father, George Alexander Hall, is recorded as living at 200 Frodingham Road, No. 1095 in the Crosby Rate Book dated 14th November 1913, which states that the property was owned by Mark Morgan Senior, one of the Governors of Crosby School.

CANADA FARM CEMETERY, IEPER (formerly Ypres), Belgium where George Alexander Hall is buried.

Fred Hare

Lance Corporal 7401
1st Battalion Lincolnshire Regiment
Died: Sunday 1st November 1914 Killed in Action

Fred Hare was born on 27th December 1882 in a two roomed dwelling at Village Street, Broughton, Lincolnshire. He was raised by his widowed mother, **Elizabeth** and her second husband, widower, John Daniel. Fred was the fourth child of a family that would eventually grow to seven children. On the 1901 census, Fred HAIR (sic) is described as *"wagon on farm ag. Horse"* at Middle Seila, Atterby, Lincolnshire living at the home of James Taylor a farmer, and his wife and family. Nothing more is known of Fred's life prior to his enlistment. This was sadly true of so many young men who lived brief, unremarkable lives until they died in their thousands in the service of their country.

But Fred's life was not as brief as many of the Crosby men. He was 31 years old when he was killed. He had enlisted at Scunthorpe as a pre-war regular soldier, listed in the 1913 Annual Report of the Lincolnshire Regiment as being a *"Private in "A" Company, 1st Lincs."* He embarked for France on 13th August 1914, following the outbreak of the First World War on 4th August 1914.

MENIN GATE, YPRES (IEPER) where the names of Fred Hare and Edwin Pittaway are inscribed side by side on Panel 21. Access to his panel can be seen on the photograph.

day, possibly together. John Pittaway, brother of Edwin Pittaway had, like Fred Hare, served in India. The Pittaway brothers and Fred Hare would have grown up together in Broughton, and Edwin and Fred may have enlisted together. Their names are on **Panel 21 of the Menin Gate Memorial, Ypres (Ieper), West Vlaanderen, Belgium.**

Fred is also commemorated on the Crosby Angel Memorial because he was a man of Crosby Parish

On the 31st October the full weight of the German offensive was unleashed. Fred was in the British Expeditionary Force at the first battle of Ypres. The remnants of the Battalion lay waiting until about 6.45 a.m. (1st November). Daylight disclosed their position and soon they were under merciless artillery fire from the enemy's guns as well as rifle fire from both flanks, while, to make matters worse, their own gunners began to shell them. From this terrible position it was imperative to withdraw, but how to do it! The order was given by Colonel Smith to dash for cover which many succeeded in doing. Unfortunately, Fred was not one of the survivors. This happened at Wytschaete. The Battalion now numbered less than 100 men, all ranks, having suffered very heavy losses the previous day during the initial attack. The enemy was firmly entrenched in considerable strength.

Hull Times 26th December 1914, *"Broughton News: Killed in Flanders*. *Much sympathy is felt for Mrs. Daniel in the loss of her son Fred who was killed in action in Flanders on November 2nd (sic). He had previously served seven years in India."*

Fred Hare is commemorated with another Crosby man, **Edwin Pittaway**, who was also 31 years old and in the 1st Battalion Lincolnshire Regiment. Edwin and Fred were killed in action on the same

GREATHEAD G.
HALL J.
HARE F.
HARVEY G.H.

PENN W.
PITTAWAY E.
PRITCHARD T.H.
RODGERS J.G.

although no relatives of his were recorded as being pupils of Crosby School. This is borne out by the fact that Fred's name is listed on the **Crosby Parish Roll of Honour,** only part of which seems to have survived. **Edwin Pittaway** had a son at Crosby School. Edwin, like, Fred, is also commemorated on the **Broughton War Memorial, near Brigg, Lincolnshire.**

Information from:
Mrs. Margery Atkinson and Mr. Jeff Baitson
(great nephew and great niece)
Mrs. Louise Price (great great niece)

George Walter Harley

Private 28604
(Formerly Lincolnshire Regiment No. 14583)
6th Battalion Duke of Cornwall's Light Infantry
Died: Saturday 27th April 1918 Died of Wounds

John and **Sarah Ann Harley** came from Shropshire and Staffordshire respectively. They married at Wolverhampton in September 1890 and it was there that their first son, **Samuel**, was born in 1893. By 1901 (census information) they were living at 105 West Street, Scunthorpe and John is described as an ironstone miner. They had three more children, **Frederick, George** and **Charlotte,** all born in Scunthorpe. The family have been traced back to the late 1700's as living in Shropshire/Staffordshire.

George, who was born on 22nd April 1897, grew up to work in the Coke Ovens Department of John Lysaght's Normanby Park Works. It is likely that his father worked there too, as he is described variously as *"steel worker"* and *"steel roller"* on the birth certificates of his two daughters **Charlotte,** born 1899 and **Dorothy,** born 1903.

It is not known exactly when George Walter Harley enlisted at Scunthorpe.

On the 26th April 1918, the Duke of Cornwall's Light Infantry Battalions were reduced to a training cadre, having lost almost 6,000 troops

and the Field Artillery had lost all their guns at the **Battle of St. Quentin** and the **Avre** in March and April 1918. Various units were temporarily attached, before the Division was moved to England for re-establishment on 17th June 1918. The Duke of Cornwall's Light Infantry had been on the Somme since 1916. It is presumed that George Harley died from wounds received at one of these two battles.

Hull Times 11th May 1918, *"Mrs. Harley, 86 Dale-street Crosby was officially informed on Tuesday that her third son, Private George Harley, Duke of Cornwall's Light Infantry, died at 12 Casualty Clearing Station, France, on April 27th from gunshot wounds in thigh and left hand received on April 25th. Private Harley celebrated his 21st Birthday five days previous to receiving his fatal wounds, and before enlisting during Christmas 1914, was employed at Lysaght's Coke Works. His elder brother,* **Private Fred Harley,** *has been a prisoner of war in Germany since the battle of Loos in 1915, and his eldest brother,* **Private Sam Harley,** *of the Durham Light Infantry, has been on the Western Front since last August. Much sympathy is felt with Mrs. Harley in her latest bereavement. On March 21st, she lost her husband."*

A Christmas Card from The Great War that many of the fighting men would have received from *"The Dear Homeland."*

George Walter Harley's last known address was 86 Dale Street. He was 21 years old when he died of wounds on Saturday 27th April 1918.

George Walter Harley is buried in **Longpre-les-Corps Saints British Cemetery, Somme, France.** In April 1918, at the turning point of the

German offensive towards Amiens, the 12th and 55th casualty clearing stations came to Longpre and a cemetery was opened close to the station, afterwards known as **Longpre British Cemetery No. 1.** Sir Reginald Blomfield designed the Cemetery.

The following burial report appears to be that of George's brother Fred who is mentioned in the Hull Times report as being a Prisoner of War at the time of George's death, "*Frederick Harley of 17 Webster Avenue age 40 buried 2nd January 1936 Crosby Cemetery.*"

It is believed that the "E. Harley" commemorated on the **Museum Wall** and **Lysaght's Memorial at Foxhills Club, Scunthorpe** is George Walter Harley. He is commemorated on the Crosby Angel Memorial because his sister **Annie**, born 1905, was a pupil there.

George Walter Harley's name, and those of his brothers **Sam** and **Frederick** (who appear to have survived) are listed on the **Crosby Parish Roll of Honour** of all who served in the Great War. This Roll of Honour was, at one time, displayed in St. George's Parish Church, Crosby.

**John Lysaght's Memorial Plaque, situated outside Scunthorpe Museum, has several names of men which are also inscribed on the Crosby Angel.
Is G. W. Harley listed as "E. Harley"?**

William Harper
Private 3945
(formerly Lincolnshire Regiment No. 17964)
18th Battalion Machine Gun Corps
Died: Tuesday 18th June 1918 Died of Wounds

The Harpers were an old established Cumbrian family recorded as residents of Castle Sowerby, Cumberland, since the early 1700's. In 1897, twenty-three year old **Isaac Harper**, a railway engine stoker, of Whitehaven, married **Sarah Donnen,** also Whitehaven born but daughter of Irish parents. Her father was an ironstone miner. Isaac and Sarah's son, **William,** was born in the autumn of 1898 in Workington, Cumberland. They named him after his paternal grandfather. At the time of the 1901 census the family were living at 12 Salisbury Street, Workington, along with their boarder, an elderly blacksmith.

Soon Isaac moved south in search of work, moving first to Skinningrove (Middlesbrough) and then to Scunthorpe, which was just entering its *"boom town period,"* when it was likened to the American Klondike Gold Rush. Isaac Harper, already an experienced iron miner, soon found work at the newly-opened John Lysaght's Works. He sent for the family to join him at No. 11 Burke Street, where they were to remain for the rest of

Empire Day (24th May, Queen Victoria's Birthday) was started in 1902 in her Memory. This Certificate was presented to Isaac Harper, William's brother, in 1916 *"... who has helped to send some comfort to the brave Sailors and Soldiers of the British Empire who are fighting to uphold Honour, Freedom and Justice."*

their lives. William had four younger siblings, **Thomas, Sarah Elizabeth (Lil), Alice** and **Isaac,** all of whom, except **Alice,** (who was blond) had deep auburn hair. Their niece recalls that the three boys all looked alike and are indistinguishable on photographs. They all transferred to Scunthorpe schools; William would have left school when he was 14 years old, but it is not known what work he took up afterwards. It is recorded that he enlisted in 1914 as soon as war broke out. He was still only 16 but had lied about his age in order to be accepted. This upset his mother very much; born an Irish Catholic, she had become a Protestant when she married Isaac. She was a very devout woman who brought up her children - five in all - the same way. William and his siblings would have been regular attenders at Crosby Church and also the Methodist Chapel on the corner of Wells Street/ High Street (site of the present British Homes Stores) where their mother was in the Sisterhood and other church and chapel organisations.

The Harpers were a musical family - Isaac played the piano and Sarah sang in several choirs. It is likely that their children did too.

William's army career turned out to be considerably longer than many of his contemporaries. He survived for almost four years - a long time in that situation. He had enlisted in the Lincolnshire Regiment, but by June 1918, there were so few men left that those remaining were being amalgamated into other units which were holding the line of the River Marne, from the 1st to the 19th June. William Harper was in the 18th Battalion Machine Gun Corps when he was fatally wounded; he died on the 18th June 1918. He is buried in the **Pernois British Cemetery, Hallay les Pernois, Somme, France.**

When William died, his mother was so distressed that she destroyed the family ancestral details she had carefully recorded over the years in her large Bible with a metal clasp on it (still treasured by the family). She had suffered a crisis of faith and swore she would never believe in God again, but assuredly she did, as her life revolved around the Church and Chapel. When her sisters came to visit, she went with them to the Holy Souls Roman Catholic Church, opened in 1911 on Frodingham Road.

William Harper's family framed his Photograph, Medals and Next of Kin disc.

Tommy as the goalkeeper in the North Lindsey Junior's Football Club 1908-9.

William Harper, in spite of four years army service, was only 19 years old when he died. **Alice Harper**, William's sister, became a teacher at Crosby School, after being one of the first pupils of Scunthorpe Technical High School (known as the *"Brown School"* because of its uniform.) It stood on the corner of Mary Street and Cole Street, but was demolished in recent years.

In 1990, **Alice** and some other family members visited William's grave in France and took photographs, a very moving moment for them all as this was their first trip abroad, and also the first time any member of the Harper family had visited William's grave since 1918.

Information from:
Mr. Rex and Mrs. Dawn (née Harper) Reeder (niece and nephew)
Mr. Ian Harper (nephew)

Thomas George Harpham

Private 21246
1st Battalion Lincolnshire Regiment
Died: Tuesday 1st August 1916 Died of Wounds

Thomas (Tommy) George Harpham, son of **Thomas** and **Susan,** was born on 11th October 1891, a genuine Scunthonian, but from agricultural stock, as were most of his contemporaries. His father was on the list of Primitive Methodist Chapel Circuit Officers and Committee, and was listed among seven names as a Schools Representative in 1900 (*Mrs. M. E. Armstrong from "An Industrial Island."*)

The Harphams were a deeply religious family, attached to the Primitive Methodist Chapel that used to be in Scunthorpe High Street, opposite Marks and Spencer's store. Their social lives revolved around Chapel activities and healthy sporting pursuits; they were well-known and well liked. Tommy's siblings were **William John** (born 1886), **Maria Elizabeth** (born 1888) **Florence May** (born 1894), **Herbert** (born 1897) **Kate Annie** (born 1900), **Charles Edward** (born 1902) **Harold Woodward** (born 1904) **Ernest Albert** (born 1906) and **Walter Henry** (born 1907).

On 11th February 1916 Thomas enlisted as a soldier at Scunthorpe, along with **Thomas William Bowden.** Thomas Harpham's army career lasted only a matter a weeks. He died on 1st August 1916 of wounds sustained at the **Battle of the Somme.** The 1st Lincolnshire Battalion were in the 21st Division; they came under sustained machine gun fire before reaching Birch Tree Wood where more stubborn resistance was met.

Headstone in Crosby Cemetery with the names of Tommy and his Mother inscribed thereon ...

Hull Daily Mail 5th August 1916, *"Private Thomas George Harpham, third son of Mr. and Mrs. Tom Harpham, 2 Sheffield Street, Crosby, is another Scunthorpe born lad to give his life in the cause of right. A printer by trade, he was for a long time in the employ of Messrs. Wilford and Kenning, but for six months prior to enlisting he worked with the joiners at the Normanby Parks Steelworks. On February 11th last, he joined the Lincolns, and he went to France, towards the end of June. He was soon in the trenches, and after successfully coming through his first engagement, did his bit in the great advance.*

Between the 3rd and 5th of last month he was wounded in the left arm and conveyed to Dublin (Castle) Hospital, where he underwent an operation. On Tuesday the sad news was received by his heartbroken parents, that he had died that day at 1.10 p.m. He was 24 years of age. Almost everybody knew Tommy Harpham, and the news of his death has cast a gloom over the few football enthusiasts that are now left in the ironstone district. A member of Mr. Symes Bible Class he first of all kept goal for the "Mites", and for two seasons he was the junior's trusty custodian. The hope is entertained that he will be buried at Crosby, this weekend."

He was buried on 4th August 1916 in **Plot B Grave No. 33 at Crosby Cemetery.** Wallis T. Heaton performed the ceremony. The inscription on his headstone bears witness to his family's strong Christian belief, ***"not my will, O Lord, but Thine be done. In Loving Memory of Thomas George Harpham dearly beloved son of Tom and Susan Harpham, who died on active Service August 1st 1916 in his 25th year."***

Thomas's Mother, **Susan Harpham,** died soon afterwards on 12th March 1919 aged 53 years and was buried with her son in the same grave. Her inscription was *"Peace Perfect Peace."*

George Henry Ross, another young man commemorated on the Crosby Angel, is buried in the same block at Crosby Cemetery. Thomas Harpham is commemorated on the Crosby Angel Memorial because it is recorded that his brothers **Ernest** and **Walter** attended the school.

Mr. Roy Gregson, (who died in October 2004) a late member of the research team for this project, was related to this family, in that **Susan Harpham (**née **Vickers)** Tommy's mother, was the sister of Roy's maternal grandmother, Maria, shown as aged 8 on the 1881 census.

Thomas George Harpham's name is also included on the **Crosby Parish Roll of Honour** which commemorates all who served in the Great War, including those who died.

Information from:
Mrs. Wendy Addy (great niece)
Mrs. Pat Freear (great niece)
The late Mr. Roy Gregson (second cousin)
"An Industrial Island" edited by Mrs. M. E. Armstrong

John (Jack) Havercroft

Able Seaman J/2163
H.M.S. "Queen Mary"
Died: Wednesday 31st May 1916 Died at Sea

John (Jack) Havercroft was born at Holton le Moor, near Caistor, Lincolnshire on Leap Year Day 29th February 1896. Few details of this brave young man's life are recorded, save for those that occurred immediately before his death at the age of just 20 years.

The fact that he was a Rack Driver prior to his enlistment on 29th February 1914, when he optimistically signed on for 12 years, is known from his Service Record. He enlisted at Portsmouth. He was only five feet four inches and seven eighths tall, with a chest measurement of thirty four and seven eighths inches; he was slightly built by today's standards. Fresh faced, with hazel eyes and dark brown hair, even the small scar at the back of his left wrist and the mole over his left collar bone are recorded.

His career commenced on the training ship, the *"Vivid I"* as a Boy Rating. It was later noted that he had grown to a height of five feet five and a quarter inches, immediately before going to sea on the H.M.S. *"Formidable I"*. He was to make one more voyage on this ship before joining the crew of H.M.S. *"Queen Mary"* where he remained until his death at sea on 31st May 1916.

Alexander (Alec) Havercroft

Ordinary Signalman J/30530
H.M.S. "Queen Mary"
Died: Wednesday 31st May 1916 Died at Sea

No details of Alec's schooling are known, but on his Naval Service Record it states that he was a joiner prior to his enlistment at Davenport on his 18th Birthday, 21st October 1915, as a Boy Rating. A report in the **Daily News dated Thursday 8th June 1916** reveals that Alec must have been born to be a sailor, having first seen the light of day on Trafalgar Day, 21st October 1897 at Holton le Moor, Caistor, Lincolnshire. Like his elder brother, **Jack,** he signed on for 12 years.

Alexander (Alec) was at five feet, minus three quarters of a inch, even more slightly built than his brother, his chest measurement of only thirty one and a half inches poignantly suggests that he was not yet fully grown. Described on his Service Record as a Boy Rating, first on the training ships *"Ganges"* and the *"Vivid I"* it was not until he joined the crew of the *"Queen Mary"* that he was listed as Ordinary Signalman. He was reunited with his older brother Jack, an Able Seaman on the same ship, the ill-fated *"Queen Mary."*

Born just eighteen months apart, sons of **Snowden** (a railway signalman) and **Lucy Havercroft,** the short lives and untimely deaths of the two young Havercroft brothers bound them

Page from an autograph book owned by Gladys Hornsby (née Sleight) a close family friend who lived at 97 Diana Street - her husband was called Harold Hornsby. Jack Havercroft's signature and drawing was done on 27th February 1916, just over three months before his death.

together for ever, when their ship H.M.S. *"Queen Mary"* was sunk twenty minutes into the infamous **Battle of Jutland.** However, the boys are commemorated on different Naval War Memorials.

After the First World War, an appropriate way had to be found of commemorating those members of the Royal Navy who had no known graves, the majority of deaths having occurred at sea where no permanent memorial could be provided. The Admiralty decided to have three identical Naval Memorials in Great Britain, sited at Chatham, Plymouth and Portsmouth, and these were designed by Sir Edward Lutyens. These were to be obelisks to serve as leading marks for shipping. **Jack** was a Pompey **(Portsmouth)** and **Alec** a **Davenport** Rating. They are commemorated on two separate Memorials but strangely both on Panels 13 respectively. A request for a posting to H.M.S. *"Queen Mary"* had been made by one of the brothers, possibly the elder one, Jack, had requested that Alec, the younger one, be permitted to join him?

Losing two sons together prompted their mother, **Lucy Havercroft,** to write to the Admiralty campaigning for brothers not to serve on the same ship. The point was eventually conceded.

"On the afternoon of May 31ˢᵗ 1916 both the German and British fleets were in the North Sea steaming towards each other. The two German groups having just left port were each headed North. Admiral Beatty with the British battle cruisers was headed East and Admiral Jellicoe with the Grand Fleet was a little way above and behind him headed South East. The picket line of German submarines had failed to intercept any British ships as they were supposed to. The whole German plan was predicated on a successful U-boat interception of the enemy battle cruisers. Jellicoe's Grand Fleet had also managed to elude the submarines. Bad weather had prevented any zeppelins from flying reconnaissance missions. Therefore Admiral Scheer had no idea that he was about to run into the entire Royal Navy. By chance a neutral merchant vessel was steaming along the line of advance of both fleets. The Queen Mary's smoke was sighted almost simultaneously by both sides who sent cruisers to investigate. She was the second ship to be destroyed, the first was H.M.S. "Indefatigable." The fleets then spotted each other at about 2 p.m. and Beatty led his battle cruisers into attack. It was unfortunate for the British that the fleets met in this way for had that merchant man not been there they would have met later and the High Seas Fleet would have been that much further from home. It was the British plan to cut off a German retreat by positioning itself between the German fleet and its home ports. It is also unfortunate for Beatty that the battle ships of the fifth battle squadron

H.M.S. *"Queen Mary"* on which the Havercroft brothers lost their lives

failed to get the signal to attack and continued towards a pre-determined rendezvous with Jellicoe and the rest of the fleet for several precious minutes. Thus Beatty's battle cruisers were drawn unsupported towards Hipper's. This was not what these ships were designed to do and they paid dearly for this misuse of force. In the ensuing exchange, the British lost the Battle Cruiser H.M.S. "Indefatigable" which was sunk and the Battle Cruiser H.M.S. "Lion" heavily damaged. By now the ships of the 5th battle squadron had turned around to engage the Germans. "Queen Mary" came under heavy fire, heavy shells from the German ships "Seydlitz" and "Derfflinger" penetrated a forward magazine and the ship blew up. Even so, there were 9 survivors of the 1275 crew. Seven were picked up by British ships, two by Germans... Fifty seven officers and 1209 other ranks were lost at sea. Amongst them were the two Havercroft boys, Jack and Alec."

At the time, the British had the Germans outgunned, and would have triumphed had Scheer not been spotted approaching from the south with his main battle fleet. This compelled Beatty to withdraw north and started the second phase of the battle. Altogether at the Battle of Jutland the British sustained 6,800 casualties, lost three battle cruisers and eight destroyers sunk. The Germans lost one old battle cruiser, one battle cruiser, four light cruisers, five destroyers and 3,100 casualties.

There were few more patriotic families in the Scunthorpe area than the Havercrofts, and they paid dearly for their beliefs with the loss of their two seafaring sons. However, their eldest son, **Fred** Havercroft, born 1891, a Company Sergeant Major with the 5th Lincolns, had a distinguished military career, and in spite of being badly wounded survived World War I. He died on 17th December 1944 of diabetes at the age of 53 years.

Mr. Taylor's Logbook, page 247, 27th July 1915, *"Three sons of the Havercroft family visited the school, two are serving on H.M.S. Queen Mary and the other is a Sergeant Major fighting in France. We sang them several songs, which they obviously enjoyed. Two other brothers, Snowden and Ralph, are scholars in the school."*

The Daily News Thursday 8th June 1916, *"Battle Toll Scunthorpe Lads Lost In Sea Fight." "Two sailor sons." "Mr. and Mrs. Snowden Havercroft of Chapel Lane, Old Crosby have lost both their sailor sons John and Alexander, both of whom were serving on H.M.S. Queen Mary. John was an Able Seaman and although only 20 years old had already seen some fighting in the Heligoland Bight Battle. Alec was just 18. Both were highly respected in the district and our sympathy is with their parents whose only consolation is that their lads died fighting. In addition, they have a son Fred, a Company Sergeant Major with the Lincolns who was badly wounded last October.*

Quartermaster Sergeant Fred Havercroft, M.M.

Fred Havercroft won the Military Medal at the **Hohenzollern Redoubt** where he fought side by side with the unfortunate Crosby lads **Daniel Cunningham, Norman Budworth, Ernest Hornsby, Arthur Newstead** and **Albert Edward Ward,** who were all killed in battle on 13th October 1915. There is a dramatic account in the **Hull Times of 16th December 1916** of Fred, who had been in the T.A. since 1912, winning his Military Medal. *"The regiment were attacking the Hohenzollern Redoubt. All the officers had been killed and the unit was beginning to be pushed back. Fred rallied the men and they achieved* *their objective, but in bayoneting one of the enemy the man's rifle went off hitting Fred in the foot. As he lay on the ground he was hit by a shrapnel and then gassed. A Grenadier Guards Officer helped him to the regimental aid post where the regimental stretcher bearer, Teddy Burgess, one time Councillor for Old Crosby, carried him on his back for about a mile to the casualty clearing station. Fred apparently said of this incident "Teddy lost some sweat on that trip!" Fred was invalided back to Blighty and was in Wharncliffe Hospital, Sheffield for six months. Afterwards he had a spell in a convalescent camp in County Cork."*

Lucy, Jack and Alec's Mother, successfully campaigned for brothers serving in the Royal Navy to be posted on different ships after the deaths of her two sons. Lucy was a District Nurse and Midwife in Crosby until 1926.

Scunthorpe and Frodingham Star 23rd December 1916, *"Military Medal For Local War Hero." "The relatives and friends of Quartermaster Sergeant Fred Havercroft will be pleased to hear that this brave fellow has been awarded the Military Medal for conspicuous bravery at the Hohenzollern Redoubt on October 13th 1915. When all the officers of the gallant Lincs. were rendered 'hors de combat' Fred took command and twice bravely led his men forward after they had been repulsed. From the second to the third line it was fierce hand to hand fighting and as our hero bayoneted one Hun the latter's rifle went off and the bullet entered Fred's left foot. As he lay on the ground he was hit in the hip*

by a piece of shell and was then gassed … his many friends in the Scunthorpe district will be pleased to hear that he has since been made a Quartermaster Sergeant. Q.M.S. Havercroft is now convalescing in Bally Conaire, County Cork where he returned last Saturday after a five days leave. The eldest son of Mrs. Snowden Havercroft of Old Crosby, better known as Curly, Q.M.S. Havercroft worked in the fourteen inch rolling mill at Frodingham before the War. He had been with the Lincolns as a Terrier since August 1909, and his wedding day was fixed for August 6th 1914, but instead of standing at the altar he was on guard duty at the docks having been mobilised the day before. However, he did marry on October 3rd at St. Peter's Hull, to Miss Ethel Tripp, whose five brothers are all with the colours. Q.M.S. Havercroft was 24 years old when he sailed for France in February 1915 and before he won the coveted Medal had many thrilling experiences. He had not been back at the trenches two hours after his five days leave in Blighty when he became acquainted with all the horrors of liquid fire at Ypres. (ibid)"

The Havercrofts' dedication to the defence of their country did not stop there. **Ernest Havercroft,** a cousin of John, Fred and Alexander, was also killed in the Great War. He was **Private No.133103 2nd Battalion Machine Gun Corps.** He died aged 19 on 10th June 1918 and is buried at **Daullens Community Cemetery Extension No. 2., near Amiens, France.**

Lucy, sister of Jack and Alec, and next in age, became a munitions worker, young **Snowden** was a member of Brigg Grammar School Cadet Corps which was attached to the Lincolns Regiment, and **Ralph**, the youngest, was in the Crosby Scouts. We are indebted to them all.

John and Alexander Havercroft are commemorated on the Crosby Angel Memorial because their siblings attended the School and their family lived in Crosby. The names of John and Alexander and that of Fred also appear on the **Crosby Parish Roll of Honour.**

Information from:
Mrs. Zelma Havercroft (niece by marriage)
Mrs. Sherry Sheppard (great niece)
Mr. Colin Havercroft
Miss Margaret Hill

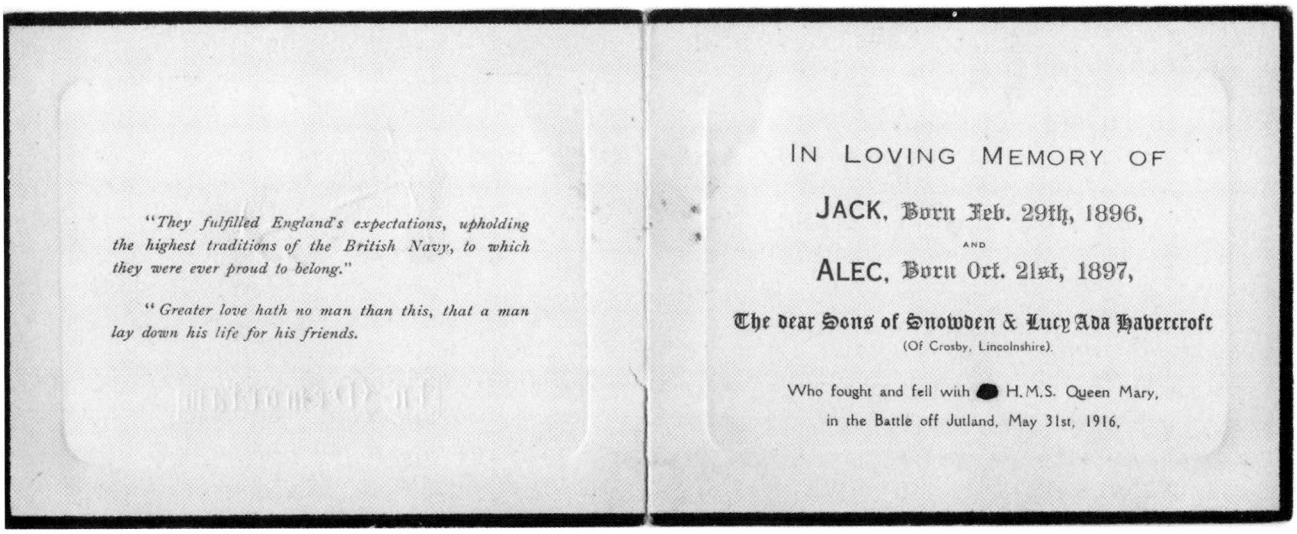

"They fulfilled England's expectations, upholding the highest traditions of the British Navy, to which they were ever proud to belong."

" Greater love hath no man than this, that a man lay down his life for his friends.

IN LOVING MEMORY OF

JACK, Born Feb. 29th, 1896,

AND

ALEC, Born Oct. 21st, 1897,

The dear Sons of Snowden & Lucy Ada Havercroft
(Of Crosby, Lincolnshire).

Who fought and fell with H.M.S. Queen Mary,

in the Battle off Jutland, May 31st, 1916,

FALL OUT

Farewell, my friends,
As we go down, together,
As we sink beneath the waves.
Our days were short,
But for Blighty we fought,
When we answered the call to arms.

Farewell, my pals,
As our lungs fill with water
As we wave our last goodbye.
We have given our lives,
And not one will survive,
From the street we once called home.

Mothers, don't grieve,
Just try to believe
That this was all God's Plan.
When the telegrams come
Hold tight to your sons,
Those children who still are free.

The Roll Call is long,
Like the words of a song
With a haunting, soulful tune.
The years, they will pass,
But for you, not for us,
While we rot 'neath the salty sea.

Farewell, cold world,
As we pass from the day,
Into endless, friendless night.
Our lives had just started,
But now we've departed …

And we will never know –
Was it worth it?

Written by **Mrs. Jenny Ferenczi** after proof reading the biographies of the Havercroft Brothers, Alex and Jack who died when H.M.S. "Queen Mary" was sunk at the Battle of Jutland 1916

Arthur Newstead

Private 2631
1/5th Battalion Lincolnshire Regiment
Died: Wednesday 13th October 1915 Killed in Action

Unlike many of his contemporaries, Arthur Newstead was truly a local lad, born in Crosby on 30th October 1896 and baptised at St. John's Parish Church, Scunthorpe. He enlisted at Scunthorpe together with other Crosby lads, **Richard Henry Davison, Norman Budworth, Ernest Hornsby, Daniel Cunningham** and **Albert Edward Ward.**

These were men recruited specifically to bring the 5th Lincolns ready for overseas service. Arthur was killed in action at **Loos, Hohenzollern Redoubt** on Wednesday 13th October 1915. He was 19 years old.

Lincolnshire Family History Society Magazine Volume 6 No. 2 June 1995, *"The County's Blackest Day"* by Eric Walter, 60 London Road, Liverpool, L3 5NF, … *"To make things worse very few of the bodies of the men who fell were ever recovered and of the 180 fatalities only 7 have a known grave. Here are just a few of the casualties from "C" Company…* **Private Arthur Newstead***, aged 18, a grocer from Scunthorpe and son of Arthur and Ruth … The names of all*

these men are inscribed on the Loos Memorial to the Missing, about a mile from the (Hohenzollern) Redoubt. The Memorial bears witness to the sacrifice of the Lincolnshire Regiment with the names of 517 Officers and Men…Thankfully the Lincolnshire Territorials never again had a day as bad as 13th October. Part of the reason was that because the attack failed, the War Office regarded the units which took part in it as 'windy' and not to be trusted and it was a long while before they were entrusted with another attack."

Arthur Newstead is commemorated on the **Dud Corner Memorial, Loos, Pas de Calais, France** together with **Ernest Hornsby, Norman Budworth, Daniel Cunningham** and **Albert Edward Ward,** who were also killed on the same day. **John Fowler** is also commemorated with them but died later. Arthur is named on the Crosby Angel Memorial because his brothers **Henry** and **Alfred** attended the School.

Another more personal memorial to Arthur exists, the following eulogy, written by his niece, Mrs Edna Barnard.

*"Arthur was the eldest child of the second marriage of Ruth Ann, née Braithwaite of Millom, Cumbria. Ruth had been married to Thomas Phillips who was tragically killed in 1893 or 1894 in a blast furnace accident at the Trent Iron Works, Scunthorpe leaving her with three small children, William John, Walter and Florrie, who was a baby. Arthur Newstead (**senior**) was his workmate and helped Ruth to return to her family in Millom. In those days there was no welfare benefit or compensation. They kept in touch and eventually Arthur became Ruth's second husband and brought up her three children as his own. The growing family lived in various rented houses in Scunthorpe between 1897 and 1913, but had spells back in Millom and in Silverdale, where Ruth had relatives. Eventually, there were five more children who survived infancy, Arthur (Junior), Nora (my mother), Belle, Alfred and Harry."*

"After becoming foreman on a blastfurnace at John Lysaght's Normanby Park works, my grandfather, Arthur, in 1913 bought newly built 95 Buckingham Street and the family lived there until 1924 when my grandparents moved to Alkborough with the two youngest unmarried

members of the family, Alfred and Harry. No. 95 Buckingham Street became the home of my parents, Nora and John Henry (Harry) Langford, where my sister and I were born."

"When the family lived in the various rented properties, the children had attended various schools. My mother had been at Ashby, Gurnell Street C of E School and like Arthur, had been at Crosby. From stories my mother told me their family life was full of fun and private jokes and sayings. As I remember my grandfather, he had a mischievous sense of humour and was always ready to entertain us with a mixture of music hall songs, interspersed with some Moody and Sankey! I can imagine he was the same with his own children. My mother said she had very happy times 'at home with the lads' as she put it."

Edna Barnard with "Uncle Arthur's Apple Tree."

"After he left school, Arthur (Junior) worked as a Grocer's Assistant at No. 1 Branch of Scunthorpe Co-op., then in Home Street, I think. He was there until he joined the army. In his spare time, judging from my mother's photographs, he was keen on football. Sadly I know little else but he was always a presence in my grandparents' home, looking down in his army uniform from a large photograph hung on the wall of the living room."

"Uncle Arthur's Apple Tree"
"As a young lad, Arthur planted a pip from an apple which grew into a young tree which was planted in the back garden of 95 Buckingham Street when the family moved there. Eventually, it outgrew its place there and so was re-planted in his father's allotments in the old pits, Normanby Road."

"After Arthur's death, his mother would not be parted from the tree, so when they moved to the cottage at Alkborough, where they remained for the rest of their lives, the apple tree went too. Following my grandfather's death in 1942, my family moved to Alkborough from No. 95 (Buckingham Street.) It is still my home and the tree can still be seen from the kitchen window. Although grown from a dessert apple pip, the fruit of the tree is rather sharp, more akin to a crab apple, but larger. It would never have been a commercial success, as the apples only keep a few days before they go brown. However, it fruits early, usually in July, and 'falls' beautifully to make pies and sauce as well making delicious jelly. Every year, a few boxes of puréed apple go into my freezer labelled 'Uncle Arthur's Apple,' a bond between me and the uncle I never knew, and perhaps an unusual sort of memorial. I am sure that had he lived, Arthur would have been a very good gardener, just like his brothers, my Uncles William, Walter, Alfred and Harry."

"The White Feather"
"One of the more unpleasant activities engaged in by the civilian population in the Great War was the presentation of white feathers - usually by older women - to any young man who looked of military age, even though he was probably too young or perhaps unfit.

Arthur was sent a white feather by one such person which caused him to sign up, even though he was only 17 and my grandfather was unable to persuade him to do otherwise. My knowledge of this is very hazy for it was only towards the end of her life that my mother talked about the incident. It was not spoken of in the family, not out of shame, but because it had so distressed my grandmother, whose two older sons were already serving in the army. I am not sure if my *mother knew who the woman concerned was, but my grandmother did. I don't think she ever recovered from the grief and anguish that the incident caused. I never knew her to look well, and she died aged 67 when I was 8."*

"There must have been other families affected in the same way, perhaps some of the families whose boys enlisted at the same time as Arthur and whose names are recorded on the Angel. A copy of the picture of the Angel with the Headmaster, Mr. Taylor, standing by, together with his staff, which included my Uncle Harry, who was a student teacher at the time, was in my mother's album. I have often wondered what was going through his mind as he stood there by his brother's memorial."

Information from:
Mrs. Edna Barnard (niece)

Arthur Norwood

Private 26435
2nd Battalion South Staffordshire Regiment
Died: Wednesday 24th January 1917 Killed in Action

Arthur Lilly Norwood was born on 29th January 1894 at Marton Lane, Hibaldstow, Lincolnshire in 1894 to **John William** and **Emma (née Lilly) Norwood**. His sister **Eva** was born the following year and his brother **James** in 1897.

Unfortunately, his mother died shortly afterwards, aged only 19 years, sadly a common occurrence in those days.

A year later, in 1899, widower **John Norwood** was remarried, to **Martha Beel**. Arthur and his siblings went to school at Hibaldstow, and Arthur attended the Church Sunday school, there, where he was presented by the Vicar with prizes for punctuality, diligence and good conduct. He was Confirmed at Blyton by the same Vicar on 26th February 1908. Prior to his enlistment at Epworth, Lincolnshire, he was working for a Mr. Garner of East Lound, Isle of Axholme and was living at Haxey. He had previously worked at the Lysaght's Normanby Park Steelworks in the Coke Ovens Department; Arthur's name is on the **John Lysaght's Roll of Honour 1914.**

Arthur's name on the Haxey War Memorial Isle of Axholme, Lincolnshire.

A report from the **Hull Times** dated **3rd March 1917** states, *"Private A. Norwood aged 23 years, Staffs. Regiment, who was so severely wounded in the thigh and side that he died on the way to the hospital. He belonged to Redbourne, Kirton in Lindsey."*

Report from **Lincolnshire Star 17th March 1917,** *"News has been received by Mr. and Mrs. John*

Norwood of Manton Lane, Hibaldstow that their son Arthur Lilley Norwood of the 5th Staffordshire Regiment was killed in action on January 24th 1917."

Two of Arthur's cousins, **Henry** and **Victor,** were pupils at Crosby School which is why his name is on the Angel Memorial. Arthur's second cousin **Alma Norwood**, whose father, also called **Alma,** who suffered from shell shock, was a Sergeant in the 1st Battalion, Lincolnshire Regiment.

Arthur's name appears on the **Haxey Parish War Memorial,** and he is also named on the **Roll of Honour, Scunthorpe Museum Wall.**

Once again there are more details of a young man's death than of his short life. Arthur is buried in **Courcelette British Cemetery, Somme, France.** The cemetery was begun in November 1916 as Mouquet Road or Sunken Road Cemetery. Arthur's was one of the original burials. He was likely to have been wounded defending the village of Courcelette after it had been captured by Allied Forces.

Information from:
Mr. David Norwood (great nephew)

Edwin Pittaway

Lance Corporal 8146
1st Battalion Lincolnshire Regiment
Died: Sunday 1st November 1914 Killed in Action

Edwin Pittaway was born in Darlaston, Staffordshire in 1883, probably when his mother Lucy was visiting relatives. **Lucy** and her husband **Henry** were *"incomers"* from the industrial Midlands, or Black Country of Staffordshire. They had almost certainly moved North to join in the iron and steel rush taking place in the Scunthorpe district at that time. Edwin had two older sisters, **Ellen** and **Jane**, and two younger sisters, **Ada** and **Elsie,** and four younger brothers, **George, John, Charles** and **Frederick,** all of whom were born in Scunthorpe.

After initially living at Glebe Terrace, Scunthorpe, the family moved out of town and settled in the village of Broughton about five miles away.

No records of the children's school days have been found, so it may be assumed that the young Pittaways attended their local village school. At the time of the 1901 census Edwin, then 18 years old, was working as an agricultural labourer, his married sister **Ellen** lived next door and younger sister **Jane** was in service to a farmer at Gokewell (Broughton).

In the spring of 1910, Edwin Pittaway was married to Scunthorpe girl **Lydia Cross**. They made their home at 54 Burke Street, Crosby. It is likely that Edwin was already a pre-war regular soldier, although he may have been a reservist who was recalled on the outbreak of War. The fact that he was in the 1st Battalion Lincolnshire Regiment indicates that he was in the British Expeditionary Force.

He was killed in action early in the war on Sunday, 1st November 1914 at the **First Battle of Ypres;** he was 31 years old. **Fred Hare** (whose name is also on the Angel Memorial), another Broughton man in the same Battalion, was killed on the same day. They are both commemorated on the **Menin Gate Memorial, Panel 21, Ypres, West Vlaanderen, Belgium** - no known graves.

Edwin's 18 year old brother, **Private 14408 Frederick Pittaway,** of the 1st Lincolns, was also killed in action, on the 6th June 1915, and his name too is commemorated on Panel 21, Menin Gate Memorial. It is believed that Frederick died in the **first attack on Bellewaarde** (between the Menin Road and the Ypres - Roulers railway,

War Memorial at Broughton, Brigg, Lincolnshire, whereon the names of Edwin Pittaway and his brother Frederick are inscribed, and Fred Hare, another man also on the Crosby Angel. The Sculptor of the Memorial was Mr. Gilbert Baynes.

Apparently he lost his legs but not in the War. There was an event to raise money for him held in Broughton village in 1914 because he had been an invalid for some ten years.

Information from:
Mr. David Pittaway (great nephew)
Ms. Elaine Mullen, researching the names on the Broughton War Memorial 2005/6

Belgium). The German trenches formed a salient. This began on the 16th June 1915. Frederick was born in the September quarter 1897.

There are four Pittaways on the **Roll of Honour in Broughton Church,** which is a list of all local men serving in the First World War, but it was only continued until about 1915.

Edwin Pittaway is commemorated on the Angel Memorial because his children, **Louis (Lewis)** and **Lucy Mary,** attended Crosby School. Edwin had been killed before Lucy started school.

Hull Times 3rd April 1915, (Edwin's brother John) *"Lance Corporal J. Pittaway, a native of Broughton, near Brigg, who has served seven years in India and returned home from there last November. He has been in many hard engagements in France, and came back to England last Thursday, having been wounded at the Battle of Neuve Chappelle, and is now at York. He is one of four brothers in His Majesty's Forces."*

Charles Pittaway was a fifth brother who did not serve in World War I as he was an invalid.

James' Headstone at Vlamertinghe New Military Cemetery, Ypres, West Vlaanderen, Belgium.

James Jabez Pogson

Gunner 820089
"C" Battery 232nd Brigade Royal Field Artillery
Died: Wednesday 27th June 1917 Killed in Action

THE CROSBY ANGEL - A COMMUNITY'S WAR MEMORIAL

James Jabez Pogson was born in 1887 at Owersby near Market Rasen, Lincolnshire, second son of **John Sherriff**, an agricultural labourer and **Susannah Pogson.** No records of James' schooldays have been found but on the 1901 census he was recorded as living at Top Farm, Lissington, Caistor, Lincolnshire, aged 14, working as a general domestic servant for John Robinson, a farmer, and his wife Mary.

Clara Pogson with her baby daughter Yvonne Hilda.

Unfortunately, little more is known of his life except that in the June quarter of 1914, in the Gainsborough, Lincolnshire district, he married **Clara J. Mabbott** (whose father was a farm labourer at Willoughton, Lincolnshire).

Hull & Lincolnshire Times (Date not stated on the article), *"News has been received at Willerton (sic) that Gunner James Jabez Pogson, husband of Mrs. Clara Pogson (née Mabbott) has been killed in action. Much sympathy is felt for the parents and the young widow, who received from his commanding officer:- 'It is with the greatest regret that I have to inform you of the death of your husband in action. As long as I have known him, he has always done his duty well, and he died doing his duty, which may be a consolation to you in your loss. You will be glad to know that his death was instantaneous, and he did not suffer.'"*

James died on 27th June 1917 and is buried at **Vlamertinghe New Military Cemetery, Ypres, West Vlaanderen, Belgium.** This cemetery was begun in anticipation of the allied offensive launched on this part of the front in July 1917. Several attacks were made during June 1917. Assaults on the German trenches on the 28th June were all preliminary to the larger operations which had been planned for 1st July 1917, the **Battle of Lens.** James' youngest brother Wilfred survived the War.

Willoughton War Memorial near Gainsborough - James' home village ...

From **School Logbook, 19th December 1915,** *"learned that **Wilfred Pogson** is in hospital with French (sic) feet and influenza."* And on **7th July 1916,** *"...on Tuesday morning **Wilfred Pogson** visited the school. He is one of our old boys* *home from France on a ten day leave."* Wilfred survived the War.

James Jabez Pogson is commemorated on the Crosby Angel Memorial because his brother **Wilfred** was a pupil at the school. James is also mentioned in the **Scunthorpe U.D.C. Roll of Honour 1917,** *"James Pogson of 28 Cemetery Road, Scunthorpe Private was wounded twice."*

James' wife Clara came from Willoughton near Gainsborough, Lincolnshire. She gave birth to a daughter, **Yvonne Hilda,** after James' death and returned with the child to Willoughton later, which is why James Jabez' name is also on the **Willoughton War Memorial.**

Information from:
Mrs. Gloria Pogson (niece)

Tom Popple is smoking a pipe on the right of the photograph.

Tom Popple
Stoker 1ˢᵗ Class 307273
(RFR/CH/B/6988) Howe Battalion R.N. Division Royal Navy
Died: Friday 4ᵗʰ June 1915 Killed in Action

Initially, Tom Popple was one of the many young men of whom little was known, however, the following details have been supplied by **Mr. Graham Popple,** (great nephew) who writes from Brisbane, Australia (22ⁿᵈ February 2005), *"I have just received the January 10ᵗʰ 2005 issue of Scunthorpe and District Nostalgia from my Sister, Wendy Fogg, who lives in Scunthorpe and have read your article "Researching memorial" on page*

2. In the list of names you have a Thomas Popple, who was my grandfather's brother."

"Tom (not Thomas) was born in Lincoln in 1885 and was the third of seven children born to **Tom** and **Susannah Popple (née Redford).** His brothers and sister were: **William** born 1882 in Great Hale, Lincs., **George** born 1884 in Lincoln, **Frances** born 2 August 1888 in Gainsborough, Lincs., **Frank** (my grandfather) born 20 January 1891 in Scunthorpe, **Fred** born 19 November 1893 in Scunthorpe and **Joseph** born 1896 in Scunthorpe."*

"In the 1891 Census the family lived in Providence Place, (N.B.: This later became Argyle Terrace) Scunthorpe, which was just off the High Street somewhere near where British Home Stores is or was."

"In the 1901 Census the family were living at 9 Robert Street, Scunthorpe, but Tom was not living there. I have found a Thomas Popple aged 15, born Lincoln, working as a farm servant in Adlingfleet, Yorkshire."

"From there I know that the family went to live at 37 Dale Street and then went to live in "The Bungalow", Old School Lane, Bottesford."

"I have in my possession a scroll that reads: '1914 – 1918 For King and Country to the Glory of God and in everlasting memory of Popple, Sto. 1ˢᵗ Cl. T., 307273 (R.F.R./CH/

B/6988). R.N. "Howe" Bn. Div. 4th June 1915. Age 29. Son of Tom and Susannah Popple of Bottesford, Ashby, Scunthorpe, Lincs. Who gave his life in the Great War that we might live and whose name is carved in stone on The Helles Memorial, Gallipoli.'"

Tom's Mother, Susannah Popple, who died in 1942.

As a young lad I remember seeing a large picture frame hung in the bungalow at Bottesford that contained a photo of Tom and his medals. I believe that this was donated to the Scunthorpe Museum in the late sixties or early seventies."

"Tom's parents have several great grandchildren and great great grandchildren still living in Scunthorpe."

Further evidence came to light via Tom's Royal Naval Service Record. Tom Popple enlisted in the Royal Navy at Chatham on 12th August 1904, signing up for a twelve year period. He was 19 years old.

On 17th September 1914, he transferred to the Royal Naval Division just one month after it was formed. The R.N.D. was made up of Naval Reserve Forces when warships of the fleet were fully crewed. The tradition of Naval personnel serving on land was long established, R.N.D. personnel fought on land alongside the Army when there was a shortfall in Infantry Divisions. They remained under Admiralty control and retained Naval Traditions, uniform and language when attempts to convert the R.N.D. to conform to Army practices failed. The R.N.D. was sent into many theatres of war, including Gallipoli in 1914. The battalions were all called after famous Naval personages.

In 1914 Tom Popple was serving with the **Howe Battalion.** Nine months later, on 4th June 1915, he was reported missing in the Dardanelles. Throughout the following year, extensive enquiries were made regarding his fate and although one man involved in "A" Company's charge on an enemy trench that day had heard someone say that *"Tom Popple had been shot,"* he had not seen him fall. Another Stoker later reported that he had seen Popple shot in the neck and *"he fell … but I did not see him again."*

The Popple family continued to hope that their son had survived; their hopes were raised once again when a man home on leave allegedly had news of him, but it was a vain hope, another straw to be clutched at, further compounding their anguish until they were informed that Tom Popple's death had been accepted by the Board of Authority, *"assumed killed in action 4th June 1915."* The waiting was over after 13 months of agonising false hope, an experience shared by thousands mourning the loss of their sons, husbands, sweethearts and brothers.

In the **Hull Times for 15th July 1916,** the following information is recorded, *"***A Crosby Naval Hero." *"A year ago, Stoker Tom Popple was officially reported missing, and on Wednesday last, the Admiralty Record Office notified Mr. and Mrs. Tom Popple, of 37, Dale Street, Crosby, that it is now assured he was killed in action when serving with the Howe Battalion, Royal Naval Division, on the Gallipoli Peninsular, on the 4th June 1915. He was their third son, and eleven years ago left his work on a farm at Sproatley to join the Royal Navy as a*

SOUTH AFRICAN MEMORIAL

1914 1918

FOR KING AND COUNTRY
TO THE

GLORY OF GOD

AND

IN EVERLASTING MEMORY

OF

ULSTER MEMORIAL

POPPLE, Sto. 1st Cl. T., 307273. (R.F.R./
CH/B/6988). R.N. "Howe" Bn. R.N. Div.
4th June, 1915. Age 29. Son of Tom and
Susannah Popple, of Bottesford, Ashby, Scunthorpe, Lincs.

WHO GAVE HIS LIFE IN THE GREAT WAR
THAT WE MIGHT LIVE
AND WHOSE NAME IS CARVED IN STONE
ON

AUSTRALIAN MEMORIAL

HIGHLAND MEMORIAL

THE HELLES MEMORIAL

Cape Helles (or Ilias Burnu) is the extreme South-Western point of the peninsula. "It was here that the original British landing was made; it was here that the greatest amount of Turkish territory was occupied; and it was from here that the last troops were evacuated". (Report of the committee of Selection, June 1921).

About 500 yards east of the Helles lighthouse is a hill called by the Turks Guezji or Kurji Baba, 150 feet above the sea, and higher than any other point in this part of Gallipoli Here is erected an obelisk, almost 100 feet high, based on a raised platform which is enclosed by a low stone wall. On a panel on one face of the obelisk are inscribed the names of the battleships, battle cruisers and cruisers which fought in the Dardanelles, and facing that panel on the low wall opposite are the names of the other vessels which took part in the fighting. On the other three sides of the obelisk are inscribed the Divisions and Brigades which fought on the peninsula, under the words HELLES, ANZAC and SUVLA, and on the wall opposite each is the detailed composition of these larger units; the G. H. Q. and Lines of Communication units are named on either side of the Suvla units.

THE HELLES MEMORIAL CONT.

This monument has two purposes. It is a Battle Memorial, and it is a memorial to the individual dead over whose bodies headstones cannot be erected. These two aspects of the memorial are stated in the inscription which is carved on the north side of the obelisk. By the Treaty of Lausanne, the Helles Memorial is established in perpetuity to overlook the land and the seas on which, for three thousand years, Europe and Asia have fought, and on which, a few years ago, the fiercest conflict of all began and ended. It is in no disparagement of the stubborn and successful valour of the Turks that its inscriptions recall the self-sacrifice of men from Western Europe, from Australia and New Zealand, from Asia and from Africa, who fought under the British flag. It is a memorial to the dead of an unsuccessful but a supremely glorious campaign. The memorial records the names of 18,968 sailors, soldiers and Marines from the United Kingdon; 1,531 soldiers from India, and 248 from Australia.

THE HELLES MEMORIAL, GALLIPOLI

stoker. Two years he spent in Malta, and then he visited Hong Kong and Jaffa, from the latter place going on a holiday tour to Jerusalem. At the end of six years he bought himself out, and obtained employment at "Klondyke" under the Frodingham Iron and Steel Company Limited. He was, however, still on the reserve, and when war broke out was called up and placed in the Naval Division with the Royal Marines. On October 4th he went to Antwerp and then to the Dardanelles. Fred Popple, A.B., Mr and Mrs Popple's fifth son, who enlisted in the Royal Marines on September 1st 1914, is interned in Groningen, Holland and has been there since the Antwerp affair in 1914."

Gideon with his wife Ellen and son Frank Edgar Roberts

Tom's Father, Tom Popple Senior 1859-1929

Tom Popple has no known grave, but his name is commemorated on the **Helles Memorial** which stands on the tip of the **Gallipoli Peninsula.** It is in the form of an obelisk over thirty metres high that can be seen by all ships passing through the Dardanelles. Tom was 29 years old when he died. The 1914 Star was issued posthumously to his next of kin.

Tom is commemorated on the Crosby Angel Memorial because his nephew, **Frank Popple**, attended Crosby School.

Information from:
Mr. Graham Popple (great nephew)
Royal Navy Service Record

Gideon Roberts

Sergeant 19471
13th Battalion Royal Welch Fusiliers
Died: Friday 9th February 1917 Killed in Action

Gideon Roberts was born in 1887 to **Robert** and his wife **Mary Ann Roberts** at Brynteg, Wrexham, Wales. The Roberts men had been miners for generations; Gideon's paternal grandfather, **Evan Roberts**, had been a lead miner and his father and uncles coal miners. However, at 14 years old, Gideon had broken the family pattern and was apprenticed to a printer, and his elder brother, **Edgar,** to a tailor. Welsh speakers all, they also spoke English.

From the John Lysaghts Wages Book of 1910, it was discovered that Gideon Roberts was a mason who had come to Scunthorpe to work on the building of the new steelworks at Normanby Park. He later worked in the Mechanical Department there.

He married **Ellen Dean** in Glanford Brigg area during the December quarter of 1911, and the couple went to live at 35 Detuyll Street, Crosby. He enlisted at Scunthorpe. The couple had one child, **Frank Edgar Roberts**, born 13th June 1912.

Badge of the Royal Welch Fusiliers.

Gideon Roberts was killed in action on Friday 9th February 1917, seven months before his son started at Crosby School.

At the time of his death, his regiment was situated North of Ypres. It is not known where exactly Gideon died as sadly hundreds of men died routinely each week from many causes not directly related to the fighting, such as being shot by snipers, or drowning in water/mud filled shell holes. Gideon is buried at **Bard Cottage Cemetery, Boesinghe, Belgium,** two miles north **of Ypres.**

Hull Daily Mail 1917, "*News of the death of Sergeant Gideon Roberts will come as a shock to his many friends in the Ironstone district. He came home on ten days leave in January, and fell killed in action within three weeks of his return. It is two years ago since he enlisted in the Royal Welsh Fusiliers and he rose to the rank of Sergeant. Roberts was a member of the Scunthorpe Amateur Operatic Society, the Scunthorpe Social and Liberal Clubs, the Crosby Working Men's Club and the Frodingham C.C.* (*Cricket Club), *but it was as a football referee that he was the widest known. He was in great demand among the Bennett Junior Football League clubs, and also was the "official" referee for Messrs. Lysaghts, for whom he worked. He*

was 30 years of age and leaves a widow and one child at 35 Detuyll Street, Crosby, for whom much sympathy is felt."

Gideon was a founder member of the Scunthorpe Operatic Society, formed in 1909, and his name appears as a chorus member in their 1911 production of Gilbert and Sullivan's operetta '*The Yeomen of the Guard'.*

Gideon is commemorated on the Crosby Angel Memorial because his son Frank Edgar Roberts attended Crosby School. He is also listed on the **Crosby Parish Roll of Honour** in St. George's Church.

A SOLDIER'S PRAYER.

Almighty and most Merciful Father,
Forgive me my sins:
Grant me Thy peace:
Give me Thy power:
Bless me in life and death,
        for Jesus Christ's sake.
                        Amen.

From the Chaplain-General.   Aug. 1914.

Prayer Card with which Gideon had been issued. This was kept inside the Soldier's Cap.

Steve Hardy, February 2002,

"*Gideon was my grandmother's first husband and they only had only child, my **Uncle Frank**. At the end of the War I am told that my grandmother was, for a short time, stewardess at the British Legion Club in, I think, Berkeley Street. She met and married a former soldier, Albert Roberts, who originated from Kirton Lindsey. They settled at 119 Buckingham Street and had two children, one of whom was my mother. Albert and **Frank** both worked at Lysaghts in the Pattern Shop. Frank lived for many years on Ferry Road. I also have in my possession Gideon's active service testament from 1914-1915, presented to him in Llandudno. I have his medals, Pip Squeak and Wilfred and, though not his, a Royal Welsh Fusilier Cap badge, and I have his wallet.*"

"*I know that 13th Battalion Royal Welch Fusiliers were part of the 38th Division and were in action at Mametz during the Somme offensive. As for Gideon's involvement, I know nothing, my guess is that he was there.*"

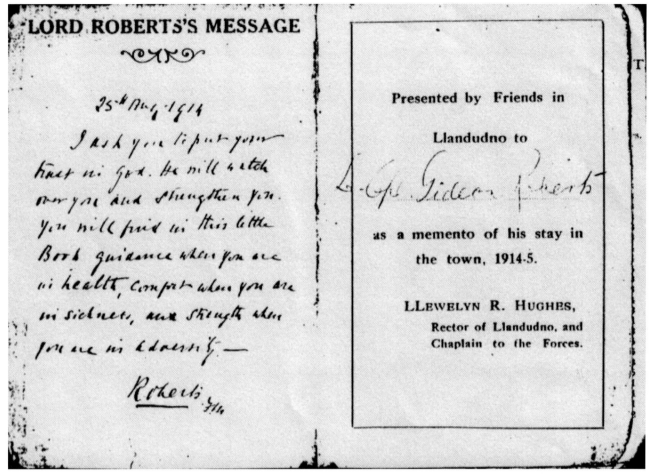

Active Service New Testament with message from Field Marshal Roberts, who was not related to Gideon Roberts!

Active Service New Testament presented to Gideon by his friends in Llandudno - probably where he did some army training -

"25th August 1914
I ask you to put your trust in God. He will watch over you and strengthen you. You will find in this little Book guidance when you are in health, comfort when you are in sickness, and strength when you are in adversity ...
(Signed) ROBERTS F/M"
(F/M = Field Marshal – top British Army rank.)

Information from:
Mr. Stephen B Hardy (step grandson)
Scunthorpe Operatic Society Archives
(Mr. Geoffrey Spilman)

Ernest William Robinson

Gunner 167060
144th Siege Battery Royal Garrison Artillery
Died: Wednesday 28th November 1917 Killed in Action

Born on 14th March 1886 at 33 Veal Street, Grimsby, Ernest William Robinson was the only son of **John William Robinson** a Master Tailor and his wife **Serena**. The Robinsons had been tailors and dressmakers for generations and Ernest followed his father into the family business as soon as he was of age.

In 1914 he married **Maude Haines** in her home town of Louth, Lincolnshire. When their son, **John Kirk Robinson,** was born on 24th June 1915, Maud Robinson was living at 46 Harrington Street, Cleethorpes, Ernest was living at 65 Taylor Street, Cleethorpes and working as a Journeyman Tailor.

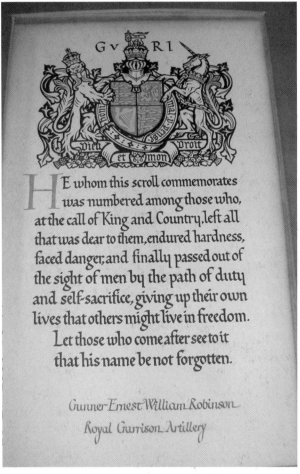

Memorial Scroll sent to the Next of Kin of World War I Fatalities.

In 1916, the couple's second son, **George**, was born and Ernest enlisted at Cleethorpes becoming a Gunner in the Royal Garrison Artillery.

Grimsby News 21st December 1917, *"Gunner Ernest William Robinson, R.G.A., is another of*

Grimsby's sons to pay the supreme sacrifice. He was the only son of Mr. and Mrs. J. W. Robinson, 25, Maude-Street, Grimsby and previous to joining the Army, was in business with his father as tailors, etc. The sad event happened on the 28th November 1917, a shell striking the shelter where Robinson and others were resting. He was asleep at the time, and death was instantaneous. He is greatly missed for he was so much needed. He leaves a wife and two young children. In a letter to Mrs. Robinson the chaplain writes:- "Your dear husband, Gunner W. E. Robinson (sic), was on duty at the battery last night. Just before midnight a shell struck the shelter in which he was sleeping, and I regret to say your dear husband lost his life. It will at least be a comfort to know that his end on earth was painless, absolutely, in fact instantaneous, and it will make you proud to know that he was at his post at the time. I had the honour of being his chaplain here, and we laid his body to rest this afternoon in a beautiful British cemetery well behind the line where no enemy will ever come. Many of his friends were present, and everything beautifully and reverently done – a brave soldier laid to rest by his soldier friends in a soldier's grave. The battery are placing a beautiful cross to mark the spot, and you may rest assured that his last resting-place will be well cared for. I am very sorry to have to write this, and we all sympathise with you far more than I can say."

Ernest William Robinson was killed in action, possibly in the **Third Battle of Ypres (Passchendaele)** and buried in **Bard Cottage Cemetery, Ypres, West Vlaanderen, Belgium**. Bard Cottage was a house, a little set back from the line, close to a bridge called *"Bard's Causeway"*, the cemetery was made nearby in a sheltered position under a bank. **Gideon Roberts,** one of the other men commemorated on the Crosby Angel, is also buried there.

At the time of Ernest's death, **Maude Robinson** was living at 13 Diana Street, Crosby, but it seems that her husband never lived at that address as he was at the war front. She later moved to 16 Dale Street. It is understood that Maude Robinson founded the Crosby Branch of the Women's Institute.

Both of the Robinson boys, **John Kirk** and **George**, were members of a church choir, possibly St. John's, Scunthorpe, or perhaps at the new St. George's Mission Church, Crosby, which had been dedicated in 1913.

At the beginning of World War II Maude moved out of town to Burton Stather, outside Scunthorpe because she was afraid of bombing. She was a staunch church woman and she attended St. Andrews' Parish Church there until she died in the autumn of 1965, 48 years after her husband, who was only 30 years old when he was killed.

Both of their sons attended Crosby School, which is why Ernest William Robinson is commemorated on the Crosby Angel Memorial.

John Kirk Robinson joined the Royal Navy and survived both the Second World War and also the sinking of his ship *H.M.S. "Kelly,"* immortalised in the Nöel Coward film *"In Which We Serve"*. George Robinson emigrated to Australia but came back to Great Britain, where he died.

Information from:
Mr. & Mrs. David S. Robinson (grandson)
Grimsby News

George Henry Ross
Private 12349
7th Battalion Lincolnshire Regiment
Died: Friday 28th April 1916 Died of Wounds

George Henry Ross, third child of **Martin** and **Emma Ross,** was born in 1894 in Messingham, one of many small villages close by the developing steel town of Scunthorpe, Lincolnshire.

Although no details of George's school days have been found, Crosby School admissions registers show that his younger brother, **Harold Ross**, born 17th September 1903, transferred from East Butterwick school on 1st October 1912, which was probably when the family moved to Crosby. The new John Lysaght's Normanby Park Steelworks opened the same year.

George Ross is commemorated on their 1914 Works Roll of Honour, as he was working in the Mechanical Department at the time of his enlistment at Scunthorpe, during the late summer of 1914.

Answering Kitchener's phenomenally successful *"call to arms"* along with George Henry Ross, were Crosby lads whose names are also inscribed on the Crosby Angel: **John Henry Dale, John William "Jack" Rimmington, John Fowler** and **Arthur Frost**. George arrived in France at the beginning of July 1915.

"The Lincolnshire Regiment" by Major General Simpson records, *"September* (1915) *opened with wretched weather: rain reduced the trenches to mud alleys, parapets began to fall in and work was in consequence, very heavy not only when in support and reserve, but in the front line also. The damage done by the enemy's shell fire was frequently extensive."*

George Henry Ross died aged 22 on 28th April 1916. On **16th May 1916** the following report appeared in the **Hull Times,** *"The funeral took place on Wednesday of Private George Henry Ross of the 7th Lincolns who died from wounds sustained in France. He was only 22, and lived with his parents at 27, De Tuyll-street,* (sic) *Crosby. He was formerly employed in the power house at Messrs. Lysaghts. He had only been in France eight weeks when he received his wound. It was on September 9th* (1915) *that he, along with Herbert Cockin of West Butterwick and young Clark of Owston Ferry, were at Loos, helping to make history. The three chums were together when some shrapnel burst, and killed*

Cockin (who was in the centre) instantly. Clark fortunately escaped injury and is still in the trenches, but a piece of shrapnel, not much bigger than a pea, lodged itself in the spine of Private Ross. After a week at the base, he was removed to King George's Hospital, London, where he died. Practically from the moment he was hit, Ross suffered from paralysis of the spine, but he also contracted pneumonia, and in October had to undergo an operation for abscesses. After his death the piece of shrapnel was taken from where it had been lodged and sent to his home. A happier memento of their son's connection with the Army is a photograph cut out of the "Christian Herald" and brought to the bereaved parents by a friend. He is there seen in the midst of a smiling group of British Tommies listening to the acknowledged "story-teller" of the camp.

On Monday the body was brought home, and the funeral took place on Wednesday, but to the regret of the commanding officer of a certain district a firing party was unable to be spared. The Scunthorpe Subscription Silver Band (the deceased's father is a member) was in attendance, and this, with the military officers stationed in the town, and the number of khaki-clad figures among the bearers and mourners gave the proceedings a semi-military character. Frodingham-road, Crosby, was lined with people when the cortege, headed by the band playing the Dead March, slowly wended its way to the Crosby Parish Church. It was met at the front entrance by the surpliced clergy and choir and the service in the church was read by the Rev. A G. Gifford, Vicar of Messingham and the deceased's old Sunday School teachers. The Scunthorpe Band headed the procession to the Crosby Cemetery and immediately behind the clergy walked Scunthorpe's three recruiting officers, wearing black armlets, Captain Colquehoun and Lieutenants Eastwood and Ackroyd. The last rites were performed by the Vicar of Crosby, the Rev. C Usher Wilson, acting-chaplain to the force, who was wearing his South African medal with two clasps. The service ended, the band feelingly played the hymn, "Lead Kindly Light." The bearers were: - Pte. Wm. Mitchell, R.A.M.C., Messrs. John Cox, Geo. Davies, Jim Cook, Robt. Cawkwell and Robt. Thompson. The principal mourners were the father and mother, Miss K. Ross (sister), Pte.

Arthur Ross (5th Lincs.), and Messrs. Ernest, Johnson and Harold Ross (brothers), Mrs. W. Whittaker (Rotherham), Mr. and Mrs. J. Coulteck and family (Dinnington), Mr. and Mrs. G. Ross and family (Susworth), Mrs. E. Ross (Doncaster) and friends. Among the many floral tributes was a wreath from his bearers and another from fellow workers of the deceased in the 'power house' at the Normanby Park Steelworks."

Reports of the funeral also appeared in the **Lincolnshire Star 6th May 1916** and the **Hull** and **North Lincolnshire Times.** George Henry Ross is buried in **Plot B No. 23 in Crosby Cemetery.** He is commemorated on the Angel Memorial because his brother **Harold,** was a pupil at the school and also because the Ross family lived in Crosby. George Henry Ross is listed on the **Crosby Parish Roll of Honour.** His name is also to be found on the **Scunthorpe Museum Wall Roll of Honour**.

George Henry Ross is buried in Crosby Cemetery, Scunthorpe.

Believed to be William Henry Rylance.

William Henry Rylance

Royal Navy Stoker 1st Class 277713
H.M.S. "Aboukir"
Died: Tuesday 22nd September 1914 Died at Sea

It is recorded that **William Henry Rylance** was born 31st January 1875 at Poplar, London, only son of Lancastrian Mill workers **Richard** and **Alice Rylance.** Nothing is known of his early life except for references on the 1881 census, where he is described as *"Scholar"* aged 6 of Stebondale Street, Poplar, London, and on the 1891 census as *"General Labourer"* aged 17 still at Stebondale Street, Poplar.

On 10th September 1894, aged 19, William joined the Royal Navy at Chatham, signing up for twelve years. He is described on his Service Record as being five feet three and a half inches tall with light brown hair, grey eyes and a fresh complexion. He trained on H.M.S. *"Vivid II"* and afterwards on the H.M.S. *"Calypso,"* H.M.S. *"Cleopatra"* and H.M.S. *"Pembroke II."*

Six years later (1901 census) William H. Rylance is listed as Stoker, single, 26 years old and a member of the crew of H.M.S. *"Prosperine"* Cruiser Third Class at Bermuda. It may be assumed that William was something of a rolling stone. His next ship was again H.M.S. *"Pembroke II"* then H.M.S. *"Sutley,"* H.M.S. *"Berwick"* and two more voyages on H.M.S. *"Pembroke II."* In September 1906, he joined the Royal Fleet

Reserve at Chatham and re-enrolled on 20th August 1910 *"to serve until 10th September 1916",* which means he would take up a civilian occupation during that period, but would be available for immediate re-call to duty in the event of any emergency, e.g. war.

William Henry Rylance married **Rose Annie Watson i**n Glanford Brigg district during the June quarter of 1911. Her father, **William,** was an ironstone miner living at Burringham. He used to walk to Scunthorpe to work every day but later moved to live there.

William and Rose's son **Richard Watson Rylance** (born in Scunthorpe) sadly died ten weeks later in the September quarter of 1911.

William and his wife lived at 16 Grosvenor Street, Scunthorpe, and he worked at John Lysaght's Normanby Park Steelworks which opened in May 1912. The larger and more ornate terrace houses on Grosvenor Street were built in 1902; known colloquially as *"Smelter's Row,"* these houses were specifically for the skilled and better paid steel men. Many naval men with their specialist knowledge of steam combustion and expertise as riggers were employed in the industry.

As a Royal Navy Reservist, William was recalled back to duty and sailed on H.M.S. *"Aboukir"* on 2nd August 1914, two days before the outbreak of World War I on 4th August 1914. On Tuesday 22nd September 1914 his ship was sunk by the German submarine U-9 off the Dover coast.

At the age of 41 William Rylance was the oldest of those on the Crosby Angel for whom we have ages recorded. He was also the first one commemorated on the Crosby Angel to die in the Great War. The loss of H.M.S. *"Aboukir"* was the first sinking of the War by German U-boats, resulting in the loss of three British armoured cruisers.

There were 17 Officers and 237 men saved from H.M.S. *"Aboukir"* – sadly, William Henry Rylance was not among the survivors.

An engineer of H.M.S. *"Aboukir"* survived and gave the following report to a correspondent at the Times, *"I was below,"* he said, *"when it happened. The weather was bad when the ship reeled under the shock of a tremendous explosion. At first we thought we'd struck a mine but we found that we had been torpedoed, probably between the first and second boilers. A great hole was torn out of her side. Men on the upper deck were killed instantly. More below tumbled up as quickly as possible, but everything was quiet and orderly. As the ship was heeling over, the order was given 'every man for himself.' It was not until then that I took my boots off. There was no question of jumping off the ship. Her deck was almost at a right angle with the water, and I just slid into the sea. I don't know how long it all took, it might have been five minutes and it might have been ten. When we were struck, the "Hogue" was not far away. She and the "Cressey" rushed to the rescue, in spite of the fact that they thought we had been mined. For all they knew they might have been rushing through a whole bed of mines. When they stopped and lowered boats for us the submarines fired their torpedoes. The "Cressey" gave them two shots from her guns, but I don't know if the shots got home. If the "Hogue" and the "Cressey" had not stopped they might have escaped. It's hard luck – but it's in the day's work, and the work must be done, or you couldn't be sitting here in safety. That's all."*

"U-9 sinks H.M.S. Aboukir, Hogue and Cressey. *The patrol by these elderly ships was much criticised, they were too old and slow with*

William's Medals "Pip Squeak and Wilfred" - 1914-15 Star, British War Medal and Victory Medal - World War I. The War Service Medals were nicknamed after three popular cartoon characters of the time.

inexperienced crews to put up a decent fight against modern German surface ships. Although the submarine threat at the time was not considered, even by critics of the patrol, the fact that the three ships did not zig zag was criticised by the board of enquiry, a practice that was widely ignored at the time and even by some ships after the loss of the three cruisers."

The U-9 also later sank H.M.S. *""Hawke"* in Aberdeen, resulting in the loss of **William Jobson Welton,** another of those men commemorated on the Crosby Angel, whose poignant letter of sympathy written to Mrs. Rylance, widow of William Henry Rylance, just three days before his own death, is as follows,

"12th October 1914
        H.M.S. Hawke c/o G.P.O. London"
"Dear Mrs. Rylance"
"it is with deepest sympathy that i write these few lines to you in your sad loss (but I trust that) you will be a brave woman as i know you will bear your loss as an English woman remember although it is hard, very hard to give up our loved ones that it is for the cause of freedom and honour that your

Chatham Naval Memorial, Kent for Royal Navy personnel with no known graves where William is commemorated.

dear Husband has laid down his life which i know that he would do willingly i know that you have lost a kind and loving Husband i have lost in him a loving comrade one of the best chums a man ever had i may tell you the morning he left to join his ship that he was still the same lively and jolly as ever if their (sic) is anything that i can possibly do for you i will gladly do it do not fret and mourn too much as you know that this is a time when i think a woman as (sic) to be braver than a man try and think of it more of an honour than a loss that he laid down his life for his King and Country his name will not be forgot but will live in history as one of England's Heroes for they died as only British Sailors can doing their duty fearlessly to the last i know that his last thoughts would be of you if there is anything whatever you want or want to know i will do all i possibly can for you for the sake of a good and true Chum i now close with deepest sympathy to you believe me i remain yours sincerely
Stoker W J Welton
H.M.S. Hawke c/o G.P.O. London"

Rose Annie Rylance, William's widow.

William Jobson Welton and William Henry Rylance were obviously friends and shipmates, although they were on different ships when they died.

William Henry Rylance is commemorated on the **Chatham Naval Memorial, Kent** for Royal Navy personnel with no known graves, and also on **Lysaght's 1914 Roll of Honour** because his last civilian job was in the Coke Ovens Department of Normanby Park Steelworks. His name is on the **Scunthorpe Museum Roll of Honour** and the **Memorial Plaque at Foxhills Club.**

The reason that William Henry Rylance is commemorated on the Angel Memorial is because he lived in the Crosby district. His name is listed on the **Crosby Parish Roll of Honour.**

Information from:
Mr. Alec Stather (nephew)
Royal Navy Service Records

(John) William Selby

Lance Corporal 3115
5th Battalion Lincolnshire Regiment
Died: Saturday 14th October 1916 Killed in Action

William ("Billy") Selby was born in Crosby on 27th November 1893, and baptised "John William Selby," eldest child of **John** and **Rebecca (**née **Dixon) Selby** of 84 Sheffield street. William had four brothers (**Harold, Rowland, Albert Edward** and **George**) and three sisters (**Nora, Ada** and **Mary).** John Selby was a cabinet maker like his father before him, but William did not follow in their footsteps. He became, instead, a painter employed by a Mr. E. Jackson of Ashby. By this time the family had moved and were living at 18 Crosby Road, Scunthorpe. William enlisted in October 1914 and was killed at the age of 22 years on Saturday 14th October 1916.

Sadly, William's father had died in an accident before William was killed in action. John was on the way to Grimsby, when the traction engine

Berles Position Military Cemetery, Pas de Calais, France.

towing the furniture van he was taking, ran over him near Melton Ross. He appears to have fallen off the precarious seating arrangement on the traction engine, when trying to retrieve his cap that had blown off his head.

Rebecca was therefore left a widow with her young family. Every November, on Armistice Day, she would place a poppy on the corner of a large framed photograph of William, in uniform, which hung in her home.

William is buried in **Berles Position Military Cemetery, Pas de Calais, France.** He was probably killed towards the end of the **Battle of the Somme,** which finished in November 1916. **John Bycroft,** another man whose name is on the Angel, is buried in that same Cemetery.

The Hull Daily Mail of Saturday 11th November, 1916 carried the following report, *"Lance Corporal William Selby, enlisted October 1914, was wounded October 1915: killed October 1916. Truly October will be an ever memorable month to the widowed mother of Lance Corporal William Selby. The eldest son of Mrs. John Selby of 84 Sheffield Street, Scunthorpe, he was a painter in the employ of Mr. E. Jackson of Ashby when the war broke out, and in October 1914 he joined the Lincolns. The following October he received a gunshot wound in his head, and last October, when he was 22 years of age, he was in a dugout in the trenches with three others, when a shell blew it in and killed all four. The Captain writes "I buried them on Saturday,* October 14th, *in the little cemetery just behind the lines, where they fell doing their duty so fully for King and Country, and as we believe in the cause of God and right. They have made the great sacrifice and remembering the Blessed Lord's words that 'greater love hath no man than this, that a man lay down his life for his friends', we may with confidence know that in that place of light when sorrow and mourning are far banished, there may be vouchsafed to them everlasting rest."* Lieutenant Mark Robinson says, *"I used to be in charge of his platoon, and I could never speak more highly of his capabilities. He was always cheerful under the most trying circumstances, and one of the most popular members of his platoon. His death was absolutely instantaneous, I shall always be proud to say that I had him for a member of my platoon."*

1917 Scunthorpe U.D.C. Roll of Honour, *"William Selby, 19* (sic) *Crosby Rd. 1/5 Lincs. Lance Corporal, wounded twice, killed 14th October 1916."*

William is commemorated on the Crosby Angel Memorial because his siblings **George, Mary** and **Ada** attended the school, and the family lived in Crosby at the time of his death. His name is listed on the **Crosby Parish Roll of Honour** which used to be displayed in **St. George's Parish Church.**

Information from:
Mrs. Sheila Williamson (niece)

Frank Edward Sellars

Private 12499
9th Battalion Lincolnshire Regiment
Died: Friday 26th November 1915 Died of illness in training

Frank Edward Sellars was born in Barton-on-Humber in 1895. His date of birth, school attended and occupation prior to enlistment is unknown, although his step sister, **Mrs. Jean Dring,** who was born in 1930, said that he was a post boy. *"There was a photograph of him with his bicycle. He was wearing a post boy's uniform and a round cap."*

Father, **Frank,** was an apprentice wheelwright in Newark, where he met and married his wife **Kate,** and they came to live in Barton-on-Humber. Frank senior was employed as a fitter at Hopper's Cycle Works, and they lived at 8 Maltby Lane. They moved to 98 Diana Street, Crosby, sometime in 1914/15, and Frank senior worked at the steelworks. Sons **Frank Edward** and **Arthur Herbert** had a sister **Muriel,** born in 1898 and brother **Alfred Ernest,** born in 1899. Alfred Ernest also enlisted in the army towards the end of the War and later briefly served in the Indian Army.

A postcard to his mother dated 15th February 1915 said Frank was billeted with a Mrs. Ridelle at 276 Burton Road, Lincoln and she was looking after him well. He was then sent to a **training camp in Cannock Chase, Staffordshire,** where he contracted dysentery.

A postcard sent by Frank Edward Sellars to his mother.

The Hull Daily Mail 4th December 1915 reports, *"Private Sellars, 9th Lincolns Son of Mr. and Mrs. Frank Sellars, late of Barton, died in Brockton Hospital, Staffordshire on Friday 26th November. The announcement of his illness reached his parents only on Wednesday and that of his death on Friday. Son of Frank and Kate Sellars of 98 Diana Street, Crosby, he was born at Barton-on-Humber, and enlisted at Scunthorpe."*

He died before he went to France. He is buried in **Basswick Holy Trinity Churchyard, Staffordshire.**

Brockton Training Camp, Staffordshire in the 1914 War, where Frank Edward Sellars was training when he contracted dysentery, from which he died before he got to France.

His death was also reported in the Hull Daily Mail, along with the details of some of the Barton -on-Humber boys who enlisted.

Jean Dring remembers: *"I was told by my father that many soldiers in the barracks had died of dysentery..."*

Frank and Kate Sellars had yet more grief in store with the loss of their second son, 17 months later…

Arthur Herbert Sellars

Private 242086
6th Battalion (TF) South Staffordshire Regiment
Died: Friday 27th April 1917 Died of Wounds

Two years younger than his brother Frank, who had already died for his country, Arthur Herbert Sellars was born in Barton-on-Humber in 1897. It may be assumed that he also went to school there.

The Hull Daily Mail of Saturday 12th May 1917 carried the following report, *"Another young townsman has made the great sacrifice, namely Private Arthur Sellars of the South Staffs. Regiment. His parents some time ago removed to Crosby but with this exception all deceased's interests and friends resided at Barton. He was an assistant in Mr. C. H. Kirby's store when called up a short time ago. He was 20 years of age and was a member of St. Chad's choir and often sang at local concerts. His parents received the first intimation of his illness, caused by wounds in France, on the 30th but on Thursday week a letter* *was received saying that on Friday 27th April he was admitted to hospital suffering from gunshot wounds in the abdomen and he died the same night."*

Arthur Sellars was buried at **La Chapellette, British and Indian Cemetery, Peronne, Somme, France.**

Arthur's name is also on the **Barton-on-Humber Cenotaph** and on the **Roll of Honour** inside **St. Mary's Church, Barton-on-Humber.**

Jean Dring says: *"From a very early age on the 11th November I would stand with my father at the Cenotaph at Crosby School, and was very aware of his sadness."*

Barton-on-Humber Cenotaph whereon the name of Arthur Henry Sellars is inscribed.

The Crosby Roll of Honour, which includes the names of all who served in the Great War, lists Frank Edward and Arthur Henry Sellars' names, as well as that of their younger brother **Alfred Ernest Sellars,** who survived.

After his wife Kate's death in 1925, Frank senior re-married **Florence Norton**, and Jean Dring is a child of that second marriage.

Information from:
Mrs. Jean Dring (step sister)
Brian Peeps and Sean Scolfield CD's Barton-on-Humber
- A Lincolnshire Village at War (1914-1918) March 2007

It is not known why he returned to Hull to enlist with the Lincolnshire Regiment, or when. The details of his death are equally scant. He was killed in action on the first day of the battle of Loos, 25th September 1915. He is commemorated on the **Ploegsteert Memorial, Cominee-Warneton, Hainant, Belgium, south of Ypres**, and has no known grave.

Charles Shaw is commemorated on the Crosby Angel Memorial because his family lived in Crosby, and his brother **Thomas** attended Crosby School. His name is listed on the **Crosby Parish Roll of Honour**, formerly in **St. George's Parish Church**.

Charles Shaw has no known grave. He is commemorated on the Ploegsteert Memorial, Cominee-Warneton, Hainant, south of Ypres, Belgium.

Charles Shaw

Private 15223
"W" Company 2nd Battalion Lincolnshire Regiment
Died: Saturday 25th September 1915 Killed in Action

Charles Shaw was born in the September quarter of 1894 at Hull in the East Riding of Yorkshire, first child of **Edwin Shaw,** a builder's labourer, and his wife **Julia.** Apart from census information, no other details of Charles' childhood years have been found. His family have been traced back to 1841, when his great grandfather, **Jordan Shaw,** was a farmer at Wintringham, in the East Riding of Yorkshire. In 1851, **Jordan** and his wife **Ann** were listed as living at Ray Slack Farm, comprising 480 acres.

However, there is recorded in the **Scunthorpe and Frodingham Star, 22nd January 1938:** *"Death of Edwin Shaw (Charles' father) of 69 Digby Street, aged 70. He had lived in Scunthorpe 26 years and worked at Normanby Park Steelworks Lysaghts as a Builders' Labourer."* Therefore it may be assumed that the Shaw family had removed to Scunthorpe around 1912. At that time Scunthorpe was a boom town, the iron and steel industry brought unimagined prosperity to incomers from all over the country.

Young Charles Shaw followed his father onto the steelworks, his last occupation was in the Coke Ovens Department at John Lysaght's Steelworks where he is recorded as *"E. Shaw"* on the **Works Roll of Honour 1914.**

Medal Card for George Sims, showing a disembarkation date as 12th November 1914.

George Sims

Private 9176
1/5th Battalion Lincolnshire Regiment
Survived the War and Died 23rd April 1921

George Sims was born at Aby, Lincolnshire in 1874, eldest child of **Thomas** and **Mary Sims,** Thomas was a lime burner and Parish Clerk of South Thoresby, Lincolnshire.

Described as *"Scholar"* on the 1881 census, it may be assumed that George and his sister **Sarah Ann** attended the local village school. They had three younger brothers, **William, John** and **Joseph** who were under school age. Another sister, **Elizabeth**, was born in 1883.

At the age of 16, George was working as a groom at the Vicarage, Alkborough, for Francis A. Jarvis, who was the vicar of Burton Stather and Rector of Flixborough. George's father had died and his widowed mother was bringing up his siblings on her own. The 1901 census shows **Mary** and two of her sons living at No. 5 Ayscough Street, Grimsby. **John** and **Joseph** had found work as a carter in a timber yard and a bricklayer's labourer respectively.

In the June quarter of 1903, George Sims married **Betsy Bonnet** at Grimsby. Betsy was 27 years old and had been in domestic service in Spilsby and in Cleethorpes. George may have met her while he was visiting his family in Grimsby, or they could have known each other previously, as she was born in South Thoresby, Lincolnshire.

The couple moved to 47 Digby Street, Crosby, and George found work at John Lysaght's Normanby Park Works in the Mechanical Department. Their first child, **Thomas,** was born on 29th January 1905, and started at Crosby School on 23rd May 1910. Betsy Sims gave birth to another son who was stillborn. He was buried 'un-named' on 1st October 1912 in Crosby Cemetery.

George Sims appears to have enlisted as a regular soldier before the War, because he was with the B.E.F. at the outbreak of war. As he had been a groom at one time, he may have looked after horses in the army when he joined the Lincolns.

Tragedy struck George and Betsy Sims when their only son Thomas died of a poisoned stomach: *Crosby School Logbook 3rd September 1914, written by Mr. George Taylor, Headmaster, "Thomas Simms* (sic) *was today interred at Crosby Cemetery. 24 school boys and myself followed the remains of the child to his last resting place. Teachers and scholars gave 17/6d. wherewith to purchase a wreath and two large photographs of the boy. One of the photographs we shall present to his mother and the other we shall hang in his classroom. The child was aged 9 years."*

George Sims was very likely overseas when his son died, and given that the Battalion were involved in the fighting retreat from Mons and the Marne, it is unlikely that he got leave for the funeral. Also, the entry in the school logbook refers to giving a photograph of their son to his mother and not to his mother and father.

Lincolnshire Regimental Cap Badge.

George was one of those men who survived the war, so he returned to his wife Betsy at 47 Digby Street, Crosby. The now childless couple had three years left together, until George died at home on the 23rd April 1921 aged 47. The cause of death given on his death certificate may have been attributable to his wartime experiences: *"nephritis - kidney inflammation and mitral regurgitation - heart valve defect."*

It is recorded that George belonged to the Old Comrades Association of the Lincolnshire Regiment to which he donated 2/6d. in 1919 and the same amount in 1920.

Presumably it was because George's death was probably attributable to his War service, and he died before the Angel Memorial was dedicated in 1923, his name was included on it. In addition, his late son, **Thomas,** had been a pupil at the school. He is also commemorated on the **Normanby Park Works Roll of Honour 1914.**

Betsy Sims remained at 47 Digby Street until she died at Scunthorpe War Memorial Hospital in 1932 at the age of 56. She was buried on 1st August 1932 at Crosby Cemetery near her boys. George is also listed on the **Crosby Parish Roll** of Honour, formerly situated in **St. George's Parish Church.**

Information from:
George Sims' Death Certificate
Medal Card
Crosby Cemetery Records

Lawrence Sissons

Lance Corporal 24164
1/5th Battalion Lincolnshire Regiment
Died: Sunday 1st July 1917 Killed in Action

Lawrence Sissons was born in Frodingham, Lincolnshire in the last quarter of 1895, but moved with his parents **Albert Henry** and **Betsy Sissons** and older siblings **Elsie** and **Harold** to 7 Porter Street, Scunthorpe. Lawrence's father worked as a labourer at the iron works. When Lawrence left school he went to work at the John Lysaght's Normanby Park Works in the Coke Ovens Department. By that time, the family had moved once again, and were living at 70 Buckingham Street, Crosby.

Lawrence's grandfather, **John**, and his wife **Jane (née Oldfield)** lived in Long Sutton, near

Holbeach, Lincolnshire, where they have been traced back to the beginning of the 1800's, working as agricultural labourers. However, Lawrence's great grandfather, **Robert,** was born at Thorney, Cambridgeshire. and he moved to Long Sutton after his marriage to **Elizabeth Hodson.**

With the outbreak of war, Lawrence enlisted at Frodingham, and was sent with his battalion to France. He was reported killed in action on Sunday 1st July 1917.

Hull Times 28th July 1917 reports, *"'We had been engaged in some arduous and heavy fighting and your son's courage and conduct throughout was an inspiring example to his comrades. Had he been spared, his name would have undoubtedly appeared amongst the recipients of honours for bravery.' So writes an officer about Lance Corporal Lawrence Sissons, the young Crosby hero who was shot through the head by a sniper on July 1st."*

"The second son of Mr. and Mrs. A. H. Sissons, 70 Buckingham Street, Crosby, he was employed at Lysaghts Coke Ovens when not with the Terriers, and when war broke out he was spending his second camp with the Scunthorpe Company of the Lincolns at Bridlington. In February 1915 he went to France and took part in the second battle of Loos and other engagements down to the Somme and the big battle round Lens."

"On the morning of July 1st he volunteered to carry a message under rifle and machine gun fire and later in the day accompanied his officer on a patrol, during which they were continuously exposed. It was while crossing a road covered by a sniper that he was killed. A gallant and cheerful soldier and a good comrade his loss will be mourned by many friends. As a boy he attended the Primitive Methodist Centenary Sunday School and was a member of the Boys Brigade in connection with the Church. He was 21 years of age."

He is commemorated on the **Arras Memorial, Pas de Calais** and also on the **Normanby Park Works 1914 Roll of Honour**. Lawrence's name is on the Angel Memorial because his younger brother **Sidney,** born in 1908, went to Crosby

Lawrence Sissons' name is recorded on the Arras Memorial, Pas de Calais, France.

School. There were also other Sissons children recorded as pupils at the school who could have been related to Lawrence.

Lawrence's elder brother, **Harold,** served in the Great War with the Lincolnshire Regiment and the Royal Engineers in France and Belgium. Harold worked for over 51 years at Appleby Frodingham Steelworks, Scunthorpe. His name, like that of Lawrence, is listed on the **Crosby Parish Roll of Honour,** formerly situated in **St. George's Parish Church,** which listed the names of all from Crosby Parish who served in the Armed Forces during the Great War, including those who died.

Lawrence and Harold Sissons' names on Crosby Parish Roll of Honour

George William Smith

Lance Corporal 9131
(formerly 17896 Lincolnshire Regiment)
47th Battalion Machine Gun Corps (Infantry)
Died: Thursday 22nd August 1918 Killed in Action

George William Smith was born on 30th April 1889 at Amcotts, Lincolnshire, first son of agricultural labourer **William Smith** and his wife **Sarah Jane**. Their first child, George's sister, was called **Sarah Ann**. The baptism of George William Smith took place on 26th May 1889 at Amcotts Parish Church, where the family were regular worshippers and where all the major events of their lives, births, marriages and deaths, are recorded. Unusually for those days, the family remained in Amcotts for many years, and in the absence of any evidence to the contrary, it may be assumed that George William Smith attended the village school, and may even have followed his father into agricultural work.

In 1909 at the age of 21, his sister **Sarah Ann** married **Jesse Oliver**, an ironworker, at Amcotts Parish Church. Two years later, 10th July 1911, their father William Smith died aged 46, and was interred at the Amcotts Churchyard. At some time between 1911 and 1915, George William moved into No. 4 West Street, Scunthorpe with Sarah Ann and Jesse Oliver, and became an ironstone miner, probably working with his brother-in-law at Redbourne Hill.

On 19th May 1915, aged 26 years and 16 days, George William enlisted *"for the duration of the war"* at Scunthorpe and began his short but eventful army career. He was killed in action on Thursday 22nd August 1918 and was buried in the **Queen's Cemetery, Boucquoy, Pas de Calais, France, on the Arras to Amiens road.**

On 18th August, 1918, the British had renewed their offensive to the North of Amiens. It was the beginning of an unbroken string of Allied victories.

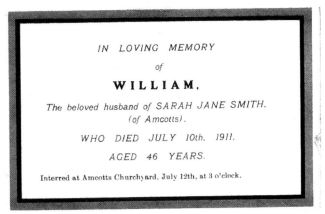

IN LOVING MEMORY

of

WILLIAM,

The beloved husband of SARAH JANE SMITH.
(of Amcotts).

WHO DIED JULY 10th. 1911.

AGED 46 YEARS.

Interred at Amcotts Churchyard, July 12th, at 3 o'clock.

"Mourning Card" sent to relatives and friends (as was the custom at that time) following the death of George's father.

George's widowed mother, who was preparing to marry again to her second husband, William Henry Spencer, received the following letter headed, *"B.E.F. Aug 24th 1918. Dear Mrs. Smith, It is with the deepest regret that I have to inform you that your son, No. 9131 L/C Smith was killed in action on August 22nd. It may be some small consolation to you to know that his end was painless as he was hit by splinters of a shell and killed instantly. I am writing to you to express for the officers and men and the company the sympathy that we all feel for you in the great loss you have sustained. Your son had not been with us a very long time but he had been quite long enough for us to realise that he was one of the best and that he was, moreover, a good leader of men. He had done extremely well in the recent fighting and would undoubtedly have been promoted. I have had many remarks by the men all showing that they too will miss him. We share with you to a small extent the loss of him. I am sorry that I am not allowed to tell you where he was killed. I remain, Yours very sincerely, J. W. Bryan Captain O.C.C Coy."*

The official letter from the Machine Gun Corps Record Office Army Form B 104-82 sent to his mother, Sarah, notifying her of George William's death.

Hull Daily Mail Saturday 7th September 1918, *"L/C George William Smith, eldest son of Mrs. W. Spencer, 34 Digby Street, Crosby was killed on the morning of the 22nd August by splinters of a shell while trying to establish communications with the front line during an advance. He was a hard working fearless man and a good leader of men. A single man, he had been in the army upwards of three years. During the two years he had*

1917 Roll of Honour Booklet cover issued by Scunthorpe Urban District Council.

Height: 5 feet 4 inches Religion: C of E
Next of kin: Mother Sarah Spencer
34 Digby Street Scunthorpe.

The Soldiers' Pay Book also contains information on:

Points to be observed on Outpost
Saluting of Officers
Pictures of Officers' Badges of Rank
How to Prevent Sore Feet
Mode of Making Applications and Complaints by a Soldier
Instructions for Cleaning the Rifle and Carbine
Instructions for Cleaning Clothing and for Washing Shirts, Khaki Clothing, Socks and Woollen Goods
Notes of Field Cooking
Furloughs (Leave), Marriage, Civil Employment on Discharge or Transfer to the Army Reserve
Soldiers' Wills, Will Pro Forma
Free Education of Soldiers' Sons.

been in France he had been twice wounded, once in the leg and once in the hand. He was killed on the same day that the news was received at Scunthorpe of the death of his brother-in-law, Jesse Oliver, Tank Corps, who was killed in action on the 8th. Both these brave men were nephews of Mrs. Fred Atkinson, West Street, Scunthorpe, who has now lost four nephews in the war. Gunner Oliver was employed at Redbourne Hill before joining up in July 1918 and leaves a wife and one child at 4 West Street, with whom much sympathy is felt."

It is recorded that George William Smith's sister, **Sarah Ann,** also remarried following the death of her husband **Jesse Oliver.**

George William Smith's name is recorded on **Amcotts War Memorial** inside the churchyard there. He is also commemorated in the **Scunthorpe 1917 Roll of Honour Booklet** as, *"George William Smith, 4 West Street. Machine Gun Corps Private wounded once."*

George William Smith is commemorated on the **Crosby Parish Roll of Honour,** and on the Crosby Angel Memorial because he lived in Crosby. Surprisingly, **Jesse Oliver** is not included on the Crosby Angel Memorial.

George William Smith was 29 years old when he died, leaving behind only his "SOLDIERS' SMALL BOOK," from which the following extracts come:

George William Smith's name is on the Amcotts village War Memorial, Lincolnshire.

Information from:
Mr. Duncan A Oliver (great-nephew)

William Thomas Spriggs is commemorated on the Pozieres Memorial, France.

William Thomas Spriggs

Private 77312
19th Battalion Durham Light Infantry
Died: Monday 25th March 1918 Killed in Action

William Thomas Spriggs was born in Scunthorpe in the winter of 1898 and baptised at St. John's Parish Church, Scunthorpe on 26th November. William's father, **Thomas Spriggs,** was a miner, and his mother, **Florence Mary Spriggs,** came from Newport, Monmouthshire in South Wales. She was said to have been a lovely woman and a great friend of Canon Greeson, Vicar of St. George's Parish Church, Crosby, which she attended in later life.

William's grandparents, **Thomas** and **Hannah Spriggs,** are buried in West Street Cemetery, Scunthorpe. Thomas was well known in the area as a Bandmaster for Scunthorpe Town.

The Spriggs family were living at 22a Frances Street when William was born. He was the eldest child; one of his two younger brothers, **Joseph,** died in infancy, and he had one sister, **Gladys.** Unfortunately, no details of William's young life, his schooling, or his occupation afterwards have been discovered.

When war broke out in 1914, the family were living at 8 Sutton Row. William enlisted at Scunthorpe with the Durham Light Infantry, date not known, probably in 1917 when he was 18 years old.

Thomas Spriggs (1852-1920) behind the big drum - the band was known as "Spriggs Band" because so many family members were in it.

On Monday 25th March 1918, William Thomas Spriggs was killed in action, and is commemorated on the **Pozieres Memorial, Somme, France.**

The Pozieres Memorial relates to the period of crisis in March and April 1918 when the Allied Fifth Army was driven back by overwhelming numbers across the former Somme battlefields, and the months that followed before the advance to victory, which began on 8th August 1918. Tanks were being brought into use in the later stages of the war and were a huge surprise to troops on both sides seeing them in action for the first time. It was rumoured that tanks represented a missed opportunity. Had the cavalry or mobile troops followed immediately in their wake, they may have got well behind German lines under their protection, which could have changed the whole face of the battle.

William Spriggs is listed on **Scunthorpe's Roll of Honour 1917,** and also his father, **Thomas Spriggs,** who was a **Corporal in the 3rd Lincolnshire Battalion.** Thomas Spriggs was discharged with shell shock, but was unable to get a pension for this.

William Thomas Spriggs is commemorated on the Crosby Angel Memorial because of family connections - relatives who attended the school. He was just 19 years old when he was killed. Louise Kate Sturman, sister of **George Robert Sturman** (whose name also appears on the Crosby Angel), married a distant cousin of William Thomas Spriggs.

Information from:
Mrs. Freda Langford (great niece)
Mrs. Elaine Leggott (great great niece)
Mr. Alan H Spriggs (distant cousin)

War Memorial at Brigg, Lincolnshire whereon John William Standerline is commemorated.

John William Standerline

Private 5148
1st Battalion Lincolnshire Regiment
Died: Thursday 22nd October 1914 Killed in Action

John William Standerline was born at Brigg, Lincolnshire, in 1878, only son of agricultural labourer **William** and his wife **Ann Standerline** of Hibaldstow, Lincolnshire. John had three sisters, **Georgina, Sarah** and **Ada** aged nine, six and five years respectively (1881 census.) In 1889 his brother **Joseph,** last child of the family, was born at Brigg.

It was customary at that time for agricultural workers and farm servants to move every two years, and in 1901 the family were living at 19 Engine Street, Brigg. The absence of John's name on the census indicates that he may already have been in the army.

John's war record shows he enlisted at Brigg, possibly as a pre-war regular soldier or perhaps as a reservist called up on the outbreak of War. Certainly at some time, he worked in the Mechanical Department of John Lysaght's Normanby Park Steelworks as he is commemorated on the **Lysaght's 1914 Roll of Honour.**

John William Standerline married Ashby born **Louisa Chaplin** in the December quarter of 1911, and at 37 years old was considerably older than many of his comrades. Shortly before the **First Battle of Ypres,** which began on 31st October 1914, the British Expeditionary Force was moving north, facing massive attacks from the Germans. John William's fighting career ended abruptly when he was killed in action on Thursday 22nd October 1914 at Mons, ten days before **Fred Hare** and **Edwin Pittaway,** who were also with the B.E.F. John William's father had pre-deceased him in 1907, but his wife Louisa was still living in Crosby at the time of his death. As Louisa is listed on the Brigg Cemetery Monumental Inscription records as having died aged 52 years on 7th December 1936, and is buried with his mother, who died aged 78 years on 22nd April 1925, it is presumed that after John William was killed, his wife returned to Brigg to make her home, perhaps with John's widowed mother. John William's name is also included on the Brigg Cemetery records together with those of his wife and mother.

John William Standerline is commemorated on the **Memorial on the Scunthorpe Museum Wall**, the **Memorial Plaque at Foxhills Club** as well as the **Brigg War Memorial.**

Because he was related to some of the pupils who attended Crosby school and was also a man of Crosby Parish, he is also commemorated on the Crosby Angel Memorial and on **Crosby Parish Roll of Honour** which used to be displayed in **St. George's Parish Church, Crosby**.

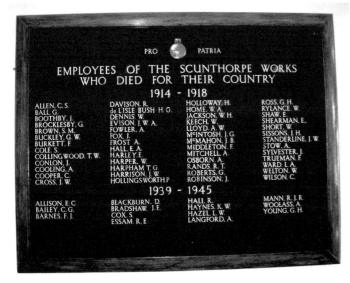

The John Lysaght's Memorial Plaque situated in Foxhills Road Club listing all employees who died in both the Great War and World War 2. The World War 1 names are identical to those listed on the Brass Plaque on the Museum Wall, Scunthorpe (see illustration adjacent to the biographies for George William Harley and William Harper on page 101.) John William Standerline's name is included on this Plaque.

Information from:
Mary E. Baker (researching the Standerline family)
Mr. Stanley Embling
Brigg Cemetery Monumental Inscription records

Walter Stow
Private 1747
5th Battalion Lincolnshire Regiment
Died: Wednesday 28th April 1915 Died of Wounds

Walter Stow was born in early 1895 at Chapel Yard, Messingham, Lincolnshire, first child of ironstone miner **Walter** and **Sarah Stow.** Walter's sister **Olive** was born in 1898 and his brother **Cecil** in 1907. At 14 years of age, young Walter became the man of the house when his 40 year old father died in 1909. His mother then married **John Taylor** in the March quarter of 1912. Nothing more is known of Walter's early life, except that he enlisted at Frodingham with the Lincolnshire Regiment, and after his basic training, somewhere in England, was shipped out to France in the spring of 1915.

Hull Times 1st May 1915, *"Still another of our local lads has been wounded at the front, this being Private W. Stow, son of Mrs. John Taylor, 27, Alexandra Road, who has received the following letter from the Brigade Chaplain – '1.2 North Midland Field Ambulance April 20th. Dear Mrs. Taylor, I am very sorry to have to report to you that your son, Private W. Stow, 1/5 Lincoln regiment, was seriously wounded last night in the arm and back. I do not wish you to think that the wound is likely to prove fatal, but it is undoubtedly a serious wound, and his convalescence will take some time.' "*

Walter Stow's name is inscribed on the War Memorial in Ashby High Street, Ashby, Scunthorpe ...

" 'As he has gone to the base hospital, I shall not be able to give you any further news of him, but doubtless others will – Believe me, yours in sympathy, Paul O. Ashby (Chaplain Lincoln and Leicester Brigade).' "

A report in the **Lincolnshire Star** dated 8th May 1915 states that Walter was seriously wounded in the arm and back and had only been in France about a month. The last his mother had heard was that he was doing well. In the **Lincolnshire Star 8th May 1915** under *"Ashby News"*, it said that Walter died of his wounds somewhere in France – he had only been at the front a few days. Conflicting reports such as these were sadly quite common in those turbulent times.

The **Second Battle of Ypres** began on the 22nd April 1915. Chlorine gas was used for the first time by the Germans.

Walter's date of death is given as Wednesday 28th April 1915. He was 20 years old.

He was buried in **Bailleul Communal Cemetery Extension (Nord), France.** Bailleul is 14.5 km.

south west of Ypres, Belgium, and was a Corps H.Q. also an important rail head, air depot and hospital centre.

Walter's last address was 27 Alexandra Road, Ashby, where his mother, Mrs. Taylor lived.

... and at Messingham, Lincolnshire, his birthplace.

In July 1915, Walter's younger brother **Cecil** transferred from Ashby Council School to Crosby, but not for long. The family left the district in November the same year.

Because of his brother's connection with the school, Walter is commemorated on the Crosby Angel Memorial. He is also commemorated on the **War Memorials** at **Ashby (near St Paul's Parish Church, Ashby High Street)** and at **Messingham.** A "William Stow" is recorded on the Roll of Honour inside Ashby Parish Church - perhaps this is meant to be that of Walter?

Walter's name was included on the **Ashby Roll of Honour** which listed all those who served in World War 1, including those who survived, and is also on the **Crosby Parish Roll of Honour.**

Information from :
Mr Lee Johnson - distant relative

River Somme, France, which is still swampy as it was in The Great War.

William Frederick Streets

Private 10100
2nd Battalion Lincolnshire Regiment
Died: Saturday 1st July 1916 Killed in Action

The details of Yorkshireman William Frederick Streets' life prior to enlistment is largely a matter for conjecture. William, whose parents were general labourer **Robert** and **Sarah Ann Streets,** was born in Hull in the winter of 1886. It is not known where he went to school or where he worked afterwards. His last known address was 12 Haycroft Avenue, Grimsby, where he lived with his wife **Clara (née Davies)** whom he had married in 1904.

It is recorded that he enlisted at Grimsby with the 2nd Battalion Lincolnshire Regiment, and was killed in action on the first dreadful day of the **Battle of the Somme,** Saturday 1st July 1916. as was also **John William Bowers. Horace Birkett** and **Charles Selwyn Foster** were killed on the 3rd July 1916 in the same action. On the 1st July 1916, thirteen divisions of Commonwealth forces launched an offensive on a line from North of Gommecourt to Maricourt. Despite a preliminary bombardment lasting seven days, the German defences were barely touched and the attack met unexpectedly fierce resistance. Losses were catastrophic and with only minimal advances on the Southern flank, the initial attack was a failure.

"History of the Lincolnshire Regiment 1914-1918" by Major General C. R. Simpson, *"They were in the 25th Brigade (2nd Lincs.) As soon as the barrage lifted the whole battalion assaulted at 0720. They were met with very severe rifle fire and in most cases had to advance in rushes and return the fire. This fire seemed to come from the German second lines and the machine gun fire from their left. On reaching the German front line they found it strongly held and were met with showers of bombs, but after a very hard fight about 200 yards of German lines were taken at about 7.50 a.m. The few officers that were left gallantly led their men over the German trench to attack the second line, but owing to the rifle and machine gun fire could not push on. Attempts were made to consolidate and make blocks, but the trench was so badly knocked about that very little cover was obtainable."*

William Frederick Streets is commemorated on the **Thiepval Memorial, Somme, France,** together with **John William Bowers, Jacob Forrest, Charles Selwyn Foster** and **Frank Clifford Sylvester,** all commemorated on the Crosby Angel.

William was 31 years old when he died. It is not known why he is commemorated on the Angel Memorial. However, there were a number of children listed in the School Attendance Registers called "Streets" who attended Crosby School. As three different addresses (33 Grosvenor Street, 88 Sheffield Street and 114 Buckingham Street) are given and *"William Streets"* is listed as the father in every case, a degree of uncertainty exists. There may well have been more than one William Streets.

William Frederick Streets' name is on the **Crosby Parish Roll of Honour,** which lists all the men of Crosby Parish who served in World War I, including those who survived.

George Robert Sturman

Corporal 7014
1st and 2nd Battalion Lincolnshire Regiment
Died: Monday 23rd October 1916 Killed in Action

(Submitted by his great niece
Mrs. Monica Cooper - née Parrott)

At the time of his death, Corporal 7014 George Robert Sturman was in the 8th Division, 25th Brigade, 2nd Battalion Lincolnshire Regiment. He was born at 24 Redbourne Street, Frodingham in 1887.

He gave his life for his country on 23rd October 1916, aged 29 years. He is buried at **Bancourt British Cemetery, Pas de Calais, France.**

Corporal Sturman was the son of **Robert** and **Mary Sturman**, who came from Norfolk to work in Scunthorpe. He was the ninth of ten children. There were eight daughters, **Mary Ann, Hannah, Lucy, Ada, Susannah, Alice, Eliza, Sarah Elizabeth,** and two sons, **James** and **George.** One child, Hannah, died in childhood.

After leaving school, he became a bricklayer's labourer at the Frodingham Ironworks, but joined the Army in the 1st Battalion Lincolnshire Regiment when he was 19 years old in 1907. He remained a bachelor.

The 1st Battalion Lincolnshire Regiment was posted to India from 1898 to 1910, so George joined them after his initial training. The Battalion was sent to Aden in 1910 and returned to England in 1912. When the War started in 1914, this Battalion took part in Battles at **Mons, Le Cateau, The Aisne, Messines, Armentieres, Ypres, Hooge** in 1915 and the **Somme** in 1916.

The 1st Battalion, presumably including George, sailed from England as part of the 3rd Division, 9th Infantry Brigade of the British Expeditionary Force at the very start of the war and landed at Le Havre on 14th August 1914. From the battles listed above, it is clear that the Battalion was very involved in the desperate attempt to stem the German advance towards Paris that was eventually halted at the River Marne.

When on 1st July 1916, the Lincolnshire Regiment was in combat at the **Battle of the Somme,** George Sturman was involved in this battle and was wounded. He was sent home to recover. He told his family that it was, *"really dreadful out there, and if I'm sent back, I don't think I shall return."* His great sense of foreboding proved to be correct.

George is buried in Bancourt Cemetery, France.

My father told us of an incident which has been recounted to family members. When great uncle George was on leave, he lived with his sister **Ada**, my grandmother, who, with her husband, **Jack Parrott**, had brought up the family (in addition to her own family) after George's mother had died in her early 40's. George's widowed

1914 - 1919

St. Lawrence's Parish Church, Frodingham - with the names of George Sturman, Norman Budworth, Charles Selwyn Foster, John Robinson and Albert Edward Ward - all on the "Angel". They are also listed on the Roll of Honour published in the Parish Magazine, December 1917 of local men who served in the Armed Forces during the Great War. The names of those who died in World War II are listed on the lower panel of this Memorial Plaque.

father lived with them in Redbourne Street, Frodingham.

They were all *"no nonsense"* God-fearing people, who had common sense and a great sense of proportion. The story is, that whenever Great Uncle George was at home, he would sometimes go out in the evenings and knock three times on the locked door to be let in on his return. This was a custom that only related to George.

After George had returned to the trenches for the last time, suddenly one evening, the customary three knocks on the front door was heard. Ada, thinking it was George, opened the door to find no one there. The family sensed that George had been killed.

In the **Hull Daily Mail** dated **Saturday 16th December 1916,** a photograph of George was published with the following report, *"George R. Sturman of the Lincolnshire Regiment, missing since October 22nd last. Corporal Sturman was an old soldier, and served nine years in the army. Any news of him will be welcomed by his sister, Mrs. Woods, Brumby Road, Ashby, Scunthorpe."* It was subsequently established that George was one of those brave men who lost their lives. The family's fears had proved to be true.

It is obvious from the war diaries for September and October 1916 that George moved to the 2nd Battalion Lincolns prior to the time of his death. The Battalion had been rotating between trenches in the Hohenzollern sector and the billets on approximately a weekly basis, as was

the custom. In the middle of October the Battalion moved to the **Citadel, near Meulte** on the **Somme.**

An attack was made on the enemy's positions to the east of **Les Boeufs** and **Guedecourt**. The 8th Division were moved to the front line on the 19th October 1916, a place of desolation, mud and water everywhere. After three days of great artillery activity, an assault was made on the 23rd October, advancing with a creeping barrage. In the afternoon, the Battalion was part of a major attack launched from the trenches near **Les Boeufs.** The first wave was shot down almost to a man. The second wave came under violent machine gun fire. The 2nd Lincolnshires appear to have been nearly wiped out.

Corporal George Sturman was awarded the following medals: The 1914 Star, presented while he was in the 1st Battalion Lincolnshire Regiment, British War Medal and Victory Medal – both posthumously awarded. Apparently he spent time in both the 1st and 2nd Battalions.

The entry in the World War 1 Roll card index showed that George first entered the Theatre of War in France, on 13th September 1914. The Commonwealth War Graves Commission commemoration lists him as being in the 2nd Battalion, and so was in that Battalion when he died.

George Sturman's name appears on Crosby School Angel Memorial and the **Crosby Parish Roll of Honour.** His married sister, **Sarah**

Les Boefs in France where George Sturman was killed - it would have been a desolate sea of mud with the villages lying in ruins, devastated by the violence of conflict .

Elizabeth, lived in Theodore Road, Crosby, therefore he would have had nephews who attended that school.

George Sturman's name is also on the **Museum Wall Memorial near St Lawrence's Parish Church, Frodingham** and on the **Roll of Honour inside the Church.**

(***N.B.*** *George Sturman's sister,* ***Elizabeth (Lizzie)*** *married* ***Harry Allcock****, who became Secretary of Scunthorpe United Football Club. They lived in Crosby, which could be why George is on the Memorial, he was also distantly related to* ***William Thomas Spriggs****, whose name is also on the Angel Memorial and whose biography is included earlier in this book.)*

Cap Badge, Manchester Regiment

Frank Clifford Sylvester

Private 13586
11th Battalion Manchester Regiment
Died: Saturday 30th September 1916 Killed in Action

Frank Clifford Sylvester was born in 1894 in Ashby, Lincolnshire, only son of **James William Sylvester**, a steelworks labourer, and his wife **Betsy**, from Hundleby, Lincolnshire.

Four large families of Sylvesters left the Welton-le-Marsh/Burgh-le-Marsh area of Lincolnshire to seek their fortune at the steelworks in the new boom town of Scunthorpe.

Frank's Father, **James William**, was to be employed for 40 years at Frodingham Works and later at the Redbourne Works. In the early days, he was a well-known figure in local football and was goalkeeper for the Old Frodingham Football Club, fore-runner of Scunthorpe United Football Club.

It is not known where his son, **Frank Clifford,** went to school or where he lived, although at the time of his death, Saturday 30th September 1916, his parents were living at 40 Laneham Street, Scunthorpe.

Frank had enlisted at Manchester and was involved in what became known as the *"Big Push"*, the third offensive on the Somme that began on the 15th September 1916 at a time when Britain was beginning to exhaust its manpower. The extreme patriotism of 1914 and the *"Kitchener's Men"* was fast evaporating.

It has been recorded that the troops were given a good tot of rum *"to get them started."* September 1916 also saw the first tanks in

Thiepval, France - the village lies to the left of the large Memorial that dominates the skyline near the trees on the right of the picture.

action at a top speed of three miles per hour; most of them broke down, or were ditched, and the fumes inside the vehicles were hazardous.

On 30th September, 1916, the 11th Manchester Regiment was in the 34th Brigade. They fought all day in a major battle for every village, farm house and copse in the struggle to capture **Thiepval**. At 4 p.m. the action was renewed and objectives nearly taken, but exhaustion took its toll of the men. Frank Clifford Sylvester was killed in action. He was 22 years old. He is commemorated on the **Thiepval Memorial, Somme, France.**

It is reported in the **Scunthorpe and Frodingham Star** of the 28th January 1939, *"the death of Mr. James William Sylvester (**Frank Clifford Sylvester's father**) at the age of 67 at his daughter's home in Lloyds Avenue Scunthorpe, where he had lived since the death of his wife Betsy, who had pre-deceased him by six months. Frank Clifford Sylvester was their only son."*

Frank's Uncle, **Joseph Sylvester,** pre-deceased Frank by two weeks. Welton-le-Marsh born Joseph Sylvester, who was **Private 18263** in the **6th Battalion, Lincolnshire Regiment,** died of his wounds at the Third Casualty Clearing Station, France, on 18th September 1916, aged 30 and is buried at **Puchevillers British Cemetery, near Amiens, France.**

Joseph's children were pupils at Crosby School, which is, presumably, the reason for Frank's name being inscribed on the Crosby Angel Memorial. This poses the question as to why Joseph's name is not also included on the Angel Memorial?

In addition to being listed on the **Crosby Parish Roll of Honour,** Frank's name is inscribed on the headstone in **West Street Cemetery, Scunthorpe, Section B120,** commemorating the death of his eight month old sister, **Madeleine Rosamund Sylvester,** who died in September 1898.

Information from:
The Late Mrs. M. Rands (cousin)
Mr. Geoffrey Rands (first cousin once removed - grandson of Joseph Sylvester who was an Uncle of Frank Clifford Sylvester).

Albert Edward Ward's name is on the Lincolnshire Regiment Panel at Dud Corner Cemetery, Loos, France - so named because of the large number of unexploded shells found nearby.

Albert Edward Ward

Private 2193
1/5th Battalion Lincolnshire Regiment
Died: Wednesday 13th October 1915 Killed in Action

Albert Edward Ward was born in 1893 at Coningsby, Lincolnshire, third son of **Joseph Ward**, whose occupation was described in the 1901 census as *"engine driver on farm",* and his wife **Georgina.**

As only statistical evidence is known, the details of Albert's short life must of necessity remain a mystery. In the absence of known school records, it may be assumed that he attended the local village school along with his brothers **Richard** and **Thomas,** and his little sister **Kate.** Like many families scraping a living in farm service, the prospect of a better standard of living on a higher wage, may have drawn the Ward family to Scunthorpe some time after 1901.

Albert enlisted, along with Crosby lads **James Boothby, Norman Budworth, Daniel Cunningham, John Fowler, Ernest Hornsby** and **Arthur Newstead.** Albert Edward Ward was, at this time, working in the Coke Ovens Department of John Lysaght's Normanby Park Works.

On Wednesday, 13th October 1915, young Albert Edward Ward aged 22 was killed in action at the **Hohenzollern Redoubt,** along with his companions from Scunthorpe (all commemorated on the Crosby Angel), **Norman Budworth, Daniel Cunningham, Ernest Hornsby** and **Arthur Newstead. John Fowler,** wounded in the battle, died later. **James Boothby,** seventh and last of this group survived until 3rd November 1915.

"The battalion on the evening of the 12th October took over the trenches in front of the Hohenzollern Redoubt. At 2 p.m. on the 13th October, the battalion attacked the enemy's trenches. They passed over the Redoubt and owing to heavy fire took a position in Little Willie and North Face. About 6 p.m. they had to retire

Hohenzollern Redoubt, Loos, France - flat open area - note the slag bank on the horizon. Loos was a coal mining area at the time of World War 1, very bleak and industrial.

to the Redoubt owing to the untenability of the former position. This position was held. The battalion showed the greatest bravery in the attack, but suffered very severely, ten officers being killed and twelve wounded. Only about 160 men returned safely." (**Lincolnshire Battalion War Diaries**).

All the boys, except **James Boothby,** are commemorated on the **Loos Memorial at Dud Corner, Pas de Calais, France.** Albert Edward Ward is also commemorated on the **Memorial on the Scunthorpe Museum Wall** and **Foxhills Club.** In addition, he is commemorated on **St. Lawrence's Parish Church Frodingham Roll of Honour,** where his address is given as Winn Street, Frodingham. He was first reported as missing.

Albert's elder brother, **Private 22845 Thomas Ward,** was killed in the Great War on 6th November 1916. He was serving in the 2nd Battalion, Lincolnshire Regiment, and is commemorated at **Etaples Military Cemetery, Pas de Calais, France (Ref. XII C 9).** One of the Crosby School *"Old Boys"* and also named on the Angel, **William Langton**, who died on 3rd March 1918, is also buried at Etaples Military Cemetery (Ref. XLIX A 7). Thomas was injured, probably in

the same military action as **George Sturman,** and taken to one of the hospitals at Etaples, a main hospital and convalescent centre, being remote from attack, except from the air, and accessible by railway from both the Northern and Southern battlefields.

In the **1917 Scunthorpe Urban District Council Booklet Roll of Honour,** both brothers are recorded as having been killed, and that they had lived at the same address, 67 Fox Street, Scunthorpe.

The Ward brothers leave behind them more questions than answers. Although there are many Ward families in the Crosby area, none have been positively linked to Albert and Thomas. Why then, is **Albert** named on the Crosby Angel, and yet **Thomas** is not?

THE CROSBY ANGEL - A COMMUNITY'S WAR MEMORIAL

Hohenzollern Redoubt Memorial, unveiled on Friday 13th October 2006 to commemorate all Regiments which took part in the Battle of Loos 13th October 1915.

Inscription on the top of the Memorial, *"In honour of the 3,763 Officers and Men of the 44th (North England) Division (TF) who became casualties at the Hohenzollern Redoubt on 13th October 1915."* The Hohenzollern Redoubt Memorial at Auchy-les-Mines, France

The memorial dedicated to the 46th Division has been set so that the apex faces the Redoubt and set so that a visitor can walk some 200 yards to the cemetery where most of the fallen who have known graves are buried. It is intended to plant flowers and a hedge around the memorial. Two bench seats taken away by Lincoln City Council dedicated to the 1/4th and 1/5th Lincolns will, on completion of the memorial, be placed in the garden.

This memorial is a dedication to all who served and fell in the Hohenzollern Redoubt battle on the 13th October 1915. The whole of division comprised of Territorial Regiments, comprising of units from Lincolnshire, Leicestershire, Nottinghamshire & Derbyshire, North Staffordshire and Monmouthshire, supported by Royal Field Artillery and Royal Engineers.

The dedication service took place just before the time the first wave went over the top. The last post was sounded after a whistle had been blown at the exact time they went over.

It was the division's first major action after its arrival on the Western Front but it was a gallant failure. The casualties incurred that afternoon changed forever the fine pre-war territorial character of the division.

The battle took place on the last afternoon of the battle of Loos, some 12 miles to the north, their objective was for "The Hump" an old mine slag heap which controlled the high ground, housing observation posts, machine guns etc.

The battle started with the usual artillery barrage early morning, after a lengthy pause, it was followed later with a gas attack, this proved to be ineffective, once again the high command demanded another pause before the troops went over the top. This gave the Germans the opportunity to occupy their positions ready for the expected attack.

The five men commemorated on the Crosby Angel who died on 13th October 1915 were: **Norman Budworth, Daniel Cunningham, Ernest Hornsby, Arthur Newstead** and **Albert Edward Ward**

Information from Lincoln Branch of Royal British Legion, by kind permission.
Photographs: Mr Christopher J. Bailey, Researcher, 5th Lincolns.

H.M.S. "Hawke" torpedoed by German U-9 Submarine

William Jobson Welton

Royal Navy Stoker 1st Class RFR/CH/B/2722
H.M.S. "Hawke"
Died: Thursday 15th October 1914 Died at Sea

William Jobson Welton was born on the 25th April 1877 at Melton Ross, Lincolnshire, the third of **Thomas** and **Jane Welton's** five children, the others being **Betsy Ann, John George, Walter Frederick Doyles** and **Frank.** The family comprised three generations as Jane's mother, **Kitty Doyles,** aged 78, was also living with them at the time of the 1881 census.

A resident grandmother, provided she was in good health, must have been a great asset to a family such as the Weltons, where the wife of an agricultural labourer was also expected to do land work, especially at haymaking and harvest time. Children, too, joined their parents, working from an early age on the land, which was their livelihood.

The 1891 census for Melton Ross, Barnetby, Lincolnshire, describes William, then aged thirteen, and his brother **Frederick** (aged twelve), as agricultural labourers.

Five years later, their father, Thomas Welton, died, leaving Jane Welton to bring up her children alone as best she could. Life was hard, as it was for countless other women in her position. Census information 1901 shows William's mother, sister Betsy and elder brother John (agricultural labourer), living at New Barnetby, eking out a living by taking in two boarders, a maltster and a railway signalman. William and his younger brother Frederick are not mentioned.

William Jobson Welton joined the Royal Navy at Portsmouth on 18th November 1896, signing on initially for twelve years' service. He was 19 years old, five feet five and three quarters inches tall, with brown hair, blue eyes and a fresh complexion.

After training as a Stoker on H.M.S. *"Victory II"*, and H.M.S. *"Mars",* he set sail on H.M.S. *"Pembroke"* in the first month of a new century, January 1900. He made many subsequent voyages over the next eight years, serving on H.M.S. *"Goliath",* H.M.S. *"Pembroke",* H.M.S. *"Northampton"* and H.M.S. *"Hawke"* until he took a break in service and came ashore for a while. He still remained in the Royal Fleet Reserve.

He married **Ellen Cook** in the December quarter of 1904 at Scunthorpe, Lincolnshire, where he came to work at the newly built steelworks of John Lysaght's.

When their only child, **George Teanby Welton**, born on 2nd January 1907, was three years old, William Jobson Welton went back to sea, on 4th April 1910. Little George began his school days at Crosby School on 9th January 1912. He and his mother were living at 41 Burke Street, Crosby.

On 7th August 1914, William Jobson Welton set sail on H.M.S. *"Hawke"* on what proved to be his final voyage. Shortly before his death, he sent a letter of condolence to the widow of **William Henry Rylance,** who is also commemorated on the Angel Memorial. They were obviously friends, and may possibly have been shipmates, both being of a similar age. Both men were Royal Naval Reservists and also worked at John Lysaght's Normanby Park Works.

A transcription of this letter is to be found in the entry in this book for **William Henry Rylance.**

THE CROSBY ANGEL - A COMMUNITY'S WAR MEMORIAL

The German U-9 submarine sank both H.M.S. *"Aboukir"* (William Henry Rylance's ship) and H.M.S. *"Hawke"* (William Jobson Welton's ship). The U-9 was the only German submarine to survive the War and ended up in Morecambe Bay, England, where she was broken up in the 1920's. The German word "U Boat" means "Unterseeboot" (undersea boat).

Three days after William wrote this letter of sympathy, H.M.S. *"Hawke"*, the ship on which he was serving, was torpedoed in the North Sea while on patrol duty, by a German submarine U-9, the same one which had torpedoed his friend's ship H.M.S. *"Aboukir"*. This was Thursday 15th October 1914.

H.M.S. *"Hawke"* was an old armoured cruiser operating as part of the 10th Cruiser Squadron assigned to the Northern Patrol. She had originally been launched at Chatham in 1891 and was one of the oldest ships still in service. H.M.S. *"Hawke"* was being used as a training ship and had many young cadets on board. She had been recommissioned in February 1913 with a nucleus crew, and had come up to her full complement on the outbreak of war in August 1914. During September 1914, she had visited Lerwick, Shetland Islands, Scotland.

On the fateful day, she was in the northern waters of the North Sea with a similar ship, H.M.S. *"Theseus"* when they were attacked. They were operating on 15th October 1914 without a destroyer screen. Unfortunately, they were slower than the submarine U-9, which was tracking them. Their position was some 60 miles off Aberdeen. At the time, H.M.S. *"Hawke"* had just turned to intercept a neutral Norwegian collier.

The U-Boat Commander was Lieutenant Weddigen. He missed H.M.S. *"Theseus"* with his first torpedo but unfortunately hit H.M.S. *"Hawke"* amidships near a magazine. The detonation was followed by a second terrific explosion, in which a large number of the crew were killed. The ship sank within five minutes and was only able to launch one ship's boat. Five hundred and twenty five men perished. Only the 49 men in the long boat were saved. They were picked up three hours later by a Norwegian steamer. H.M.S. *"Theseus"* was under strict Admiralty orders not to attempt to pick up survivors, as only several weeks earlier there had been a disaster. On that occasion, on the 22nd September, both H.M.S. *"Hogue"* and H.M.S. *"Cressy"* had also been torpedoed when going to pick up survivors from H.M.S. *"Aboukir"*. The officer in charge of the submarine that had sunk these three ships had again been Lieutenant Otto Weddigen.

Had they had sufficient time to launch other lifeboats from H.M.S. *"Hawke"*, then undoubtedly more would have been saved by the Norwegians. It is recorded on his Service Record, that William *"drowned in North Sea after H.,M.S. "Hawke" was sunk by a German submarine"*, which indicates that he had managed to leave the sinking ship..

William Jobson Welton's name is included on the Crosby Angel Memorial because his son George was a pupil at the school and the family lived in Crosby. He is also commemorated on the **John Lysaght's 1914 Roll of Honour,** the **Memorial on the North Lincolnshire Museum Wall, Scunthorpe,** the **Memorial Plaque** at **Foxhills Club, Scunthorpe,** and **Panel VI on the Chatham Memorial Register 1914 - Memorials to Naval Ranks and Empire.**

A Barton-on-Humber man, Chief Petty Officer Thomas Henry Bate, L.S.M. G.C.M., also died when H.M.S. *"Hawke."* went to her watery grave.

On 30th October 1914, seven year old George Welton left Crosby School and returned with his widowed mother, Ellen, to her home in Melton Ross, Barnetby, Lincolnshire.

William's second cousin, **Private 203590 Thomas Welton, 2/5th Battalion West Yorkshire Regiment (Prince of Wales Own),** the son of his grandfather's brother, died on 20th July 1918 and is commemorated on the **Soissons Memorial, France.**

Information from:
Mr. Terry Clipson (distant relative)

HIGH STREET, SCUNTHORPE.

A 1912 Postcard of Scunthorpe High Street. Beckett's Bank (doorway with triangular arch above its doors) is to the right of the picture and was on the corner of Trafford Street and High Street. St. John's Parish Church is off left.

Arthur Shannon Wilson

Private 53637
10th Battalion West Yorkshire Regiment
(Prince of Wales' Own)
Died: Tuesday 11th June 1918 Killed in Action

Arthur Shannon Wilson, first son of the **Reverend Charles and Mrs. Usher Wilson,** was born into a war zone in Colesburg, Cape Colony in 1900 during the second of the South African (or Boer) Wars. This war began in October 1899 when Kitchener was Governor General of the Sudan. At first the operations of the British troops in Cape Colony were unsuccessful; disastrous losses were sustained. Lord Roberts was sent out to be Commander in Chief with Kitchener as his Chief of Staff.

When Kimberley, Ladysmith and Mafeking were relieved and a Boer leader, Cronge, was compelled to surrender, the war appeared to be practically over in 1900. Lord Roberts went home, leaving Kitchener in charge as Commander in Chief. But there followed two years of fiercely fought guerrilla warfare which was brought to an end by Kitchener's effective but draconian scorched earth measures. Boer

women and children were rounded up, some 20,000 of them died in concentration camps along with many Africans. For this Kitchener was much criticised.

After his ordination in 1895, The Rev. Charles Usher Wilson and his wife made their home in South Africa where he became a priest, assistant master and chaplain at St. Andrew's College, Grahamstown, curate of St. Paul (Port Elizabeth) and chaplain to the forces in South Africa 1899-1902 (Queen's Medal with two clasps). He then became rector of Colesburg and Aliwal North, and acting chaplain to the Royal Navy on H.M.S. *"Cochrane"* 1909-1911. It is not known why he returned to England to become the curate of St. Martin's, Lincoln, where the family remained until 1912.

The following item appeared in the **Lincolnshire Star dated 11th October 1913,** *"Sir Berkeley Sheffield Bart. the Patron of the new ecclesiastical district which has now been carved out of Scunthorpe Parish has offered the living to the Rev. Charles Usher Wilson, curate of St. Martin's, Lincoln, who has accepted it and*

THE CROSBY ANGEL - A COMMUNITY'S WAR MEMORIAL

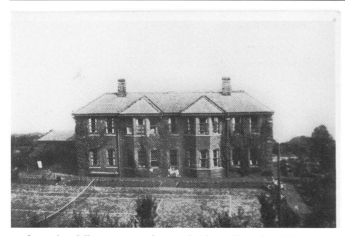

Crosby Vicarage where Arthur lived with his family - his father was vicar of the fledgling St. George's Mission Church.

will take charge of the district after Order in Council for its formation, has been obtained. Mr. Wilson was ordained in 1895 and has thus been in orders 18 years."

In 1913, the Rev. Charles Usher Wilson took the living of St. George's Mission Church, Crosby. Young Arthur was 13 years old and the family had increased. **James M. S. Wilson**, another son, was born on 19th July 1909, a year after Crosby School opened. The school was only yards away from Crosby Vicarage, the family's home and next door to St. George's Mission Church, which was dedicated on 6th December 1913. Rev. Wilson was its first vicar, although the church had been opened since 28th October 1907.

Arthur's brother, James, became a pupil of Crosby School on 24th September 1917 *"from private tuition"*. He left on 1st April 1920, having won a free scholarship to Sleaford Grammar School. The paths followed by the two brothers could not have been more different. After a brief working life at Beckett's Bank, High Street, Scunthorpe, (on the corner of Trafford Street), Arthur enlisted at Scunthorpe with the West Yorkshire Regiment in 1917. Proud, perhaps, to follow his father into military service if not into Holy Orders.

His army career ended on Tuesday 11th June 1918 when he was killed in action. He is buried in **Acheux British Cemetery, Somme, France**. The graves there cover the period from April to August 1918 when the German offensives brought the allied line within eight kilometres of Acheux.

The Hull Daily Mail dated 22nd June 1918 reports, *"Private Arthur S. Wilson, West Yorks., eldest son of the Rev. C. and Mrs. Usher Wilson, Crosby Vicarage, was killed in action on June 11th. He was attached to a Lewis gun team. He was not 19 years of age, and was in the Scunthorpe Branch of Beckitts (sic) Bank, and won the Boxing Shield for his Company in the Res. Batt. at Rugeley last year."*

Arthur's short life was overshadowed by war; born in the thick of the Boer War, he was destined to die at war in another foreign country half a world away in France. He was one of the youngest men to die; there were two other Crosby men who died at the age of 18: **Richard Davison** and **Alexander Havercroft,** who were commemorated on the Angel Memorial. Arthur is commemorated on the Crosby Angel Memorial because his father was the vicar at the Crosby Mission Church and his brother attended the school.

Lewis Gun, the type which Arthur used.

Arthur's name is also listed on the **Crosby Parish Roll of Honour.**

Arthur's father, The Rev. C. Usher Wilson, left the parish of Crosby to take up the living at Sutterton in South Lincolnshire in November 1920, where he served for 21 years. He died in Surrey in the spring of 1955 aged 84.

Fifty one years later, the following interesting item appeared on the Internet in 2006,

"On the last Sunday of April the Church of the Ascension in Lady Grey celebrated its centenary, with Bishop Thabo Makgoba presiding.

Research in the Cory Library in Grahamstown reveal that the foundation stone (still visible) was laid on March 31ˢᵗ 1906 by the **Revd Charles Usher Wilson**, *rector of Aliwal North.*

£550 was needed to build and furnish the church, and by the time of the dedication service on 25 August 1906, most of this had been collected. A notable feature of the foundation of the Church of the Ascension was the contribution of the local Dutch Reformed Church: the plot on which the church stands was given by a Mr. and Mrs. Coenraad Potgieter, and other contributions came from this source, indeed "from all quarters". The building includes two vestries, the second intended as an overnight bedroom, complete with fireplace, for the use of visiting clergy.

The dedication service referred to above was presided over by **Wilson,** *assisted by Robert Voyie Morgan, rector of Barkly East. Fitting, for while the church was to remain a chapelry of Aliwal North until 1980, it was then transferred to the care of St. Stephen's Barkly East. It is noticeable that no Bishop presided at this dedication in 1906; the Bishop of the time,*

Charles Edward Cornish, was on overseas leave. Church officers in 1906 were: O. Von Broembsen and C. Lilford. In 1907: Dr. F. Towne and E. Cowley. The present chapel wardens are Eddie Ranft and Gloria Brine. (Adapted from an article first published in the Barkly East Reporter.)"

Information from:
Newsletter of the Diocese of Grahamstown, Cape Province, South Africa June-July 2006 Volume 29 No. 3. Website: http://www/diocesegrahamstown.co.za/umbuliaso/umb2006.03.htm.
Mr. David Blake, B.A. (Hons)., M.A., A.M.A., Curator, RACgD Museum c/o Amport House, Amport, near Andover, Hants. SP11 8BG (Crockford's 1949.)
Mr. Dennis Howlett

This photograph, taken in the 1950's, shows the location of Beckett's Bank *(opposite Scunthorpe Parish Church, built in 1891 by Rowland Winn, Baron St. Oswald of Nostell Priory, a great local benefactor.)* It is believed the bank had left the town by the end of the Great War.

THE PARISH CHURCH, SCUNTHORPE   K 5436

Chapter Five

Time Line

**Actions in The Great War in date order with names of
Those Commemorated on the
Crosby Angel who died between**

1914-1919

THE CROSBY ANGEL - A COMMUNITY'S WAR MEMORIAL

1914 4th August   <u>War Declared</u>

8th August   **Crosby Parish Council's concern about possible unemployment owing to stoppage of work in the district due to the War*

10th August   **Recruitment at Crosby Hotel for Home and Foreign Forces Service*

23rd August   Battle of Mons - Retreat

6th - 9th September   Battle of the Marne

AT SEA   22.9.1914   H.M.S. *"Aboukir"* sunk in North Sea torpedoed by German U-9 Submarine.   22.9.1914 **William Henry Rylance**

12th September   **478,893 men in Britain volunteered in six weeks for armed service*

14th - 28th September   Battle of the Aisne

18th September - 16th October   Battle of Flanders

October   **War Relief Fund Crosby School starts monthly deposits in Yorkshire Penny Bank*

AT SEA: 15.10.1914   H.M.S. *"Hawke," "Cressey,"* and *"Hogue"* torpedoed off Aberdeen by German submarine U-9.   15.10.1914 **William Jobson Welton**

13th October to 2nd November   Battle of Armentiers   22.10.1914 **John William Standerline**

12th October -17th November   First Battle of Ypres   24.10 1914 **George William Calvert**

     1.11.1914 **Fred Hare** and **Edwin Pittaway**

1st November   Battle of Wytschaete

November-December   **Arrival of Belgian refugees into Scunthorpe district*

16th December   **Bombardment by 4 German Cruisers off Scarborough, Whitby and Hartlepool*

1915   5.1.1915 **Parkinson Cook** (<u>name not on Angel Memorial</u>)

*Slump in local Building Trade in Scunthorpe district

10th - 12th March   Battle of Neuve-Chapelle

     28.4.1915 **Walter Stow**

17th April   Capture of Hill 60

May   **Crosby Parish Council proposed special fund raising efforts for Red Cross*

May   **Crosby Parish Council petition Government to intern or deport all aliens of enemy origin*

9th May   **The first local men recruited in Kitchener's army left for France*

22nd April - 4th May   Second Battle of Ypres

5th June   **Normanby Hall to be used for wounded Soldiers' Convalescence*

AT SEA   Dardenelles Howe Battalion, R.N.: 4.6.1915 **Tom Popple**

     9.7.1915 **John William Cowling**

July   **Crosby Builder Mr. Jackson's Munitions Factory opened*

19th July   **112 soldiers/sailors' dependants paid allowances by Frodingham Iron & Steel Co. Ltd., Scunthorpe*

August   **Recruitment at Crosby Hotel, Normanby Road, Crosby*

11th September 1915   **Crosby Councillor Thurston, received £1 from Pigeon War Committee. His pigeon had carried an admiralty dispatch to France, where it had been four times*

25th September - 5th October   Battle of Loos and Champagne

25th September   Bois Grenier   25.9.1915 **Charles Shaw**

26th September   Loos   26.9.1915 **John Fowler**

13th –19th October   Hohenzollern Redoubt   13.10.1915 **Norman Budworth, Daniel Cunningham, Ernest Hornsby, Arthur Newstead, Albert Edward Ward**

	3.11.1915 **James Boothby**
AT SEA : H.M.S."Anglia" Hospital Ship Sunk by German Mine	17.11.1915 **William Henry Dymond**
	20.11.1915 **Richard Henry Davison**
Died of dysentery at Training Camp	26.11.1915 **Frank Edward Sellars**

10th December   *Mrs. Taylor. George Taylor's wife, made 13 plum puddings/dozens of mince pies for France for National Christmas Pudding Fund*

1916

29th January   *First Tank trials in Britain*

31st January   *First Zeppelin Raid on Scunthorpe (Mr. Taylor's Logbook)*

14th -15th February, 2nd March   Action of the Bluff

2nd March   *National Conscription commenced: those born between 1886-1896*

9.3.1916 **Arthur Frost**

27th March - 16th April   Fighting at St Eloi

19.4.1916 **Walter Martin**

28.4.1916 **George Henry Ross**

21st May   German Attack on Vimy Ridge

AT SEA: 31st May   Battle of Jutland   **H.M.S. "Queen Mary"**

31.5.1916 **Alexander** and **John Havercroft** (brothers)

1st July -18th November   Battle of the Somme   1.7.1916 **John William Bowers** and **William Streets**

3.7.1916 **Horace Birkett** and **Charles Selwyn Foster**

During this period many actions were fought. They included:

1st-13th July   Battle of Albert

2nd- 4th July   Capture of La Boiselle

20th - 25th July   Attack on High Wood

1.8.1916 **Thomas George Harpham**

1st September   *War Savings Association for local schools discussed in Scunthorpe*

12th September   *Crosby Council protest to Great Central Railway working on nights following air raid warnings, due to possibility of railway engine fireboxes being visible to enemy airships*

23rd July - 3rd September   Battle of Pozieres Ridge

4.8.1916 **John Dale**

14.8.1916 **John Bycroft**

2nd - 22nd September   Battle of Flers-Courcelette   15.9.1916 **John Cowan**

26th - 28th September   Battle of Thiepval   30.9.1916 **Frank Clifford Sylvester**

7th October   *Crosby Parish Council try to exempt its Clerk from Military Service*

7th October - 5th November   Attacks on Butte de Warlencourt

14.10.1916 **William Selby**

23rd October   Zenith Trench Les Boefs   23.10.1916 **George Robert Sturman**

December   *Unoccupied land taken over for allotments to feed the nation due to convoys of food supply ships being torpedoed by the enemy*

1917

Rowland Winn had become the largest single iron ore producer in the country, producing 1/12th of all output

Sporadic food riots during the year due to shortages

20th January   *Total of 78 razors for the army collected by Crosby School*

23rd January   Raid at Neuville

24.1.1917 **Arthur Lilly Norwood**

29th January	Raid at Butte de Warlencourt	
		2.2.1917 **Thomas William Bowden**
February	* *National Voluntary Food Rationing*	
7th February	Capture of Grandecourt	
		9.2.1917 **Gideon Roberts**
		10.2.1917 **Jacob Forrest**
March	*"War Bread" introduced to reduce consumption of imported grain*	
23rd February - 5th April	German retreat to the Hindenburg Line	
9th April - 3rd May	Battle of Arras	
9th 14th April	Battle of Vimy Ridge	
9th - 14th April	1st Battle of the Scarpe	
23rd - 24th April	2nd Battle of the Scarpe	
		27.4.1917 **Arthur Herbert Sellars**
		28.4.1917 **John William Rimmington**
28th - 29th April	Battle of Arleux	
May	*Rate of Allied shipping losses due to German U-boat attacks is 64%*	
12th May	*Crosby Council Vote of Condolences to Council Chairman, F. B. Rimmington, following the death of his son, John, on active service*	
24th May	*The King's Proclamation on Food Economy read at Crosby School*	
14th June	Battle of Messines	
		27.6.1917 **James Jabez Pogson**
July	*Eggs for the Wounded Campaign supported by Crosby School Boys*	
July	*Crosby Parish Council expressed concern regarding lack of suitable accommodation available for Government draft of 3,000 workmen into the district*	
July	*Wiebeck field made available to Crosby children as playground.*	
1st July	Attack on Lens	1.7.1917 **Lawrence Sissons**
31st July—10th November	Battle of Ypres (3rd Ypres)	
August	*Crosby Parish Council Concern regarding lack of sugar supplies compared with elsewhere*	
16th—18th August	Battle of Langemarck	16.8.1917 **George Alexander Hall**
22nd—25th September	Battle of Menin Road Bridge	
26th—30th September	Battle of Polygon Wood	
9th October	Battle of Poelcappelle	10.10.1917 **George Allison Hudson**
12th October	First Battle of Passchendaele	
26th October—2nd November: Second Battle of Passchendale		28.11.1917 **Ernest William Robinson**
November-December	*Horse Chestnut collections for acetone production (Cordite)*	
20th November—7th December	Battle of Cambrai	
23rd November	*Church Bells in Great Britain rung to celebrate Victory at Cambrai*	
20th—21st November	The Tank Attack	
21st November	Recapture of Noyelles	
23rd—28th November	Capture of Bourlon Wood	
30th November—3rd December	The German Counter Attacks	

1918

Sunday 6th January	*National Day of Prayer & Thanksgiving: Rev. C. U. Wilson, Crosby Vicar, invited Crosby Council to attend Parish Church Morning Service*
6th February	*Votes for women with property over age of 30 years granted by Act of Parliament and to all men age 21 - Representation of the People's Act*
January	*Council request for Military Service exemption of resident doctor, Dr. Clark, because of the manufacture in the area of munitions, iron and steel for shell and other War purposes by many workers.*

9.3.1918 **John Robinson**

April

National Meat Rationing introduced

21st March—5th Apri:	1st Battle of the Somme	25.3.1918 **William Thomas Spriggs**
21st—23rd March	Battle of St. Quentin	
25th – 26th April	2nd Battle of Kemmel Ridge	27.4.1918 **George Walter Harley**
27th May	Third Battle of the Aisne	28.5.1918 **Alfred Garrett**
		30.5.1918 **Herbert Alfred Daniels**
		11. 6.1918 **Arthur Shannon Wilson**
		18. 6.1918 **William Harper**

July

Most foodstuffs rationed - households must register with retailers

21st—23rd August	Battle of Albert	22.8.1918 **George William Smith**
18th September—9th October	Battle of the Hindenburg Line	20.9.1918 **Wilfred Short**

The Final Advance—1918
17th October—11th November in Picardy

17th – 25th October	Battle of Selle	3.11.1918 **William Langton**

2nd October—11th November in Artois

28th September—11th November in Flanders

11th November   Armistice

*Fisher Education Act raised school leaving age to 14 years
(before this children could leave school at aged 13 years wit h an
"Exemption Certificate")*

19th July 1919   *Peace Celebrations—Bonfire on Old Show Ground, Scunthorpe*

23.4.21 **George Sims****

(1)   **G. Cook's** name is on the Crosby Angel but is not listed on this Time Line because he seems to have been MISSING for some time then returned and married in 1919.

(2)   **Parkinson Cook** lived in Crosby but is not commemorated on the Crosby Angel; it is conjectured that he was omitted from the Angel, as he lived in Crosby but he was killed in action.

(3)   ****George Sims** – came back from the War, but died **23rd April 1921 at 47 Digby Street Age: 47**

World War 1 Army Ancestry (fourth edition) by Norman Holding, revised and updated by Iain Swinnerton
Published by the Federation of Family History Societies (Publications) Ltd.
15-16 Chesham Industrial Centre, Oram Street, Bury Lancashire BL9 6EN fourth edition 2003
ISBN No. 1 86006 179 6 www.familyhistorybooks.co.uk Copyright : Norman Holding and Iain Swinnerton

Chapter Six

The Home Front

Life in Crosby during World War I

By

Rachel Butler

Crosby's 'Home Front'

What was remarkable about the 1914-18 or Great War was the sheer scope of the conflict. It was the first time on a global scale that civilians were directly affected by their county's decision to fight. This was a war where **everyone** in society was involved: from soldiers to housewives to school children. The 1914-18 war demanded a whole new rethink of how to cope in war-time, and demanded the co-operation of everybody in society to make any new policies work. We can trace the governmental and popular initiatives through the local newspapers and other sources (Mr. Taylor's **Logbooks**) to find out how Crosby, and the country, went about fighting from the **'home front'**.

Army Recruiting Poster with Lord Kitchener's image.

The first few weeks of war in late summer 1914 quickly demonstrated that this was to be a conflict which was to involve not only those voluntarily fighting for King and country, but the 'general public' too, *"The crowds that gathered so enthusiastically outside Buckingham Palace were less aware than their King of the terrible catastrophe that was beginning to unfold. Few appreciated that the war would be no longer a matter simply for the professional services; that... the social and domestic life of the nation would be transformed with ordinary people subjected to regulation, discomfort and privation such as had not been experienced before. But on the night of 4th August it was assumed that the war would not last more than a few months…"* (AQHF,2004:24).

Once it was generally understood that this war was going to last quite some time, and that it was unlike previous conflicts, it was realised that new strategies were needed to support and aid the war effort. **The Times** ran a column of '*Practical Patriotism - How to be useful in Wartime*', which, among other things, listed defence organisations and the growing number of charities to which gifts could be sent.

Help on the Home Front

Soldier's envelope—the writer was thanking a Crosby School pupil for sending him a pair of socks that she had knitted ...

Tens of 'worthy causes' were set up, mostly nationwide initiatives, which spread their word via columns in the local newspapers, in Crosby's case the **Lincolnshire Star**.

These collections, which usually worked through local drop-off and pick-up points, included **Razors for the Army**: Mr. Taylor writes on 20th January 1917 that, through fundraising in Crosby School, *"The total of razors collected for the Army is now 78"*. There was also the **Vegetables for the Navy** appeal; the **Star** dated 26th November 1916 notes that "*Mr. Fred Glasier Jnr., who is working the Winterton Depot at the Brigg Branch of the Vegetable Production Committee... has received a letter of thanks from Mrs. Landers, the Hon. R.N. Noke, R.N., H.M.S. "Achilles" and Lieut. A.E. Johnston, H.M.S. "Sappho", who both expressed their gratitude and appreciation for the splendid gifts received of fruit and vegetables. Mr. Glasier wishes to thanks the Boys Brigade for their excellent work in collecting the fruit and vegetables weekly"*.

Princess Mary's Gift Box Christmas 1914 - sent to His Majesty's soldiers and sailors following a public appeal, containing tinder lighter, a pipe, cigarettes and tobacco, with alternatives for non-smokers, and a Christmas card.

In the same vein, there was a **National Christmas Pudding Fund** for the troops: the **Logbook** records, *"Dec. 10th 1915: Mrs. Taylor has made 13 plum puddings and dozens of mince pies to be sent to France. These we shall pack up to dispatch to the trenches in France (launch of pudding fund in Star)".*

There were also collections for those invalided in fighting. The **Eggs for the Wounded** campaign was also reported in the **Star**, with regular updates: on 14th April 1917 the paper said that the local collection, supervised by a Miss M. Fowler from Winterton, had 446 eggs to hand in to the nearest depot, in Barnetby. Crosby School itself gathered a huge amount of eggs. The following passage from the **Logbook** shows how much was brought in in a very short time, *"July 7th 1917: 36 eggs sent to London. July 21st 1917: Today we sent 48 eggs to London. July 27th 1917: I took 36 eggs to the railway station for Hospital use".* Crosby School was obviously a 'drop off' and collection centre for the local community.

One collection made by the school, however, seems a little unusual at first glance. During research a few references were found in the **Logbooks** to the gathering of acorns and chestnuts, *"Nov. 26th 1917: The boys have collected 24 lbs. of chestnuts and six or seven sacks of acorns. With the acorns we have fed two pigs, one of which belongs to the school. The chestnuts we shall send to the Director of Propellant Stores".* A further reference only helps to deepen the mystery, *"Dec. 10th 1917: Today we sent 24 lbs. of chestnuts to Kings Lynn for ammnitin (sic) purposes".* What possible use chestnuts could be as ammunition - firing them at the enemy when you run out of shells, perhaps?!

The answer came to light in a seemingly totally unconnected piece of literature, **Young Betjeman** (Bevis Hillier, 1988, Cardinal), about the Poet Laureate John Betjeman. In reference to his time at school during the Great War, he also mentions the collection of chestnuts for ammunition. An inconspicuous footnote helps clear the whole matter up, *"The* **Imperial War Museum**'s *Information Sheet, no.7, 'The Collection of Horse Chestnuts, 1917', reveals that the horse chestnuts were needed to produce the acetone that was used, with ether-alcohol, as a solvent for manufacturing cordite, the basic propellant for shells. The fact sheet adds, "Nobody really knew exactly why they were collecting horse chestnuts. The Government was, naturally, reticent to reveal the motive behind its scheme since the Germans could very well copy this novel form of acetone production".* That's why it was so difficult to get to the bottom of!

Harry S Truman, U.S. President (left) and Chaim Azriel Weizmann, a qualified chemist born in Belaruse, Russia, in 1874 became a naturalized British subject. As Director of the Admiralty Laboratories 1916-19 he discovered acetone for war purposes - hence the chestnut collections! He became first President of the new State of Israel 1949 - 1952.

Collections such as those mentioned obviously come from a desire to **help those helping us** -

THE BEST MONEY BOX

SAVINGS CERTIFICATES
GO INTO THE
EMPIRE BANK
20/- FOR 15/6 IN FIVE YEARS ~ 26/- FOR 15/6 IN TEN YEARS

making sure the troops fighting for us overseas have decent food and, just as importantly, that symbolically, they are placed at the heart of their nation even though absent from it at the moment. It is the nation saying thank you.

Crosby's Efforts

Crosby as a community made many appeals for the troops. Most collections were of everyday but indispensable items such as cigarettes, extra provisions, extra clothing; things taken for granted in times of peace and prosperity, but which make living seem that much harder when they are not available. The **Star** newspaper, 10th October 1914 notes that, *"Crosby WMC raised £19 from concerts and sent to Drum Major Woodley at Luton, 100 packets of Gold Flake cigarettes and 200 ounces of tobacco for the 300 local men who have responded to the call of their country"*.

In another area of Crosby, Lady Sheffield, President of Lincolnshire Needlework Guild (and wife of Sir Berkeley Sheffield, local M.P. and one-time landowner of Crosby Parish, who resided at Normanby Hall) expressed the desire for her guild to help in the war effort too. At the national level The Queen herself, *"... appealed to all the needlework guilds in the country to send in underclothing for soldiers and sailors..."* (AQHF, 2004:27). In Crosby, *"It was decided to form a branch (of the Guild) ... and to make garments suitable for men at the front and for the families of soldiers and sailors at home"*. This was the fostering of the **'do your bit'** attitude with regards to wartime collecting which re-emerged in the 1939-45 conflict, *" 'It is earnestly hoped that every woman in Crosby will do something to help in the great work of providing comfort for those engaged in the war and for their dependents at home".* (**Star,** October 1914).

In December of the same year, another needlework guild in Scunthorpe, the Frodingham branch, was also able to report a great effort on the part of their members in making a practical difference to the life of 'Scunthorpe lads at the Front', *"Re. Soldiers and Sailors etc. Total number of garments sent to Lady Sheffield: 23 nightshirts, 129 dayshirts, 41 helmets, 50 handkerchiefs, 42 cup covers, 468 pairs socks, 13 Helpless Case shirts (disabled), 76 vests, 10 caps, 36 mufflers, 19 bandages, 2 towels, 29 belts, 2 pair bed socks, 4 pair cuffs, 3 bed jackets, 10 pair mittens, 2 blankets, 9 petticoats, 9 children's garments, 18 tins Vaseline and boric powder, 1 swab, plus a quantity of cigarettes".* (**Star**, December 1914). Such newspaper reports help to depict with what enthusiasm the Scunthorpe parishes took it upon themselves to help in W.W.I.

Crosby Boys' School and Collecting

It is obvious that Mr. Taylor was one of the main organisers of these efforts in the Crosby Parish - his **Logbooks** are punctuated with descriptions of various fundraising ideas, many thought up by the headmaster himself. In the first few weeks of the war this amounted to mostly **raising funds** as not much more could be done at this point: *"October 1914: We deposit 9s. 9d. in the Yorkshire Penny Bank monthly for the local War Relief Fund. The teachers pay a sum calculated from their salaries in accordance with the rules drawn up by the local committee".* However, his financial fundraising continued throughout the war, *"Sept. 1st 1916: Tonight I was present at a meeting at the Empire Theatre. The formation of War Savings Association was discussed. We have decided to form an association in connection with our school. All the Head Teachers were elected as members of the committee."* Every teacher did their bit, *"Oct. 13th 1917: The House to House collection was made today*

THE CROSBY ANGEL - A COMMUNITY'S WAR MEMORIAL

The purchase of War Bonds helped to finance the war effort.

in Crosby Parish by Crosby Boys' School Teachers. We collected £27 2s. 4½d. Last year we collected £22 17s.1½d. on the first day".

Old Boys' Appeals

Some collections were of a more **personal** nature to those at the School, *"Jan. 25th) (1915) :Today I packed up 5 good cardigans and jackets and sent them to five of our **old boys** who have joined Kitchener's Army. I also wrote each lad an inspiriting (sic) letter. We have fifteen or sixteen boys under Training and it is our purpose to send comforts to them from time to time. Children bring half pennies and pennies to School to make this purpose possible".*

*"Dec. 10th 1915: This week we have sent 13 sweaters and 13 pairs of gloves to **Sergeant Hall, Sergeant Sleight, Pte. T.H. Winfrey, T. Beverley, Tom Ellis, Tom Hunsley, - Taylor - Bowers and T. Watson** all in the B.C. x 28 Provisional Battalion stationed at Southend on Sea. Mrs. Taylor paid for the gloves. I sent £5 17s. 6d. to Manchester for the sweaters. Boys have so far brought £2 2s. 6½d. in pence, and the Chairman of Managers gave me a 1 pound note"* Mr. Taylor never forgot the 'higher' needs of the soldiers, *"Sept. 6th 1915: This week children have commenced to bring in literature to the school to be sent to the Old Boys at the Front".*

Visitors from 'The Front'

His 'Old Boys' obviously felt affectionately towards their old headmaster; the **Logbooks** record happy wartime visits to their old school, *"20th December 1916 - **Jack Rimmington, Wm. Langton** and **Frank Standish** visited the School at 3 o'clock. The boys gave them a grand reception. **William Langton** is still suffering from wounds received in the Somme. **Jack Rimmington**, who has never had a leave for 19 months, told the schoolboys that their parcels and magazines were greatly appreciated by the Old Boys at the Front".*

*"18th October 1918 - this afternoon a Crosby Warrior **Sergeant Pidd** was presented with a Military Medal by the Rev. Usher Wilson in the boys' playground, which was suitably decorated for the occasion. The boys sang appreciative songs and the girls performed very pretty dances to the evident enjoyment of **Sergeant Pidd**, who has been in the War since its commencement. There was a huge concourse of people… The ceremony was a great success".*

Mr. Taylor and his Family Fundraising

"The Star" Saturday 30th October 1915 - after the Battles of Loos and the loss of a third of the B.E.F. "Kitchener's Army" before Conscription was introduced in 1916.

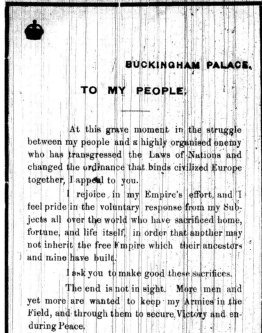

The Lincolnshire Territorials marching past St. John's Church, Scunthorpe in 1914 to the Railway Station which was then situated off Brigg Road. No doubt the Crosby lads were among them.

George Taylor was a whirlwind when it came to generating funds for the war effort; from the **Logbooks** you get an impression of a driven, caring man who felt a deep responsibility in giving to and in helping those less fortunate than himself and his family. His whole family was involved: **Hull Daily Mail**, 7th September 1918, *"Some few months ago I called at the Crosby Boys' School, and was pleased with the zeal which the Headmaster, his assistants, and the boys were devoting to the gathering of waste materials. I understand from the waste materials already sold 110 War Saving Certificates have been purchased, and, in addition, £10 has been given to the Prisoner of War Fund… This week, by kind invitation, I called at 24, Gurnell Street, the residence of Mr. G. Taylor, headmaster, to see the natty things made by the nimble fingers of his two little daughters, which, by now, I expect, will have realised a nice round sum for the Red Cross. Some of the articles displayed a good deal of ingenuity on the part of Mrs. Taylor, who has been imbued with a zeal corresponding to that of her husband for converting waste into profitable sources of revenue for war sufferers. Marvellous doll's caricatures of the Dutch style had been evolved out of a marble, a bit of wire, and rag... and all the rest that make up the wonders of doll-land. Letter racks and work-boxes, all fashioned out of the waste from the shopkeeper, showing what can be accomplished with willing hands and inventive genius".*

Not content with simply collecting others' donations, he and his wife put some of their own money in too, *"Oct. 29th 1917…66 War Savings Certificates have been bought by the teachers. In addition to this my wife and myself have bought over £400 worth of 'War Loan'.*

Crosby and the War: World Events and Local Responses
1914: Belgian Refugees

World wide events impacted upon the day to day life of Crosby School. The **invasion of Belgium** in late 1914 meant that many Belgian people came to Britain to escape German rule. Refugees were accepted into Scunthorpe voluntarily by the local community, The **Star** dated 3rd October 1914 states that, *"Father Askew sent a letter to Belgium offering to fix up Belgium families in Scunthorpe. Letter forwarded to their ministers in England who were much obliged by the offer and would certainly accept".*

Events were held in Crosby to welcome the refugees, *"Belgian refugees' concert at Crosby Hotel partook of a big demonstration in favour of the Belgian refugees now amongst them... They had only two houses at Dragonby at present but were going to have four "*. Mr. Taylor's **Logbooks** note that a few of the refugees were of school age, *"Jan. 25th 1915: This morning I admitted two Belgian boys who are living here as refugees. One is 8 years of age and the other 10 years of age. I have put both in Standard 7 under a very good teacher until they can better understand what is said to them"*. Mr. Taylor's tireless fundraising didn't forget those still suffering in their homeland: *"July 17th 1916: Today we have sent £1 12s. 5½d. being collected for the starving Belgian children in Belgium. This money has been brought to school in pennies and halfpennies"*.

George Taylor, from what we know of him from the **Logbooks,** cared very deeply about local and national issues, *"October 12th 1914: ... the news of the fall of Antwerp caused me much pain, not for the loss as far as it affected the final result of the campaign but for the further suffering of the Belgian people"*. His fundraising initiatives were a very rewarding way of easing the suffering he experienced.

1916: Zeppelin Attack

As mentioned in the introduction, the 1914-18 war was very unlike those previously seen, with fighting on many fronts, including the military and the domestic. Britain, therefore, was a frontline in this new kind of battle, a battle that involved unrestricted warfare and military attacks. Locally, Scunthorpe suffered a couple of Zeppelin raids, mid-war in early 1916, which are written about in the **Logbooks,**

"January 31st 1916: Tonight a German zeppelin visited the town. It dropped an explosive bomb and an incendiary bomb on Ravendale Street. That was the commencement of the bombing. Seven explosive bombs and 61 incendiary bombs were dropped in all. Very little damage was done as the vast majority of the bombs fell in the allotments. Three men were killed and two pigs. Eight or nine men were injured. No one was killed indoors".

"Feb. 1st 1916: Less than half the children were present. Hundreds of people with their children fled their homes last night and stayed in the fields. It was decided to close the school for the day".

"Feb. 10th 1916: An Air Raid Alarm was circulated through the town. I was asked to put out the lights... A general exodus of women and children commenced to country districts".

"Feb. 18th 1916: Attendance has been considerably reduced owing to families temporarily leaving the district on account of the air raids".

Again, in August, it is noted that, *"August 1st 1916: There was an air raid last night. Eight zeppelins entered the country. There was no school this morning"*.

A Zeppelin, illustrated on this recruiting poster, illuminated by a searchlight, was a German airship and made no noise as it travelled across the sky. It was a sinister, silent foe.

Fortunately only a couple of farm workers were killed in the Scunthorpe Zeppelin raid, along with some animals, but the entries go to show how ordinary life was disrupted and affected in new and potentially life-threatening ways (in other raids on the East coast, in

Whitby and Scarborough, there were many fatalities). People in 1914-18 had to cope with the idea that they could be killed going about their ordinary pre-war daily activities.

1916: Food Crisis

Food became a major crisis point on the home front as the war went on because of the new method of unrestricted warfare carried out by both sides. The Germans decided to carry out a plan of sabotage on foodstuffs from overseas due for the British domestic market. They sabotaged via the torpedoing by U-boats of Allied food ships. This strategy was carried out with the hope of literally starving the British into defeat. It was noted that, "*On the eve of war, 2/3rds. of Britain's food, measured in calories, came from overseas*" (AQHF, 2004:189). In more detail, "*The German Admiralty believed that their strengthened U-boat fleet could sink 600,000 tons of British shipping every month. This, they calculated, would knock Britain out of the War in 6 months... This was war against British civilians*" (AQHF, 2004:190).

The British Government recognised that it had a potential crisis on its hands; the **Star** dated Oct 1915 quotes a member of Government, *"To Feed Ourselves: Sir Horace Plunkett said if there was one factor in German efficiency which had defeated our main policy it was Germany's capacity to feed herself"*.

In statistical terms, the German attack on 'our daily bread' was working - by **May 1917**, the rate of sinkings without warning had tripled to 64% - 3,000 Merchant seamen died in 1917. The British diet was severely under attack, "*46,000 tonnes of meat was lost at sea in 1917. Between February and June 85,000 tons of sugar sunk. At one point, only 4 days' supply was left. Stocks of wheat and flour were so low that they would only last for another 2 months* " (AQHF, 2004:190).

The Health of the Nation

What made things worse was the fact that, when war began, those who could afford to do so stocked up and hoarded many essential foodstuffs, which meant that some people were much better off in terms of diet, "*As a result of such panic buying, wholesale prices rose quickly.*" The **Hull Daily Mail** reported that, "*in Grimsby the price of wholesale flour had risen from 27 to 40 shillings per 20-stone sack. Invariably such rises hit the shops, and prices of staple foodstuffs briefly spiralled, the price of bread nearly doubling.*" So not only were some people hoarding foods, it was mostly the same kind of people, wealthier people, who were the only ones able to afford what food was not hoarded away! The **Tottenham and Edmonton Herald** dated 19th August 1914 reported, "*the case of a lady who walked into a grocer's store in Palmer's Green and spent the huge sum of seventeen pounds. So effectively did she empty the shelves that it was forced to close for three days*" (AQHF, 2004:16).

Queueing

This appeared to be an outrageous situation for those working class people who could not afford the rising prices. Not only did the average person have to pay extortionate prices for staples, they had to queue for hours to pay for the privilege; Mr. Taylor reported the situation, "*Nov. 30th 1917: Attendance has fallen as low as 86.8%. In addition to boys working on land and fever cases... a few have lost their marks owing to having to stand in the queue at shop doors waiting to be served.*" "*Dec. 7th 1917: This week many boys have been absent through standing at shop doors in queues waiting to purchase food.*". The queues had to be heavily policed, some queues formed as early as 5 a.m., and children were frequently used to find and keep a place in the queue.

T. Erett and H. F. Leeman's shops, Frodingham Road, opposite Crosby School - typical shops of the Great War. Note the rabbits along the frontage of the corner shop!

In the Autumn of 1917, queueing became a major issue; for example, on the 17th December, "*Over 3,000 people waited for margarine outside a shop in south-east London - 1,000 people left empty-handed*" (AQHF, 2004:217). Resentment was growing within certain areas of the working class; it seemed, and indeed was the case, that they were the worst off with respects to food supply and availability, "*Inevitably, the main victims of food shortages were the poorer members of the working classes in both city and countryside. Because it was cheap, **bread** was vital to their diet, and 80% of the wheat to make it was imported*" (AQHF, 2004:191).

The growing tension worried the government: "*An article in November 1917 in the **Socialist Herald**, describing 'How They Starve at the Ritz', caused a storm. It was revealed that a **Herald** reporter had been able to buy a six-course meal including four rolls, hors d'oeurve, smoked salmon, and a wide choice of soups, fish, meat entrées and desserts, and unlimited servings of cream and cheese... (the report) was mass-produced as a leaflet*" (AQHF, 2004:216). To heighten the tension further, reports of uneven treatment over food with regards to the working classes had filtered through to the boys at the front-line, "*...popular resentment increased. **It was picked up by the censors vetting the letters home written to soldiers by their families - hundreds of thousands of them mentioned the food problem and food queues. Morale suffered - especially when the soldiers returned home on leave**"* (AQHF, 2004:219). The feeling was that one soldier was worth as much as another when it came to giving their life for their country so why should the families of the working class soldiers come off worse in food measures?

"*What many of the returning soldiers were hearing was that the sacrifices were not being shared fairly or equally at home. The problems of a class-divided society were coming back to haunt the Government, and in 1917 the divisions and conflicts seemed more damaging than at any other time*

165

before. Some believed they were so serious that they might undermine the war effort altogether" (AQHF, 2004:219). Something had to be done to quell the unrest beginning to arise; from spring 1917 there were sporadic food riots in places such as Liverpool, Hoxton, Fulham - areas with a sizeable working class population.

Solutions: Allotments and Voluntary Rationing

The **convoy system** was brought in with regards to shipping - where military ships accompany the fleets of merchant ships to protect them from attacks. A new government came into office late in 1916, and shook things up, "*Lloyd George took office on 7th Dec. 1916…5 new depts. of state were set up: shipping, labour, food, national service and food production, and within months the government was able effectively to deploy a substantial machinery of state control* " (AQHF, 2004:96). Among these controls issued by the state, the Government issued a plan to make any available green patch into an allotment, thus increasing the supply of fresh fruit and vegetables. **Schools** were vital in this scheme; playing fields were dug up and planted, "*In December 1916, with losses at sea steadily increasing, local authorities had been given powers to take over unoccupied land for allotments. Horticultural advisors from the Government's Food Production Department urged public schools, hospitals and asylums to turn over all available land to help feed the nation*", "*By the middle of May (1917) an additional ½ million acres had been put under cultivation*" (AQHF,2004:98). The King himself directed that potatoes, cabbages, and other vegetables should replace the normal geraniums in the flowerbeds surrounding the Queen Victoria memorial outside Buckingham Palace, and in the royal parks.

Mr. Taylor, as expected, was not slow to react to this initiative. He records,
"*March 16th 1917: Took a party of boys to work upon a plot of land this afternoon.*
March 17th (Sat) 1917: About 20 boys went to work on plot of land again this afternoon."
"*May 11th 1917: Began to plant the seed potatoes… Mr. Chamberlain a local potato dealer gave me sufficient seed to plant about 5 perches. This is an extra piece of land which the Parish Clerk told me we could work. The profits of this will also go to the Red Cross Fund.*"
"*July 12th 1917: Tonight we planted 150 more cabbage plants on our land.*"
"*Oct. 1st 1917: Today we sold to the children who had dug the school plot 34½ cwts. Potatoes at 6s. per cwt. The total realised was £10 6s. 0d.*"
."*October 1st 1917: …The total yield of our plot of land was 38½ cwts. We have several hundred plants of the cabbage family still growing on the land which plants were brought by two school boys.*"
"*Oct. 11th 1917: The Managers have decided that in addition to boys already working on land, 25 other boys may go to work for Mr. Ferraby of Crosby Grange Farm. They began this morning.*"

The requisitioning of land to grow foodstuff on helped to supplement the average diet greatly; it was reported that, "*From June onwards, under the new Food Controller, Lord Rhondda, the food system was gradually brought under effective state control. This led to greater efficiency on farms, and essential foods were grown. The aim was to give a massive boost to arable farming and the production of wheat, barley and potatoes*" (AQHF, 2004: 104).

However, much more needed to be done to improve diets. At first the government was loathe to

interfere in the lives of the citizens to the extent of forcing any kind of rationing on them, "*It was ideologically opposed to a system of compulsory rationing, and preferred a voluntary solution… In February 1917, Lord Devonport, the new Food Controller, introduced a voluntary rationing scheme. Everyone was encouraged to reduce their consumption, with appeal for restraint and meatless days*"…"*Each citizen was implored to eat only four pounds of bread, 2½ lbs. of meat, and 12 oz. of sugar each week*" (AQHF, 2004:100).

'War Bread'

The strategy the government tried to implement was to create a huge publicity campaign, "*followed in newspapers, on billboard posters and in Government propaganda films*", to promote the eating of meat over the eating of grain, as grain, "*was predominantly imported, (and) meat... was mostly produced at home*" (AQHF, 2004: 192). The government intervened, finally, in more tangible ways too; from March 1917 something called 'war bread' was baked. This was a specially created loaf in which, "*a higher proportion of raw wheat was used and other grains like maize and barley were mixed in. Even potatoes were added*'" (AQHF, 2004:196). This was a strategy following on from that outlined above; to reduce the use of imported grain in loaves.

Also, of course, it was much easier to get hold of (and afford) a loaf than a decent (or, indeed, any) piece of meat. However, this 'war bread', although worthy, was not high on many people's lists of favourite foodstuffs, "*The new War loaves were more nutritious, but were a mixed blessing, as they tasted unpleasant and were unpopular with the customer (with reports of cutting a loaf to find half a potato stuck in it)*" (AQHF, 2004:196). The **Star,** dated 9th June 1917, however, dismisses the loaf's detractors, "*The contention is that the constitution of the war loaf set up stomach ailments either from their poor quality or from the fact that the baking has been insufficient. People who eat the war bread - and eat it in as large quantities as honour and conscience allow - without feeling the slightest ill effects...they consider the new bread capital eating and would be extremely glad if they were allowed by voluntary rationing to eat more of it.*"

To reinforce the measures already implemented, in May a **Royal Proclamation** on the saving of grain was read. The **Logbooks** note this event, "*May 24th 1917: To celebrate Empire Day the children sang patriotic songs, recited patriotic poetry, listened to addresses on the Empire and wrote essays on the subject. The King's Proclamation on Food Economy was read to the children*". Parliament also passed the Unreasonable Withholding of Foodstuffs Act to ensure that no one hoarded food beyond what was personally consumable.

Following on from the doctored war bread, in September the Government's Food Controller set maximum prices for **all** bread, "*...(the price) involved a direct state subsidy to millers and bakers amounting to about 45m pounds a year*" (AQHF, 2004:206), as a strategy to stop black-market capitalisation of shortages. The Government also introduced a **bread subsidy**, trying to ensure more equal distribution of basic foodstuffs, "*The tax-paying classes found themselves paying extra to make sure the less well off could afford to eat. Bread, which had doubled in price since 1914 to 1 shilling for a 4lb. loaf, was reduced to 9d.*" (AQHF, 2004:206).

Autumn 1917: Success

All of the above initiatives meant that the situation was gradually coming under control, "*By Autumn and Winter of 1917 real progress had been made, ensuring that the nation would not be starved into submission...Britain was winning the war at sea. Direct Government intervention in the food supply system was proving a success. The drive to reduce profiteering, improve productivity on the land and achieve greater self-sufficiency in food was starting to work. The good potato harvest later in 1917 had halved prices*" (AQHF, 2004: 208). However, problems remained. Some areas were faring far better in obtaining, sharing and distributing food than other places. Pressure was mounting for a nationwide, and compulsory, rationing scheme after other areas saw how efficiently such schemes worked.

Compulsory Rationing

The much-desired rationing was finally introduced in the February of 1918, and, "*By April, all of Britain was required to have meat rationing. All districts, whether rich or poor, got equal shares of meat, whether of good or poor quality*" (AQHF, 2004:208). Equality in the allocation of foodstuffs was eventually achieved. Very quickly the system was established, "*By July...every household had to register with a retailer who supplied the appropriate rationed goods, in particular sugar, butter, margarine and lard which were all compulsorily rationed, and tea, cheese and jam rationed according to the decisions of local food committees...Shopping confidence returned to families who knew their allocation of food was safeguarded and did not depend on hours of waiting in line. As a result, feelings of resentment receded*" (AQHF, 2004:208).

Potential civil unrest was quelled; just as the famous quote from Napoleon states that, "*An army marches on its stomach*", it can be said that, '*A nation's survival (in every sense; physically, culturally, politically) depends on full stomachs.*"

The Home Front and the Angel Memorial

There is a direct link with the Angel Memorial and national and local food initiatives. A final quote from the **Logbooks** explains the link extremely clearly, "*21st Jan. 1917: Owing to the difficulty of securing meat the Managers decided that the school pig should be killed. Today he was transformed into pork. He weighed 15 stones and was sold at 17s. 6d. per stone to Mr. Mark Morgan, who presented the pig to the school. The money realised is to be divided between the Red Cross Fund and the Old Boys Monument Fund*". (This appears to be the first mention of the **Angel Memorial** in Mr. Taylor's Logbooks).

From the earthly to the angelic!

Bibliography:
The Illustrated London News: Social History of the First World War
(J. Bishop, 1982: Angus and Robertson)
All Quiet on the Home Front: An Oral History of Life in Britain During the First World War
(van Emden & Humphries, 2004 : Hodder Headline)
The Lincolnshire Star, 1914-18
Hamlyn Children's History of Britain (Grant, 1978: Hamlyn)
The First World War: An Illustrated History (Taylor, Penguin, 1974)
Crosby Boys' School Logbooks (Mr. George Taylor)
Photograph of H.F. Leeman's shop from Mr. Donald Leeman
Photograph of U.S. President Harry S Truman and Dr. Chaim Weizmannry
(Harry S. Truman Library, U.S.A. permission obtained).
Posters used by kind permission of the Imperial War Museum

Chapter Seven

Crosby

the Men Knew

Reminiscences of an Imaginary "Old Timer" who lived through the second half of the 1800's to the Great War of 1914-18

By

Susie Broadbent

YOUR PRAYERS ARE ASKED FOR THOSE WHO HAVE GONE TO SERVE OUR KING & COUNTRY BY LAND AND SEA AND AIR

OUR ROLL OF HONOUR
Parish of Crosby

CROSBY BUILDINGS

A................Crosby School
B................Crosby Church, Later to become St. George's Church
C................Crosby Vicarage
D................Primitive Methodist Church, now known as Centenary Church
E................The Holy Souls Roman Catholic Church
F................The Co-operative Stores in Crosby
G..............The Grosvenor Public House

The addresses of the Men who lived in Crosby - numbered on the Map :

1.	62 Mulgrave Street	Horace Birkett
2.	51 Mulgrave Street	John Bycroft
3.	73 Sheffield Street	John Cowan
4.	75 Sheffield Street	Jacob Forrest
5.	76 Sheffield Street	Daniel Cunningham
6.	29 Sheffield Street	John Fowler
7.	55 Sheffield Street	Alfred Garrett
8.	2 Sheffield Street	Thomas George Harpham
9.	58 Sheffield Street	Ernest Hornsby
10.	47 Mulgrave Street	George Allison Hudson
11.	29 George Street	Walter Martin
12.	91 Grosvenor Street	Jack Rimmington
13.	16 Grosvenor Street	William Henry Rylance
14.	84 Sheffield Street	William Selby
15.	69 Digby Street	Charles Shaw
16.	47 Digby Street	George Sims
17.	34 Digby Street	George William Smith
18.	96 Buckingham Street	Arthur Frost
19.	37 Dale Street	Tom Popple
20.	86 Dale Street	George Walter Harley
21.	95 Buckingham Street	Arthur Newstead
22.	35 Detuyll Street	Gideon Roberts
23.	27 Detuyll Street	George Henry Ross
24.	70 Buckingham Street	Lawrence Sissons
25.	114 Buckingham Street	William Streets
26.	11 Burke Street	William Harper
27.	54 Burke Street	Edwin (Edward) Pittaway
28.	23 Burke Street	John Robinson
29.	41 Burke Street	William Jobson Welton
30.	85 Diana Street	Norman Budworth
31.	13 Diana Street	Ernest William Robinson
32.	98 Diana Street	Arthur Herbert & Frank Edward Sellars
33.	236 Frodingham Road	Thomas William Bowden
34.	200 Frodingham Road	George Alexander Hall
35.	Chapel Lane, Old Crosby	Alexander & John Havercroft
36.	15 Old Crosby	Wilfred Short
37.	The Vicarage, Frodingham Road.	Arthur Shannon Wilson
38.	82 Berkeley Street	Richard Henry Davison
39.	47 Grosvenor Street	James Boothby

Scroll quotes from the Holy Bible New Testament—Ephesians Chapter 6: v.10-17
The Whole Armour of God –
Helmet of Salvation, Shield of Faith, Breastplate of Righteousness, Sword of the Spirit,
Girt about with Truth and Feet Shod with the Preparation of the Gospel of Peace.

HELMET of SALVATION

BREASTPLATE of RIGHTEOUSNESS

SHIELD of FAITH

SWORD of the SPIRIT

GIRT ABOUT WITH WITH THE PREPARATION

TRUTH & FEET SHOD OF THE GOSPEL OF PEACE

CROSBY THE MEN KNEW

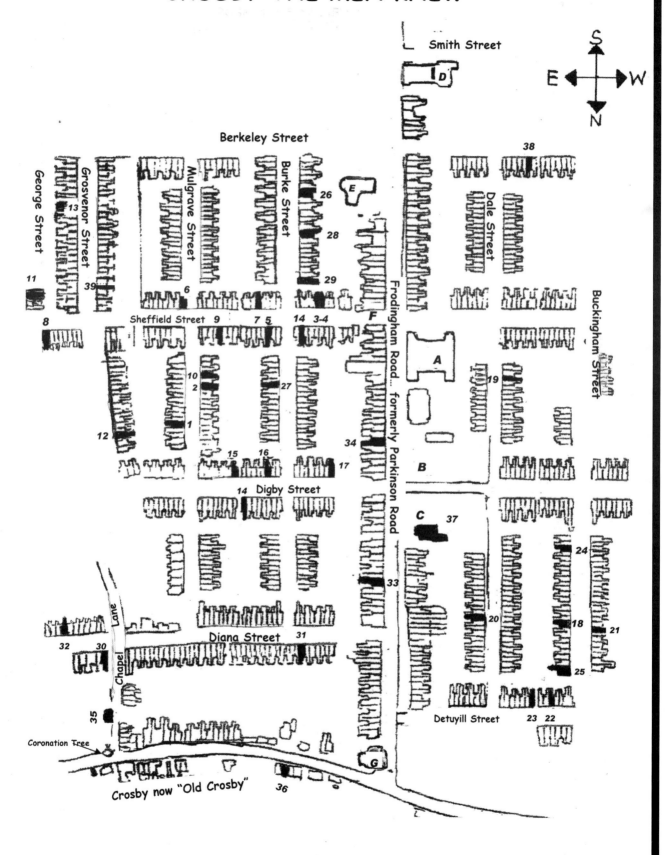

The numbers in the streets refer to the houses corresponding to the names of the Men who lived there, shown on the Roll of Honour on the opposite page.

Frodingham Road, formerly Parkinson Road. The homes of Thomas William Bowden and George Alexander Hall, men whose names are on the "Angel" were situated in this street. The spire of the Centenary Methodist Church opened by Lady Sheffield in 1908, can be seen on the left, situated on the corner of Smith Street ...

… and further along Frodingham Road, on the corner of Berkeley Street, was Holy Souls Roman Catholic Church, built in 1910, as a place of worship for the influx of newcomers into the district who came to work at John Lysaght's and other local steelworks in the town. Note the trees at the end of the street, now Ferry Road ...

CROSBY VILLAGE: THE PLACE WHERE THE BOYS LIVED AND CALLED HOME

Crosby School, Frodingham Road before the Angel was erected on the corner of Sheffield Street! H. F. Leeman's shop on the right - note the lack of motor traffic.

A factual account of the days gone by through a fictitious discussion between a young boy and an old Crosby-ite gentleman during the 1920's:

So you want to know about Crosby young 'un, well that's a tall order, I mean where do you want me to start? Well, I have lived here all my life, and I'm tellin' you I'm right proud of it, our family has been in Crosby for best part of nigh on a hundred years, give or take a few. There's not much we don't know about these 'ere parts and fowk. Of course, I've kept lots of bits and pieces over the years, photos and the like, some's come down through our lot, I seem to be the custodian of it all.

They used to grow flax and hemp around these parts when my Grandma was a lass, they used to steep the flax in the dykes for over a fortnight. It were called retting, and my grandmother said it stank to high heaven. They used the Hempdykes you know, the ones down off Crosby warren. Afterwards the fibres which had been separated into linen fibres were dressed and spun and finally woven at the home-steads. That were a long time ago. And in the early days, 1850's, the 60's and beyond, our Crosby warren was overrun with rabbits, beautiful they were, silver grey, so soft and silky. It were just off Pinfold lane, now called Winterton Road as it's on the way to Winterton.

Do you know of the *pleugh jag?* Plough jag, we had one here in Crosby and in Scunthorpe. It were a grand sight, men and women parading up and down in all their best. One man would dress like a horse all hidden under a costume with his eyes peeping out, and he'd run around after folks scaring 'em, then the plough lads would start their capers. What a day!

THE CROSBY ANGEL - A COMMUNITY'S WAR MEMORIAL

You want me to start with the time around the putting up of the Angel next t' Crosby Juniors? You don't want to know of the old stuff, well, to me it is interesting but I get your drift. Is that because of your father losing his uncle, his name being on the Memorial? You say he won't talk about it, is there no wonder, it were like a living nightmare … who would die next? You dreaded t'telegraph boy with his messages of death. In the streets, people shook their heads and prayed he'd pass them and theirs ... for a rap at the door set you on edge. 'Who was it?' After all, if it were family or friends, they'd call out and then come in. Yes, bad days, for a long, long time, for well over four years, lad. (Even after that the pain still went on for many, some lads were missing, some prisoners, and of course the wounded were everywhere, and the dead a heartache never to heal. The lads who came back, who survived, it wasn't easy for them either. The horrors they saw, the pain, those shell-shocked and near demented and half-starved. Even now many still live in a hellish terror and may never recover.)

Crosby Road in the early 1900's - now Normanby Road with the Big Social (built in 1908) opposite the period design Crosby Hotel. The Crosby Hotel was built in 1910 and used as a World War 1 recruitment office. It can be seen in the left background on the corner of Berkeley Street.

It did not seem so long since all the lads were queueing up outside the Crosby Hotel to join the Army, determined to fight against the dreaded Hun, to save hearth, home and loved ones, it was the Crosby Hotel that was the recruitment office.

Do you know that the men in the forces had all sorts of names for things? Sort of like cockney slang. Well, I can give you a full list of them, so pin your lugs back and take a note. Here is the slang from the Great War, soldier style:

'Dog and Maggot' - Of course, that's bread and cheese.
'Canary' - that was an army instructor, he had a yellow band on his arm.
If you spilled your dinner down your front, the stains were called - *'Canteen Medals.'*
Getting rid of the lice, which most every one had - was called *'Chatting.'*

You must have heard your father call his cigs, *'Coffin Nails?'*
Full kit parade was - *'Christmas Tree Order.'*
Those big Army boots were - *'Daisy Roots.'*
The army Chaplain - he was called a *'Devil Dodger.'* I knew that would make you laugh!
A *'Dingo'* - well sadly some one who went mad.
You know the soldier runner who delivered messages? - he were called a *'Duckboard Harrier.'*
So that's as many as I can bring to mind at the minute.
During the war there were casualties here about. It was a night in January, the last day I reckon, in 1916, when a steely Zeppelin came over. Anyway, he dropped at least 20 high explosive bombs and half a hundred incendiary bombs! Well, the Lord must have looked down on us all, for if they had hit the works we would have all been blown to Kingdom come. As it was, a bomb dropped in Redbourne yard and killed poor Thomas Danson of 2 Park street and Jack C. Wright, of 23 High street, Ashby. Then Mr. Wilkinson Benson was killed in Dawes lane, he lived in Ethel Terrace. What a terrible shock and loss to the community.

A view of Frodingham Road on Peace Day Celebrations on 19th July 1919.

And it's a true tale that Mrs. Markham whose husband founded the Co-operative store movement in Scunthorpe, her being 86 years young at the time, was getting ready to retire for the night, when one of those incendiary bombs was dropped over the Trent cottages. It came through her roof alight, and, cool as a cucumber, she ups and throws a bucket of water over it! A neighbour then rushed up the stairs and without more ado, promptly threw the bomb out of the window, where it alighted next to the Trent Iron Company's offices! What a presence of mind hey! otherwise the whole neighbourhood – boom - would have been blown to blazes.

After the war was over life was so difficult, as we had that there Spanish flu to fight next, it killed millions of people, men, women, and children. After surviving through so many trials we British

A street party held in Crosby, to celebrate the end of the First World War.

feared what was next. There wasn't much work around, some lads worked labouring, digging through Occupation lane, cutting it out, so as to make the road which is now called Doncaster Road, the main road into these parts.

Children's Memorial Crosby

This is what Mr. George Taylor, the headmaster, wrote in the school Logbook for Saturday 19th May 1923: "The School Monument *(sic)* was today unveiled by Sir Berkeley Sheffield Bart. M. P. Thousands of people gathered together to witness the ceremony. The Police Force, the British Legion Band, the British Legion, the Fire Brigade, the Nursing Association, the Local Education Committee and all the clergy of the district walked in procession from the Primitive Chapel, High Street, Scunthorpe. Mr. Talbot Cliff, the High Sheriff and Sir Berkeley Sheffield joined the procession. The whole ceremony was very gratifying and bestowed fitting honour upon the young lads who had fallen."

The unveiling of the Angel, what a day!!!! Any one who was anybody came just to be there at the ceremony. They came to pay their respects, to see the result of all their hard work, the collections, that went on for years of all the waste, cans, bottles, paper and the like. There was George Taylor, or should I say Mr. Taylor to you, Headmaster all these years of Crosby School. He was so proud, stood there, not one to push forward you know, a modest man, so caring. What he did for his lads, well I tell you some one should write it all down. God Bless him! It was him as arranged for the collections and all they entailed. He sent so much to each and every one of the lads you know at the Front, for all those long years of war, baccy, cigs, comforters, warm socks, clothing and the like, and when each fell, it was as if they had been his own. He did not have a son, but he did have three bonny daughters, though he had his own cross to bear when one died of an illness.

The day of the unveiling brought many mixed emotions you know, there were some parents who could not bring themselves to see the unveiling, the pain was far too much even these five years on. Umh … All those boys, denied the right to a future.

So you see, lad, we have a lot to be thankful for, lets hope we never see the like again. Look now at the Angel and be proud. Sorry, you'll have to give me a moment to compose me self. I tell you it took a lot of getting used to 'our Angel', we had seen the school seventeen years without her, and now she graces the corner. Remember, when the lads lived she wasn't about, they perished and she is our reminder of Crosby lives lost ...

THE CROSBY ANGEL - A COMMUNITY'S WAR MEMORIAL

We would all have gladly never had her and kept our dear boys. But there you have it - she is a strong symbol of what and who has gone before. I bet you and your pals say 'see you at angel corner' when you want a meeting up with them? Yes, I thought you did. Even us older 'uns do the same.

What else did you want to know about? Oh the shops. Well, I can't say I'll remember 'em all, folks were always coming and going, it were a busy time. There were thousands living in Crosby, you've never seen the like of it, all the building of new houses left, right and centre. All had to be fed, clothed, shod and so on. Many of the homes, you know yourself, took in lodgers. Doing that helped pay the rent and, to be honest, folk needed a place to put their heads down.

Did you know, fellah m'lad, that the amount of folks who lived in Crosby around 1900 were about three hundred, same as ten years and twenty year afore? Can you guess what it was when the Crosby boom started? Well, by 1910, there was over six times that, well over three thousand folk. Can you believe it? So you see, life did change quite a lot. Folk came from away, not just from down by the Trent, but from over it, and from all over this country. I couldn't understand some of the twang, even if I stood on my head. The people kept coming, and still are, for the work. Though I do often long for the old days when I knew everybody and they knew me, my mother and father, grand-dad, uncles and the like. How life changes.

Shops? You want to know what shops were here in around 1913, when the Crosby Old Boys were here, before that dreadful war started? It's a tall order to think that far back, so I tell you what, I'll go up and down the streets in my head as if I'm walking around, that will be easiest to do.

Oh! By the way, **Frodingham Road** wasn't always called that. Way back about 1909 it was changed from Parkinson Road, named after the Rev. Parkinson. And High Street from Belgrave Square to the top, used to be Frodingham Road. I must say it caused all sorts of a rumpus, especially with the postman! (*Chuckle, chuckle*) Let's get on:

Top end: ADE & WALTERS, Stone & Marble masons, they put up the Angel you know, and wrote all the names on it (what a wonderful job they did, eh!) It's the jewel in our crown.

Now I'll start at the other end, by Clayfield Lane (*now called Doncaster Road in 2008*)

1 Frodingham Road	Edward Brown, joiner
	next to Miss Rose Clayton, Sweetshop
3 Frodingham Road	Henry Peck, Newspapers
7 Frodingham Road	Walter Gibbins, Pork butcher
9 &11 Frodingham Road	Thomas Heald, Grocer with Drapery next door.
14 Frodingham Road	Mrs. Alice Grasar was a Tobacconist &
	Mr. William Grasar he was the Printer
18 Frodingham Road	Mr. Nutall & son, Milkman
20 Frodingham Road	John Vasey, Plumber
22 Frodingham Road	William Northall, Fried Fish Shop
24 Frodingham Road	Arthur Davey, he dealt in Corn & Flour
26 Frodingham Road	Arthur West, Chemist

28 Frodingham Road	Albert Bowskill, Crockery shop
30 Frodingham Road	William Barr, Barber
41 Frodingham Road	Walter Kirby, Grocer
42 Frodingham Road	Thomas Erett, Greengrocer
43 Frodingham Road	Alfred Jefferson, Butcher
44 Frodingham Road	Herbert Leeman, Grocer
45 Frodingham Road	Mrs. Rachel Cox, Shopkeeper
46 Frodingham Road	James Copeland, Cycle Repairer
49 Frodingham Road	Robert Lockwood, Grocer
51 Frodingham Road	Joseph Goodyear, Newspapers
50/52 Frodingham Road	Crosby & District Working Men's Club, Albert Geary Secretary (Frodingham Road Club)
53 Frodingham Road	George Smith, Greengrocer
55 Frodingham Road	Peter Windle, Sweetshop
56 Frodingham Road	Robert Marshland, Sweetshop
59 Frodingham Road	Mrs. Mary Jane Mason, Draper
Scunthorpe Co-operative Society (Crosby Branch)	
63 Frodingham Road	William Gurnell, Butcher
86 Frodingham Road	Wilfred Spencer, Shopkeeper
98 Frodingham Road	Jabez Brown, Undertaker

Scunthorpe Co-operative Society Crosby branch was on the corner of Sheffield Street and Frodingham Road, diagonally opposite to Crosby School.

What a beautiful day it was the day they opened our own Co-op store in 1908, I remember it so well. It was built by Mr. H. J. Thompson the local Scunthorpe builder and designed by Mr. W. H. Buttrick. Our own Mr. John Crawshaw declared the store open, he being a pioneer of the Co-operative movement in our parts. When all the speeches had been said there was a public tea in the Primitive Methodist Schoolroom, and later a concert in the Public Hall, a grand 'do' you know. In dark days or not, every penny counts and "divi" adds up.

Now I'll tell you of the companies about then.
> Frodingham Ironworks
> New Calyx Drill & Boring Company Limited
> Crosby Mines Office
> Redbourn Hill Ironworks
> Scott Walter Limited, Iron Masters
> Sheepbridge Iron & Coal Company Limited (W, J .Hudson, Manager)

Doctor Clarke lived at Eniscoe house, Frodingham Road.

The homes of George Walter Harley and Tom Popple, men whose names are on the "Angel" were in Dale street, which led off Berkeley Street.

Who were the farmers hereabouts? Let me think ...
> Ferriby - he farmed and lived at Crosby Grange
> Alfred Foster, at Neap house
> Thornton Foster, Le Moor
> Tommy Kell, Conesby
> Arthur Sheardown, and William Sheardown, Old Park Farm
> George Waite, down at Neap house
> Albert Sleight, Miller, Crosby Road

Well as you know we have all the side streets running off Frodingham Road. They also had shops in these streets, so let me think …

Right, here we go ...

Berkeley Street,
14 Mrs. Mary Jackson, Baker - I remember her lovely cakes
17 George Tate, Shopkeeper
31 Mrs Annie Hadley, Shopkeeper - she could sell you anything
37 Edward Hall, Assistant Overseer and Clerk to the Parish Council - he knew a thing or two
67 Herbert Tate, Fried Fish Shop
71 Charles Hurd, Butcher
73 Bert Quarton, Fishmonger - lovely fresh Grimsby fish!
77 George Taylor, the Coal man
101 Miss Grace Daubney, a Dressmaker
109 Charles Hall, Shopkeeper
125 Thomas Johnson, Coal man

Dale Street,
63 Edwin Ebbatson, Shopkeeper

**Looking down Sheffield Street, where several men lived whose names are on the "Angel" :
John Cowan, Daniel Cunningham, Jacob Forrest, William Selby, John Fowler, Alfred Garrett,
Thomas George Harpham and Ernest Hornsby. Seen from the corner of Frodingham Road,
with the Crosby Angel standing guard outside the school.**

Sheffield Street,
36 Morley Johnson, Grocer
62 Harry Cheeseman, Barber
63 Fred Robinson, Shopkeeper
67 Frederick Harrison, Draper
96 Samuel Broomhead, Fried Fish Shop

Burke Street,
1 Richard Hood and his sons, Builders
.

Grosvenor Street,
2 Mrs Mary Drinkall, Baker
20 George Morse, Shopkeeper.

Digby Street,
21 George Johnson, Bootmaker
23 David Spavin, Butcher
32 Mrs Amy Painter, Shopkeeper
53 Henry Parkin, Grocer
66 Fred Morley, Grocer

What do you think of that, then, young 'un, not bad for an oldie remembering all them! Then there was John Wadd, he were the blacksmith, and Jonathan Dent, a right good joiner if ever you saw one. 'Course life was at a slower pace, none of them motor vehicles, all horses, carts and the like, with plenty of manure in them days! Always someone out with a bucket and shovel to get the good hoss muck up!

The Coronation Tree is to the left of this photograph of Old Crosby planted to commemorate the Coronation of King Edward VII in 1902. Wilfred Short, whose name is on the "Angel," lived in this street. To the left is Chapel Lane where brothers Alexander and John Havercroft lived.

You know the Coronation Tree, at the junction of Chapel Lane and Old Crosby? It is said to have the old Crosby Stocks stone beneath it, stocks being used in days long gone for correction of wrong doers.

Well let me tell you a story. Young **Ernest Hornsby,** one of our lads that fell, he was a relative of old Mr. James Hornsby, who passed away in 1915 aged 82. Well, old James who were a rat catcher, he were also known for being a poet; folk from far and wide knew of him, and he wrote about the Coronation tree, to commemorate King Edward's Coronation. He also wrote about the fact that the stock stone was unearthed and removed to that site where it sits beneath *"the shady green bower of the Coronation Tree."* He even wrote about Miss Dorothy Sheffield's wedding day in 1902 to the Honourable Gerald Portman. I say "wrote" but he spoke it, for he could not read or write, he used to get people like the teacher at the Dame school to do the writing. He became quite famous and his daughter worked for a Lord of the Realm. You ask your Mother about him, maybe she can recite some of his stuff. In the early years, I reckon around 1909, there were a great gathering of the Hornsby clan, well over two hundred and fifty of them, offspring of five Crosby brothers, what a sight to behold!

The Hornsby family gathering 1909 outside the family home - James the Ratcatcher is arrowed - his brothers, left to right are hatted gentlemen on the same row Frederick, William, John and George.

There were quite a few old fellows around as I recall before the war; there was old Mr. James Ellis, he were 91 and had lived through the reigns of George III, IV and V, William IV, Edward VII and our dear old Queen Victoria. The others I remember were John Morley, coming up 90, and George Todd, near on 90 - grand old blokes with many a tale and yarn to tell.

Do you know I nearly forgot about Mr. Salim & Mrs. Eliza Wilson, you know, they live at Kathish Villas here at 246 Frodingham Road. What a stir when they married in 1913. I bet most of the 'Old boys', were there in the crowds. You know he were referred to as "The Black Prince". It was not a young match, for they were both passed the meridian of life. The bride was Mrs. Eliza Alice Holden, a widow, and her daughter, as also was a Miss Polly Heald, were her bridesmaids. I did not know the best man; he was a friend of Salim, a Missionary from Barnsley way, I believe. They married in the Scunthorpe Methodist Chapel, *(In 2008 this is now the Centenary Methodist Church, at the corner of Smith Street and Frodingham Road.)* Mr. Wilson were a real gentle man who had endured such a hard life. He was born in the Sudan and his given name was Hatashil Masha Kathish. His father was killed, and Salim was enslaved. The poor man endured so much pain. He became a Christian and he trained as a missionary

MR. & MRS. KATISH (WILSON)

in this country. You know how kind he is to you young 'uns - always has a goodie for you if you behave yourself. So maybe if you are polite, you could ask him some questions about his life, and he might oblige. Yes, I know you all refer to him affectionately as "Darkie" or "Black Man Wilson", and he knows that, for that is what he is.

What else can I tell you about Crosby, well I can look in this here directory that were given to me for safe-keeping. It's called *Kelly's Directory of Lincolnshire 1913*. In it you can look up any town, village or hamlet and it tells you all about the place.

For **CROSBY** it says:
'A township which for ecclesiastical purposes forms part of the parish of Scunthorpe. It is about 1 mile north from Frodingham station on the Great Central railway and about 10 miles north west from Brigg, in the North Lindsey division of the county, parts of Lindsey, east division of Manlake Wapentake.' So, lad, you now see where we are. Now I'll continue ... we're *'in Scunthorpe petty sessional division, Glanford Brigg union and Scunthorpe county court district.'* That's all about law and order.

'Scunthorpe has a mission hall in connection with the church of St. John the Evangelist, opened in 1908, seating 300 persons; it is served by the clergy from the Parish Church.'

Now to Crosby itself: *'The Catholic church of the Holy Souls was erected in 1910; there is also a Primitive Methodist chapel, built in 1836. A cemetery of one and a half acres was formed in 1906 on land given by Sir Berkeley G. D. Sheffield Bart., and has a mortuary chapel; it is under the control of the Parish Council. Sir Berkeley Sheffield Bart., of Normanby Park, is lord of the manor.'* His Lordship released all the land hereabouts for building, and we remembered him in the naming of our streets. We've a lot to be thankful for having a decent roof over our heads. I continue ...
'Extensive mining operations for ironstone are being carried out by lessees on the lands of Sir Berkeley G. D. Sheffield Bart., of Normanby Park, and Frank Chatterton Esq. of Somerby Hall, who are the principal land owners. The population is increasing rapidly in the township.' (Didn't I say

The original Crosby Parish Church, dedicated to St. George, nicknamed "Tin Tab" because it was a temporary iron clad building. The men would have known it well, especially Arthur Shannon Wilson, eldest son of The Rev. Charles Usher Wilson, its first vicar. Arthur's name is on the "Angel" because he lost his life in World War 1 (see his biography on an earlier page.)

that to you?) *'The area is 3,179 acres of land, 2 of water, 9 of tidal water and 2 of foreshore; rateable value £42,200.'* So there you are; Crosby according to Mr. Kelly, no less, all official. Don't it make you think?

Frodingham Road celebration of the Coronation of King George V on 22nd June 1911 - the circular window of Holy Souls Roman Catholic Church, opened the same year, can be seen to the right of the photograph.

We ought to talk about the Iron and Steel works, and the fact that they alone made all the difference to Crosby and the other four villages. Now come on lad what are the other four? That's right, Scunthorpe, Brumby, Frodingham and don't forget Ashby, even if it is quite a walk away. Well, it made a difference to this whole area of Lincolnshire, they came in from the farming villages and even beyond the Trent, most would walk, you know, calling it 'Shanks' pony'. What a sight hey, all the men's mufflers wrapped around their necks, ready to soak up the sweat of the long hard day. Why, it made us a boom town, you know, like in the gold rushes in Australia. So you see, for without these here works, we would be telling quite a different tale. Who would have thought a little bit of ironstone would have given something like a gold rush, for that is just what it was like. Everyone wanted to be here, to start a company and get rich, then the companies came and some fell by the wayside and went. I'll tell you of the ones I remember:

Primitive Methodist Chapel, Diana Street, opened in 1885. Closed in March 2008 due to falling congregation. It will continue to be used for Christian work in the district. The families of Norman Budworth, Ernest William Robinson and brothers Frank Edward and Arthur Herbert Sellars lived in this street.

In **1864** the first furnace was blown in, it being the Trent Iron Works.

In **1865** the first furnace was blown in, at the Frodingham Iron Works.

In **1866** there was the North Lincolnshire Iron Works.

In **1870's**, quarrying in the area in open cast mines. Around this time in 1871, there were no Crosby men labouring in the iron works. The daily labour rate was around half a crown a day, as I remember, not a lot, but more than most had.

In **1872** the Redbourne Hill Iron and Coal Company and the Lincolnshire Smelting Company were formed.

In **1874** the Appleby Iron Company, known as the 'Scotch' company was here.

Trent Iron Works, Scunthorpe in the 1800's

Have you heard of the 'sanders' me lad? No! Well these were the blokes who stripped the sand and soil, this was real hard work, I know, for you got four shillings a day, that was real graft, there again all work was graft, look at them in the works, nearly roasted, talk about blood, sweat and tears. Nearly swore then lad, I beg your pardon.

Did I tell you that before your school was opened we used to have a Dame school at the top end of Frodingham Road? It had up to twenty children of all ages attending, so you see even then we were educated. That is in the three R's, *'reading, 'riting, and 'rithmatic.'*

Also at the top of Frodingham Road, held in the reading rooms, we had the Parish council that met and looked after the interests of our 'Crosby' Parish. Why you know of young **Jack Rimmington** who perished in the war, he's on the Angel? Well, his father, Mr. Frederick Butcher Rimmington, he was a strong parish councillor who sorted things out. All issues, gas lighting, water and the sewage (that was a big problem in Crosby, I remember the smells!) It all had to be sorted and costed with the peoples concerned. Remember a lot was happening, with all the house building and the making up of proper roads. All the work undertaken, it does not just happen, good planning lad, good planning is what makes it happen. You know they fought tooth and nail for long enough about amalgamating (that means joining) with Scunthorpe to become one council. It had to come, though, as Scunthorpe became more wealthy and powerful than Crosby and if you can't beat 'em, you join 'em.

You'll have to excuse me now son, I'm feeling quite tired, me brain is stalled and look at the time! You and me will get scalped! Any time you want to talk, just ask. You know, I could say they were the good old days, but yon Angel shows us we lived through Hell too. Thank the Lord the war has ended and we have peace. So long son, so long ...

Stone laying ceremony of Crosby Church, 21st June 1924, consecrated and dedicated to St. George, replaced the "Tin Tab."

Stone laying, Crosby Church, 21/6/24.

Acknowledgements and Sources of Information

The "Friends of the Crosby Angel" wish to express their appreciation to all those who have kindly assisted in any way with this publication, including those who have allowed us to use copyright material. We hope that all have received an honourable mention herein, but if we have omitted to mention everyone, we sincerely apologise. Each biography also includes acknowledgements specifically relevant thereto.

Mr. Charles Anderson, Researcher, World War I
Mr. Christopher J Bailey, Researcher, Lincolnshire Regiment
Mr. Geoffrey Bryant, M.B.E., Author, Barton on Humber, Lincolnshire
Dr. Ian Dewhirst, M.B.E. Local Historian, Keighley, Yorkshire
Mr. George Hankinson
Mr. Keith H. Harrison, B.A. WEA Tutor, Local History
Mr. Paul Harrop "Direct" Magazine, North Lincolnshire Council www.northlincs.gov. uk
Mr. Chris Horan, "Nostalgia," Scunthorpe Telegraph
Captain D J Lee B.E.M. J.P. Lincolnshire Regimental War Diaries
Mrs. Mary Leitch, Immingham, Lincolnshire—author of "Whatever Happened to Joe?"
Mrs. Vanessa. R. Lond, Photography, Isle of Axholme War Memorials
Mr. Bryan Longbone, WEA Tutor, Local History
Mr. George Lord, Photographer, Scunthorpe Camera Club (photographs of The Angel)
Mr. George Mann, Publisher
Ms. Elaine Mullan, Researcher, Broughton War Memorial
Dr. David Sutton, UK Director, WATCH copyright project www.watch-file.com
All Saints Church Magazine, New Brumby, Scunthorpe
St. Hugh's Church Magazine, Old Brumby, Scunthorpe
Humberside Federation of the Women's Institute
Bartlett's Battlefields, Broomhill, Edlington, Horncastle LN9 5RJ www.**battlefields**.co.uk/
(Messrs. David Bartlett, Michael Kelly and Christopher Wesley)
Census records 1841 to 1901
Commonwealth War Graves Commission website www.cwgc.org/
Crosby Rate Books 1914-1918 (John Wilson, Archivist, Grimsby Archives)
        http://www.nelincs.gov.uk/leisure/archives/
Miss Suzanne Bardgett M.B.E. Imperial War Museum, Lambeth Road, London SE1 6HZ
Isle of Axholme Family History Society
Kingston upon Hull Central Library & Local Studies, Albion Street, Hull HU1 3TF
Lincolnshire Archives, Rumbold Street, Lincoln
Museum of Lincolnshire Life - Sara Basquill and Stephen Rowan
North Lincolnshire Library, Carlton Street, Scunthorpe, Lincolnshire
North Lincolnshire Museum, Oswald Road, Scunthorpe: Mr. David J Taylor Local History Assistant
School Admissions Registers and Log Books for Crosby School covering the period 1908-1933
Soldiers Died in the Great War CD series
War Memorials Trust, 4 Lower Belgrave Street, London SW1W 0LA
World War 1 Army Ancestry (Fourth edition) by Norman Holding, revised and updated by Iain Swinnerton
Published by the Federation of Family History Societies (Publications) Ltd. 15-16 Chesham Industrial Centre,
Oram Street, Bury Lancashire BL9 6EN Fourth Edition 2003ISBN No. 1 86006 179 6
www.familyhistorybooks.co.uk Copyright: Norman Holding and Iain Swinnerton (Time Line Information)
www.ancestry.co.uk website)
Barton-on-Humber website www.**barton**upon**humber**.btinternet.co.uk/
The Long Long Trail www.1914-1918.net
        authored by former Chairman of the Western Front Association, Chris Baker
"The History of the Lincolnshire Regiment" by Major General C R Simpson C.B.
National Archives website www.**nationalarchives**.gov.uk/
"The History of World War 1" by Andy Wiest, published by Grange Books 2001 ISBN 1-84013-419-4 Grange
Books PLC The Grange Kings North Industrial Estate, Hoo, near Rochester, Kent ME3 9ND.
International Genealogical Index www.familysearch.org
FreeBMD website http://www.freebmd.org.uk/
http://www.ancestry.co.uk/

APPENDICES

(i) Crosby Parish Roll of Honour
It appears that two further pages are missing.
(ii) Wesleyan Church Memorial plus Transcription.
(iii) Newspaper account of its Unveiling and Dedication.

The three surviving framed Rolls of Honour for Crosby Parish listing all those who served in His Majesty's Forces during the Great War (sadly they are incomplete).

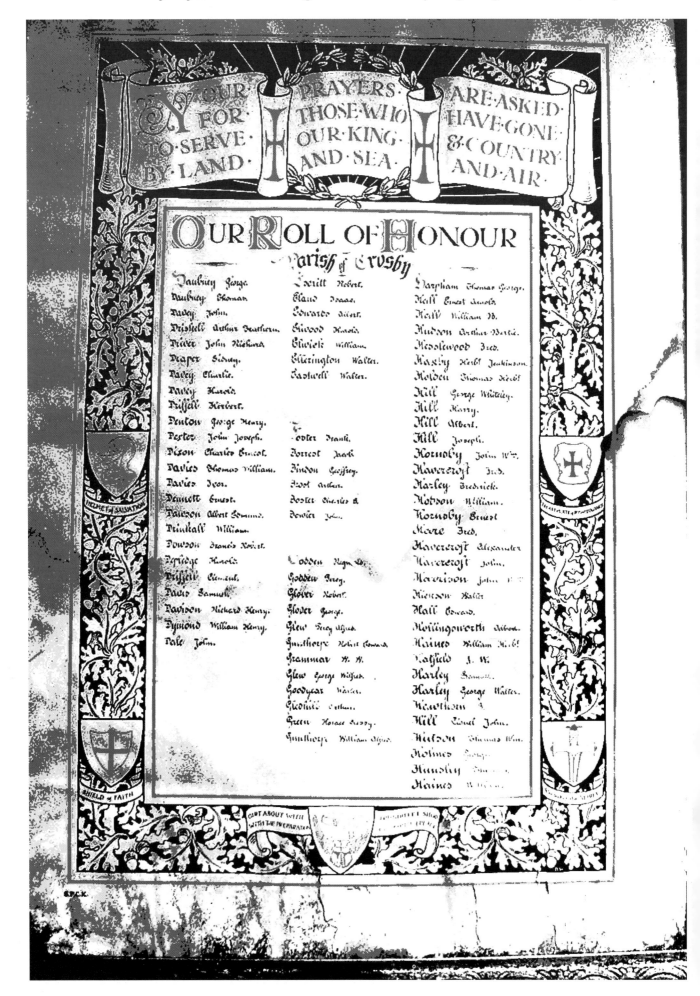

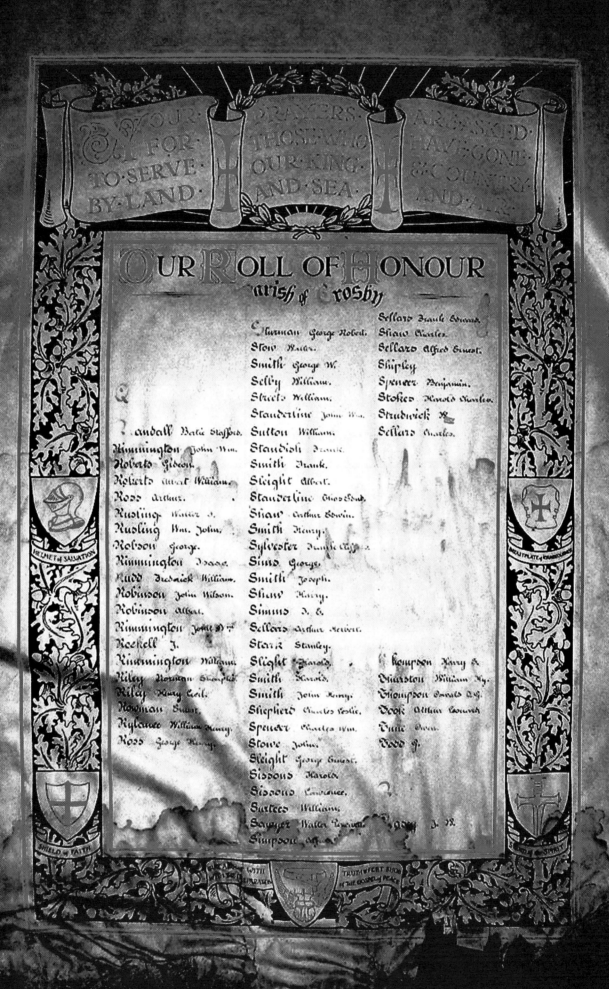

Your Prayers Are Asked
for those who have gone
to serve our king & country
by land and sea and air

Our Roll of Honour

Parish of Crosby

Wright G. W.   Young Thomas.
Walker Arnold.
Walker Norman.
Walker Edward Wm.
Nogin John William.
Nogin Albert Victor.
Whitby Stanley George.
Watson James Richard.
Watson Thomas William.
Wright John Jacob.
Whitesmith Rowland.
Whitesmith Stanley.
Winfrey George William.
White Percy.
Windley Stephen.
Allcockson Robert.
Wright
Wilson Arthur Shannon.
Welton William J.

The Wesleyan Church Memorial Plaque, originally situated in the Trinity Methodist Church on the corner of Wells Street and High Street, Scunthorpe (where the present British Home Store stands.)

Transcript of the Wesleyan Memorial Plaque aforementioned
(The names printed in **BOLD** are also inscribed on the Crosby Angel)

𝕿𝕺 𝕿𝕳𝕰

𝕲𝕷𝕺𝕽𝖄 𝕺𝕱 𝕲𝕺𝕯

And in

Sacred Memory

Of the undermentioned Members
of this Church and Congregation who
gave their lives in the Cause of Freedom
during the Great War. 1914-1918

ARRAND, Edmund Bernard
AXE, Walter
BELLAMY, Frank William
BUDWORTH, Norman
CLEGG, Cyril Thompson
COWDELL, Cyril
CROSS, Charles William
DODDS, John Reginald
FISHER, John William
HALES, Alfred

HANBY, William James
HARPER, William
HEATON, Eric Rupert
HINDMARSH, Albert
HOLT, John
MADDISON, Albert
MARRIS, John Henry
MARSHALL, Richard Henry
PLATT, Edwin
PLATT, Herbert
POGSON, James Jabez

POPPLE, Tom
RUSLING, William
SELLARS. Frank Edward
SELLARS, Arthur Herbert
STAMPE, George Henry
SYLVESTER, Frank Clifford
TURNER, George
VESSEY, William John
WATKIN, Robert
WOOD, Thomas Neal

Greater Love hath no man Than This

**WORLD WAR 1939-45
L.A.C. DAVID EAST DOUGLAS
23rd August 1940**

The "Star" Saturday January 17th 1920.

Scunthorpe Fallen

Weslyan Memorial Tablet Unveiled

Impressive Service

The Weslyans of Scunthorpe have been among the foremost to show appreciation of its 28 adherents, who fought in the war. The roll of honour has been affixed in the chapel, and the men who returned, welcomed and entertained months ago. However, to keep the memory of those green, who made the supreme sacrifice, a beautiful brass tablet has been erected over the rostrum, the unveiling of which was impressively carried out on Sunday afternoon, in the presence of a numerous congregation.

The service was conducted by the Rev F W Smith, Ashby, and the tablet was unveiled by the Rev R. F. Priestley, M.C., of Misterton, late of Ashby, who served in the war both as a private nd as a chaplain and for his conspicuous bravery and devotion to duty was awarded the Military Cross. He appeared in his chaplain's uniform, with ribbons, on Sunday. The service throughout was most impressive and there was a large congregation. Mr. Richard Smith was at the organ and the proceedings opened with the singing of the hymn, 'Jerusalem the golden'. Prayer was offered by the Rev R. F. Priestley and the lesson was read by the Rev F. W. Smith. The hymn 'God of the living in whose eyes' followed, at the end of which the Rev R. F. Priestley unveiled the tablet: 'To the Glory of God and in ever grateful and loving memory of those whose names are inscribed thereon'.

He then read the following inscription which is on the tablet: 'To the Glory of God and in sacred memory of the undermentioned members of this church and congregation who gave their lives in the cause of freedom during the Great War 1914-1919. Edmund Bernard Arrand, Walter Axe, Frank Wm Bellamy, Norman Budworth, Cyril Thompson Clegg, Cyril Cowden, Charles Wm Cross, John Reginald Dodds, John Wm Fisher, Alfred Hales, Wm Jas Hanby, Wm Harper, Eric Rupert Heaton, Albert Hindmarsh, John Holt, Albert Maddison, John Henry Marris, Richard Henry Marshall, Edwin Platt, Herbert Platt, Jas Jabez Pogson, Tom Popple, William Rusling, Frank Edward Sellers, Arthur Herbert Sellers, George Henry Stampe, Frank Clifford Sylvester, George Turner, William Thos Vessey, Robert Watkin, Thomas Neal Wood, "Greater Love Hath No Man Than This."

Returning to the pulpit, the Rev R. F. Priestley said that when he received this very nice letter of invitation to come and take some part in that afternoon's service his mind went back to September 1914, very shortly after the war had broken out, when he commenced his labours in the Scunthorpe and Brigg circuit. Even then many had responded to the call that every one of them was feeling. For twelve months it was his privilege to serve and help as well as he might the different congregations there, and then at last it came his own turn to go. Now they were gathered together just to express very simply and very briefly and very lovingly the gratitude not only to the boys whose names were on the tablet but to the boys who have returned and are now in our towns and homes. He counted it a very great honour indeed to be asked to conduct that solemnly impressive service. It was good indeed to see those tokens of remembrance. All that their boys did and endured they would never know, it was beyond all telling. He had been privileged to some extent to share their experiences, to be with some of the great host represented by those names. He was with some when they died, with others when they were hit, and others he had helped to dig out when they were buried. It was just the greatest privilege in his life to be able to help them in any way whatever but his saddest lot as a chaplain was to write to the people at home the dread news of the passing of a loved one, letters that would bring stunning shock and despair. Oh! but the letters he got back in return were just bonny beyond words. They showed their sorrow, their bitter grief, but they showed too the great brave heart. The pride was felt that their dear one had proved himself a man, and he had them all *(referring to the let* - a pathetic little bundle but very precious to him.

That was a memorial service and whenever anyone was brought in contact with sorrow his mind always went instinctively and first of all to One who had borne in His own heart and in His own life the sorrows of the world. Some of those present were mourners and he would ask them if they had taken the One who could sympathise and help to the utmost with the sorrows of your heart. The war had given to him (the speaker) a clearer realisation and a richer experience of the values of Jesus Christ. They were united in that memorial service and he asked them if it was to stop there. They should show their gratitude to the world for its heroes and sufferers, and to those who had been comrades of those whose names were on the tablet- to their friends and relatives, to the citizens generally who had produced such as those. He beseeched them to be worthy of those who had made that sacrifice for them.

> 'Be worthy of your noble dead
> So shall your hearts be comforted
> He is not lest who goes before
> But standing in the open door
> He wants you there with outstretched hands
> Love's dearest, best ambassador'.

He also beseeched them to not only make that a memorial service, but a covenant service to pledge that the thing that that they gave their lives to win shall yet be, and the thing that caused them to suffer and die like that shall never be again.

> The call of my country's God; come
> Is the call of my country's dead.

Having put war behind them they must strive equally hard to build up again the life of the world. They wanted that message to thrill through the nations by the lips of men -.

> See to it, then, Ye builders of the peace
> And build with bold surprise,
> Life's new-won liberties
> Build this fair kingdom as he first
> designed
> To His unending glory, and the welfare of mankind.

In conclusion, Mr Priestley said that was a solemn service but it would not be altogether a sad one if they decided in their own lives so to live that this England of ours should be a new Jerusalem; that there shall be Peace on Earth and that in whatever part of the community they represent so to live their lives that the coming of this Kingdom of God would be hastened. Their sacrifice will not then have been made in vain.

The final hymn was 'For all the Saints who from their labour's rest.' A verse of the national anthem and the Benediction brought to a close a memorable service.